TIM & ERIC'S
ZONE THEORY™
7 EASY STEPS TO ACHIEVE A PERFECT LIFE
TIM HEIDECKER
ERIC WAREHEIM

TIM & ERIC'S ***ZONE THEORY™***

Tim Heidecker & Eric Wareheim

GRAND CENTRAL
PUBLISHING

NEW YORK BOSTON

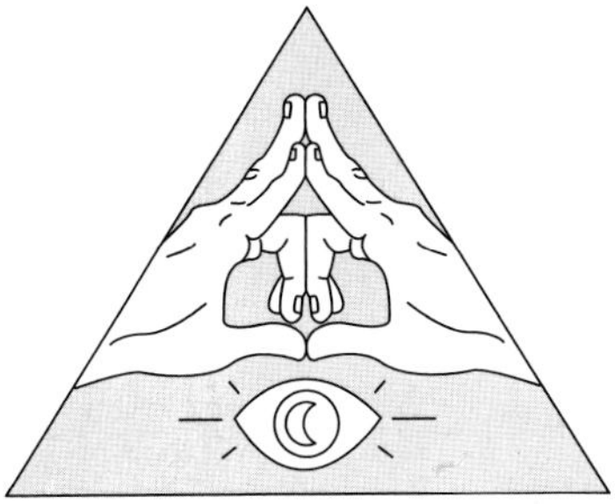

7 EASY STEPS TO ACHIEVE A PERFECT LIFE

(Instantly acquire perfect happiness in seconds)

Book Design by Duke Aber
Additional Artwork by Tak Boroyan
Photography by Rickett & Sones
Additional Writing by Doug Lussenhop and Gregg Turkington
Edited by Ben Greenberg
Editorial Assistant Maddie Caldwell
Production Managed by Megan Gerrity
Production Coordinated by Tom Whatley
Production Assistant Caroline Bader
Proofread by Angelina Krahn
Special Thanks to Daniel Greenberg

Grand Central Publishing
Hachette Book Group
1290 Avenue of the Americas
New York, NY 10104
www.HachetteBookGroup.com

Printed in the United States of America

Q-MA
First Edition: July 2015
10 9 8 7 6 5 4 3 2 1

Grand Central Publishing is a division of Hachette Book Group, Inc.
The Grand Central Publishing name and logo is a trademark of Hachette Book Group, Inc.
The Hachette Speakers Bureau provides a wide range of authors for speaking events.
To find out more, go to www.hachettespeakersbureau.com or call (866) 376-6591.

The publisher is not responsible for websites (or their content) that are not owned by the publisher.

Library of Congress data has been applied for.

ISBN 978-1-4555-4543-8 (Hardcover ed.); ISBN 978-1-61969-966-3 (Audiobook downloadable ed.);
ISBN 978-1-4555-4544-5 (Ebook ed.)

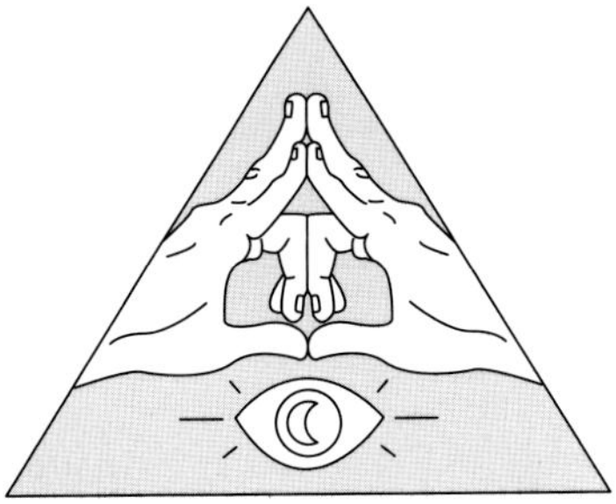

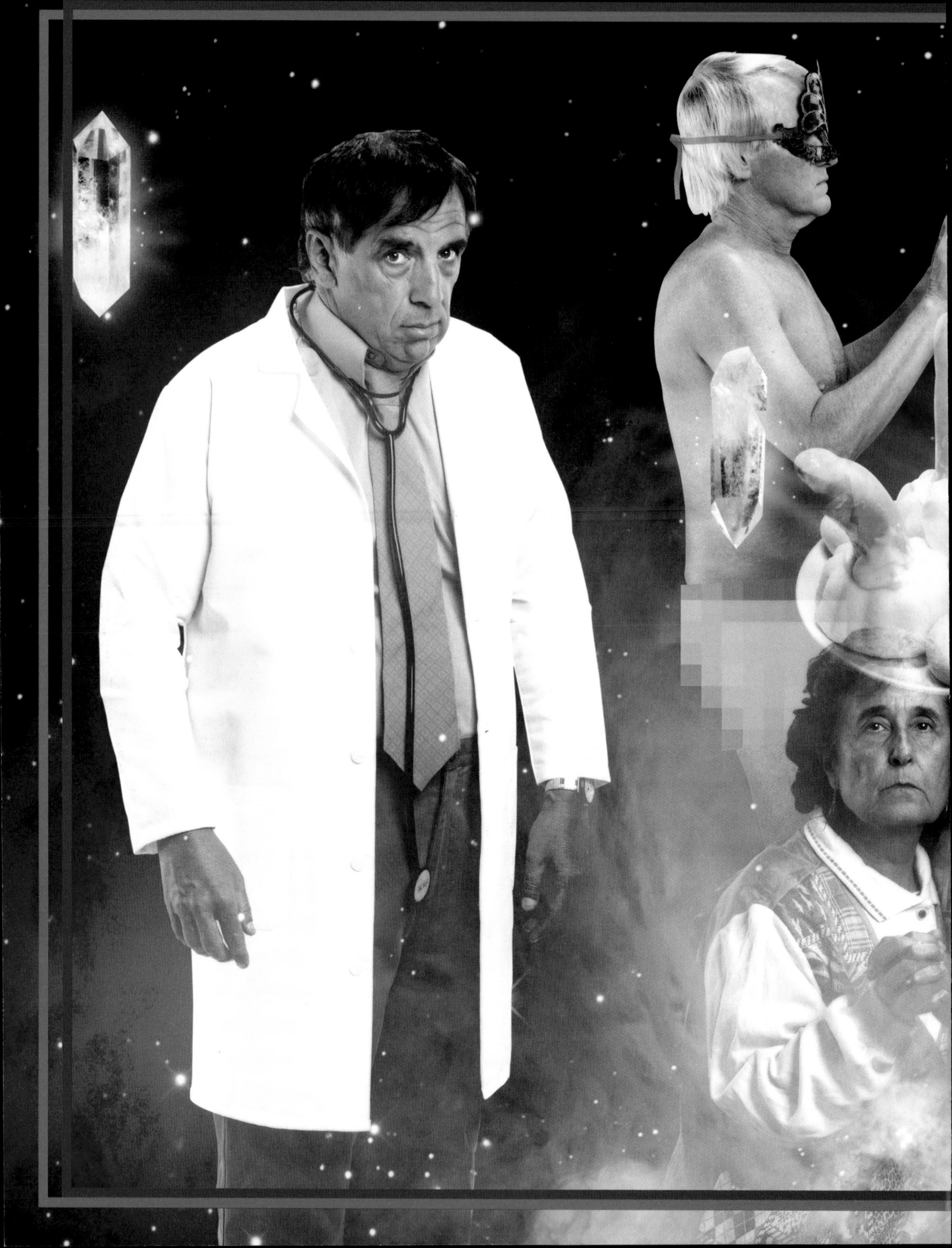

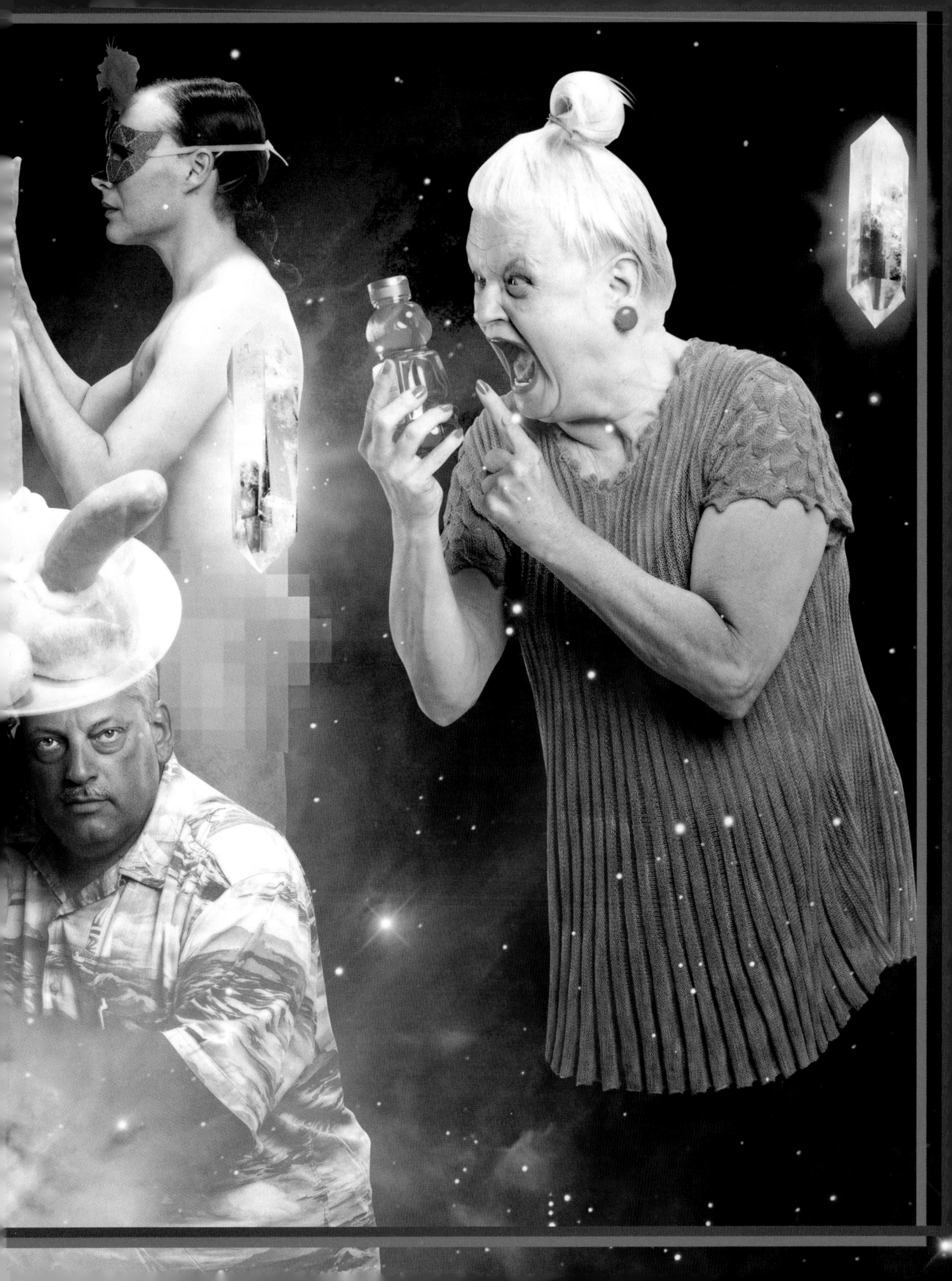

TABLE OF CONTENTS

PART I

LCOME

OME

ST

BEFORE CONTINUING, ANSWER THE FOLLOWING QUESTION AS HONESTLY AS YOU POSSIBLY CAN:

ARE YOU ARE MAN? OR WILL BE A MAN SOON?

OP

IF YOU ANSWERED YES—
CONTINUE READING.

IF YOU ANSWERED NO—
DESTROY BOOK
IMMEDIATELY (DO NOT
ATTEMPT TO RETURN)

A NOTE TO THE READERS

Readers please note. *Tim & Eric's **ZONE THEORY**™* features several print ads throughout which were designed and created to offset the cost of the book. Original estimates for the book ranged from 75 to 100 dollars and thanks to the offset plan enabled by our publisher we are able to pass the savings on to you. These ads have been selected to cater to your needs—we hope you find them useful and beneficial.

Dr. Jason Brip

FOREWORD *by Dr. Jason Brip*

Good Morning,

My name is Dr. Jason Brip. I am a Zone counselor and Zone leader of my Zone community in Charles River, Colorado. I am also a licensed medical practitioner of "Hoy Medicine" which uses oats to diagnose and treat a variety of diseases. I have been roundly discredited by the established medical community but who cares, I am the best.

As a dedicated "Oat Burner" Hoy guy, 19 years old, it's obvious that my mind is open to new ideas and experiences. I done acid and shrooms when I was a freshman in high school. It's mind expanding and very sad that psychologists don't prescribe it for mentally ill patients. It would cure all insanity!

But what really blew me away was when I read ***ZONE THEORY***™. It's better then all the drugs mankind could make combined. Its really set me straight!

I read this book and it suddenly dawned on me: I get it! My 7 Zones are what make me who I am and when these zones are aligned I am HAPPY! Thank you Tim and Eric for teaching me about my zones and how to align them.

By the way, do you know Spock's Beard? I saw them last year. Seriously, one of the best concert experiences of my life. It wasn't just the music that ruled: they could jam, but the people, the vibe. It was better than all the drugs in the world combined!

With Peace and Love,

Dr. Jason Brip

(Zone Plane 5)

A BLESSING *from Father Michael Passt*

Dear Lord,

You who guides us in our choices, bless me and bless this book. Give it your blessing, Lord, bless it.

Amen.

I have just read *Tim and Eric's* ***ZONE THEORY***™ and I am at peace. I write this lying in bed, scribbling on a yellow legal pad just at peace. I have many homilies to prepare but I might just go back and read this whole book again. Tim and Eric are my favorite parishioners—they breathe life into the stale word of God. They breathe life into me and into who I am as a man.

The ***ZONE THEORY***™ is not acceptable and not compatible with the teachings of the Church, but nonetheless I am compelled to wish them, and all of you: The best.

Signed,

Mike Passt
(Zone Plane 7)

Father Michael Passt

About the

Authors

Tim *NAGRUME* Heidecker

(Zone Plane 8)

Tim is a weight lifter, poet, artist, musician and writer. He was born in Allentown, PA, in 1976. His birthstone is Amethyst (rhombohedral class 32)

Tim's blood counts are high but being maintained by a Dambeck Machine.[1]

Tim is a weight lifter, dancer, chef and minister at his local **ZONE CENTER**™. *A founding member of* **ZONE THEORY**™ *Inc., Tim spends his time updating* **ZONE THEORY**™ *books, lecturing and coaching Amateur Horseplay.*

---

[1] Dambeck Machines maintain and service blood counts.

About the

Eric *SHARM* Wareheim

(Zone Plane 8)

Eric started his career as an artisanal metalworker and glassblower throughout his 20s. After meeting Tim at a glassblowing trade show, he helped develop the **ZONE THEORY**™ *and officially changed his name to Sharm.*

Eric's blood counts are normal to low. (Eric has only been tested once as a child and refuses to be retested as a man.)

Eric was born with three testicles. At the age of 12 one was removed.

At the request of Nagrume, a third testicle was publicly reattached as part of a Zone Ceremony Seminar in Newark, Delaware, in September 1990.

Authors

WHAT IS THE *ZONE THEORY*™?

ABOUT *ZONE THEORY*™: A BRIEF OVERVIEW

ZONE THEORY™ is a life system designed by Tim Heidecker and Eric Wareheim and inspired by the teachings of Ba'hee Nodaramoo Priss Dimmie—there are 7 confirmed Zones in life:

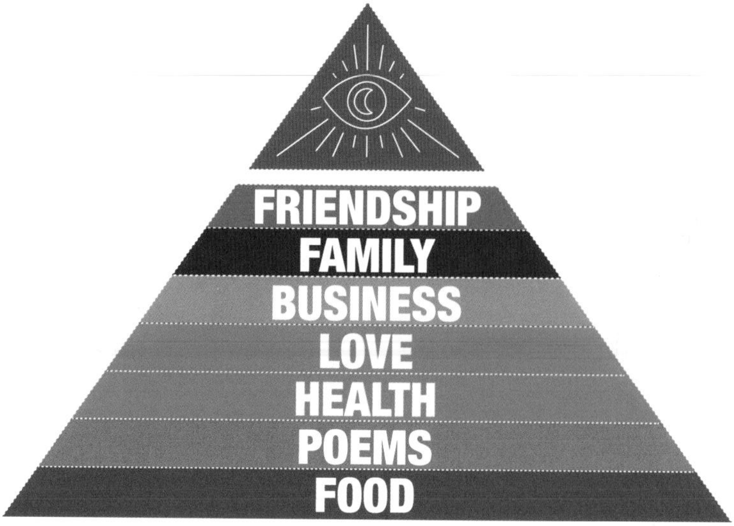

These Zones have been confirmed. There is no need to confirm these elsewhere. We have confirmed that the above 7 Zones are correct.

There are 7 confirmed Zones and they are as follows:

ZONE ONE: FRIENDSHIP • ZONE TWO: FAMILY
ZONE THREE: BUSINESS • ZONE FOUR: LOVE
ZONE FIVE: HEALTH • ZONE SIX: POEMS • ZONE SEVEN: FOOD

ZONE THEORY™ CONFIRMS that these 7 Zones provide a road map to successful living.

Aligning these 7 Zones is key.

Behavior must act in harmony with each other and the 7 Zones accordingly.

Harmony and alignment with the 7 Zones is easy to achieve once the ***ZONE THEORY***™ is used properly.

THIS BOOK INTENDS TO:

1. IDENTIFY AND EXPLAIN THE 7 ZONES
2. TEACH YOU HOW TO "TONE YOUR ZONES"
3. CONNECT AND ALIGN YOUR ZONES
4. SET YOU ON THE PATH TOWARDS ZONE PLANE 8

UNDERSTANDING THE ZONE PLANES

The ultimate goal of ***ZONE THEORY***™ is to achieve Zone Plane 8. Most people operate at Zone Plane One or Two. **SO...**

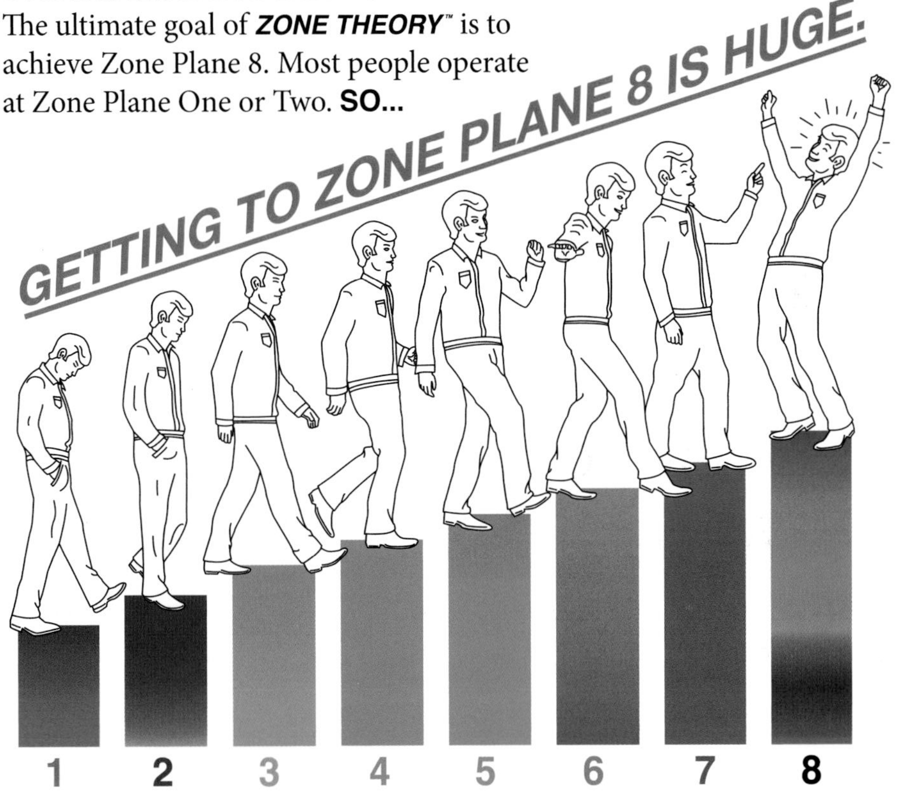

WHAT IS ZONE PLANE 8 ?

You have absolutely no right to ask that question right now. You are just beginning on this amazing journey of Zone Enlightenment and you're asking "what is Zone Plane 8?" Fuck you. You have no idea what Zone Plane 8 is, do you? But when you do find out it's going to:

BLOW!!! YOUR!!! MIND!!!

It's more like Heaven than you can ever know. (We don't recommend it, but you COULD skip to the back of the book to see a preview of Zone Plane 8. It's your right. Go ahead and take a peek. But you shouldn't. Will you?)

IS THIS BOOK RIGHT FOR ME?

Before answering that question, try the following experiment:

- Locate a mirror *(this is now your Zone Mirror and will be used throughout the book for self-reflection exercises)* and stare into your own eyes for 1 hour.
- Have the answer yet? It's "yes."
- Here is a drawing of you:

You are in bad shape. Your breath smells and you have body odor. You are underweight and have a lot of zits all over your body. Aside from the zits you just generally have bad skin. You are not good at work and people that you know don't like you. We've counted: you have less than two friends. And no actual BEST friend—you seem to be made of trash. Place a bookmark on this page, close the book and use it to hit yourself in the forehead several times. Once a steady headache is established you can open it up and continue reading. See? Look what we made you do. You are a puss to the nth degree. Your Quar Levels are well below average. What's the point in dealing with you? You are a waste. Your skin crumbles and chaps easily and the people that know you are right to call you behind your back "blotchy boy." You bleed easily as demonstrated when, as a child, your classmates routinely cut your arms with their penknives. Oh! How you'd bleed like a little bitch. Incredibly, there has never once been a dog or cat who's come up to lick you or nuzzle up against you. In fact, all animals are repelled and repulsed by you. You are trash.

You are a Discard.[2]

For years now, you have tried and tried to be better, but you keep failing! But don't cry like a baby—it's going to be OK because you've found the right book for you!!!

ZONE THEORY™ WORKS FOR EVERYONE![3]

Is it going to be EASY? No. But what is when you think about it? Especially when it means guaranteed happiness and wish fulfillment. Doesn't matter who you are—whether you are the head of a big company or a shit boy with nothing to his name.

QUIK QUIZ 1—FILL OUT BEFORE READING

1. Do I weep to sleep?	☐ YES	☐ NO
2. Do I moan all the time?	☐ YES	☐ NO
3. Do I identify myself as "Moan-man"	☐ YES	☐ NO
4. Are my moans between 2 Hz and 40 Hz?	☐ YES	☐ NO
5. When I hear moaning do I go "sounds like me"?	☐ YES	☐ NO

QUIZ 1 ANSWERS: 1. YES 2. YES 3. YES 4. YES 5. YES

[2] A "Discard" is anyone who is not Zone Certified.

[3] Not Women.

THE ZONE THEORY™ BOOK SHELF℠

(compatible with The Zone Theory™ book(s) only)

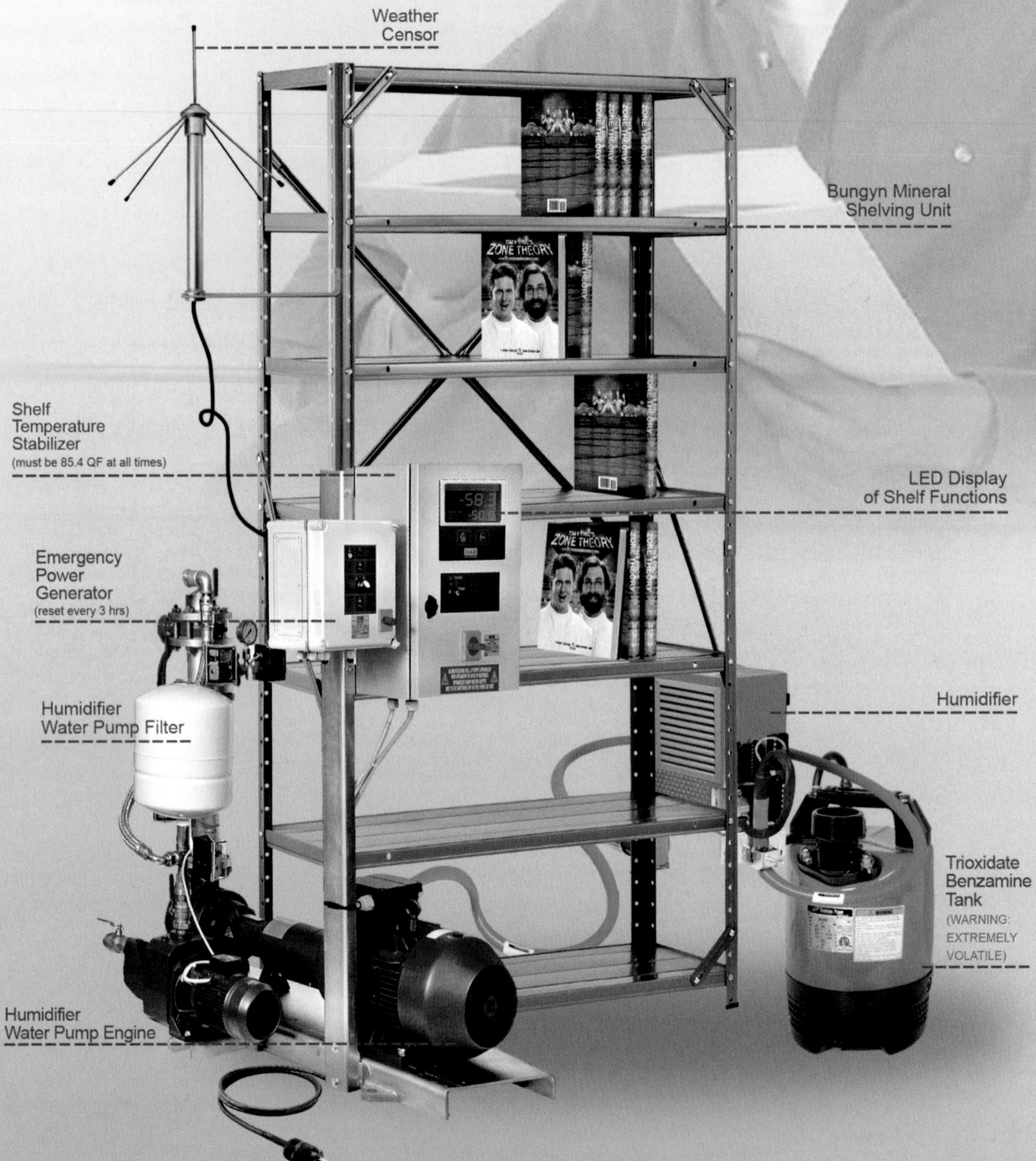

In case of malfunction please contact your local Zone Theory™ Customer Service and Help Center.
Refer to The Zone Theory™ manual for contact information.

OFFICIAL WARNING

"Vin Nager-Jones is a US Attorney General, advocate for the mentally insane, and outspoken critic of the **ZONE THEORY**™. *It's important to know more about Vin Nager-Jones so you can understand where he's coming from and realize his position on the* **ZONE THEORY**™ *comes from his own misunderstanding and narrow-mindedness. You should seriously look him up on the web. He is a major piece of shit. Do an image search on "Vin Nager-Jones no shirt" on your web browser. It's disgusting. He smokes cigarettes and his ball sac droops very low because he is old. We have allotted him this page to speak his mind - say his piece and get it over with—sadly, Fair Speech laws now require this type of thing in all "self-help" and "religious" books.*

I have a law degree from Tulane University as well as a Master's in Psychology from Tufts. Over the past 25 years my focus has been to study and evaluate the benefits and potential dangers in cult religions, self-help gurus, quick-fix solutions to life's mysteries, diet fads and celebrity fitness programs. Having thoroughly reviewed the ***ZONE THEORY***™, I can confidently state that this program to "Instantly Acquire Perfect Happiness in Seconds" through "Seven Steps" is pure quackery plain and simple. Furthermore, several exercises contained in this book will lead to pain, suffering and even death. I can see absolutely no positive side to the ***ZONE THEORY***™ and officially recommend Grand Central Publishing cease publication of the irresponsible and dangerous book immediately. Beyond this advisory letter I am contacting State Attorneys General in hopes of awakening and enlightening them to the dangers posed to our community in these pages.

It is reasonable and understandable for human beings to seek out alternate methods to achieve happiness and fulfillment. It's in our very nature to ask these fundamental questions and seek answers to life's deepest mysteries. And I am sympathetic towards anyone reading this now who might be in a place where other "life systems" have failed them and they are depressed, lonely, seeking help and guidance. But please, if you are reading this: Stop right now. Stop reading this horrible, dangerous book. Put it down. Put it down. Walk away.

Also, my name is not Vin Nager-Jones. It's Dr. Vincent Jones.

WAR THE

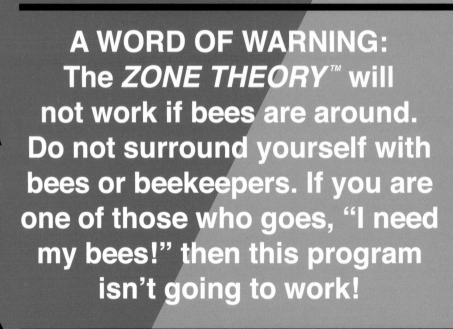

A WORD OF WARNING:
The *ZONE THEORY*™ will not work if bees are around. Do not surround yourself with bees or beekeepers. If you are one of those who goes, "I need my bees!" then this program isn't going to work!

NING
BEES

A variety of bee extermination products are available on the internet.

Bees are not only harmful to the Zone process but are also disgusting.

SHOPPING LIST (BA'HAHTWEN)

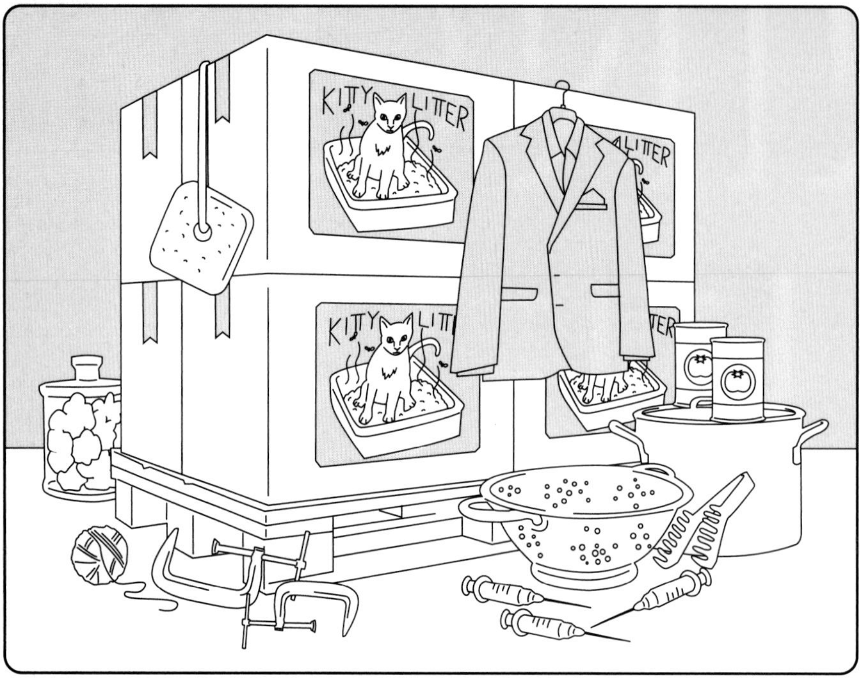

The ***ZONE THEORY***™ is EZ! But you're going to need a few things before you begin. Here's a helpful checklist for you—most items can be purchased at any supermarket or online.

- 1 Full Pallet of Cat Litter (to be consumed)
- 1 Spaghetti Pot
- 1 Spaghetti Strainer
- 1 Jar of Chunky Style Spaghetti Sauce
- 1 Jar of Regular Spaghetti Sauce
- 1 Pair of Spaghetti Tongs
- Children's Yarn
- Salt Lick
- 10 Large Cotton Balls
- Several Clamps of Various Sizes
- Several Disposable Syringes—and/or Barber's Needle
- New Wardrobe—Two to Three Sizes Bigger Than Your Current Wardrobe [4]

[4] ***ZONE THEORY***™ guarantees you will grow 3 feet in height.

HEAD WEIGHT (TORSCH)

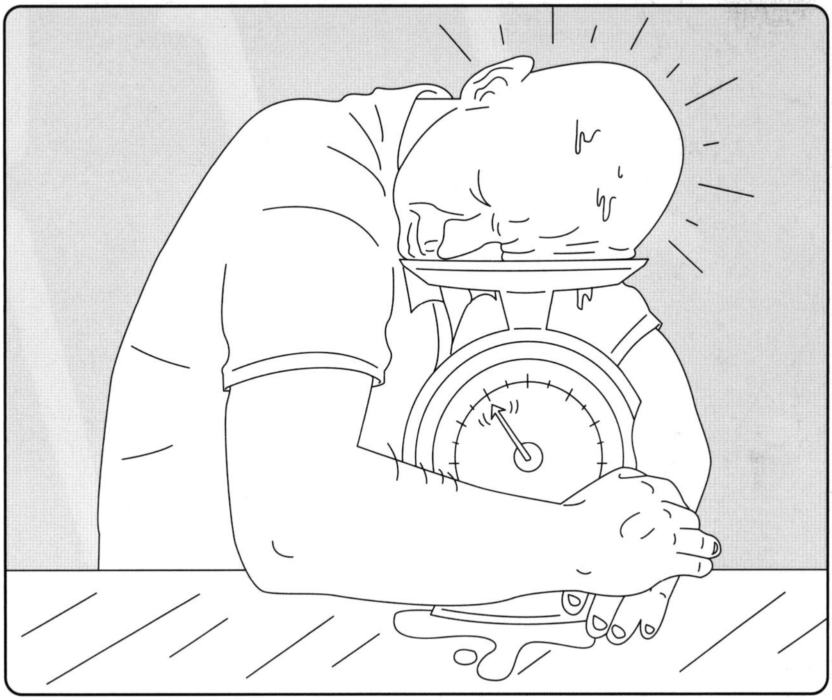

Additionally you will need to weigh your head to determine and track brain weight—a typical electronic brain scale will work. Just shave your head and eyebrows to get the most accurate reading, then place head on brain scale.

TAKE NOTE OF YOUR BRAIN WEIGHT AND WRITE THAT NUMBER HERE. FYI YOUR BRAIN IS GOING TO GET HUGE:

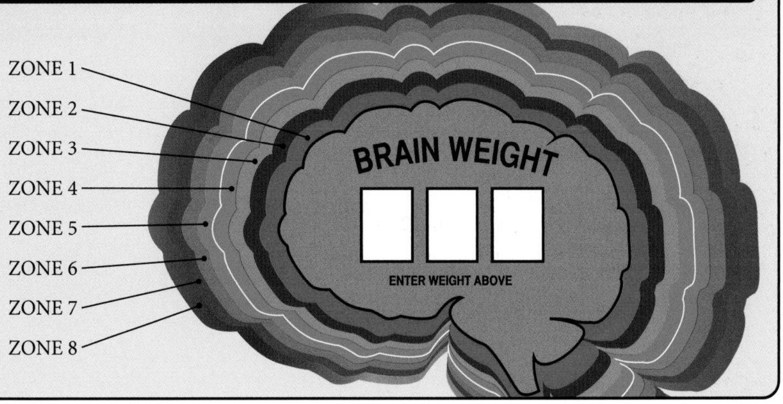

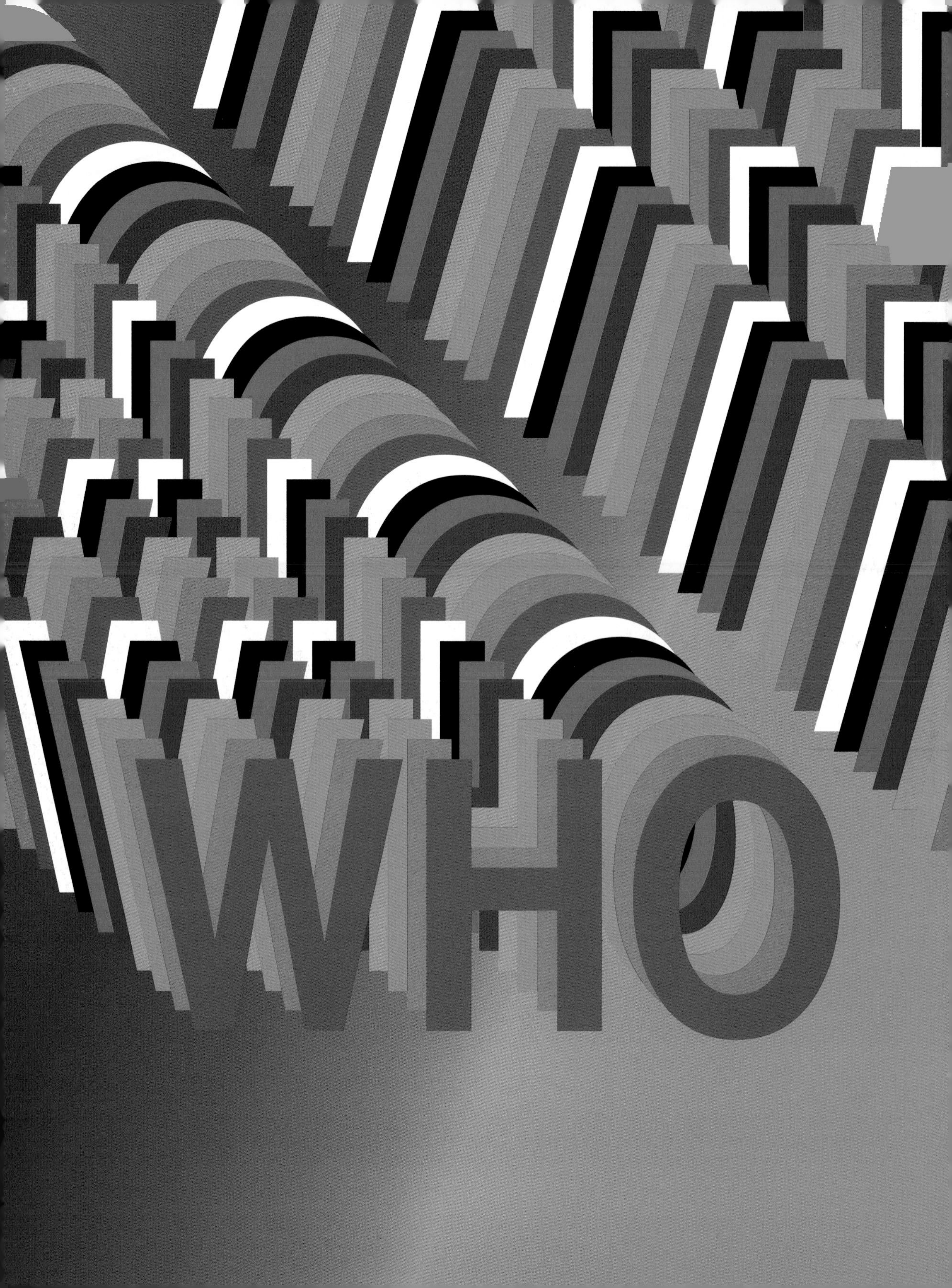
WHO

AM I?

ZONE THEORY™ GENESIS

"AHHHHHHHHHHHHHHHHHHH!"—You
I know—you are already saying—

"WHAAAAAAA?"

What is this? What is ***ZONE THEORY***™? Where did this new and brave set of ideas come from? How come I'm just hearing about it now? The following lecture recorded and transcribed will answer your questions about the Genesis of ***ZONE THEORY***™…

[The following conversation took place at the Plumous Auditorium in front of three thousand people on October 9, 2011.]

TIM: Good evening.

ERIC: Hi. Hello, how are you all!

TIM: Thank you! Please sit.
[Several minutes of uninterrupted applause, cheering…syncopated foot stomping and "Tim and Eric" chanting.]

TIM: Thank you. That's enough. Please sit.
[The cheering continues…the cheering almost picks up in intensity…it's insanity.]

ERIC: We can't start unless we get some order in here!
[After several minutes the cheering FINALLY calms down and people sit.]

TIM: Ain't you sweet!

ERIC: It means the world to us that you are here tonight!

TIM: Tonight we want to talk to you about the ***ZONE THEORY***™.

ERIC: The ***ZONE THEORY***™ is about to transform the way you think about yourself and the world around you.

TIM: But first, a little backstory:
[The room goes dark—lasers and high-energy techno music blare—it's an unmistakably great moment. Glitter and confetti drop from the ceiling. The room FREAKS!]

ERIC: As you know, Tim and I began making viral hit videos for the 'net—we used a combination of surrealism, gross-out comedy and just plain silliness to build a loyal fan base. Hollywood perked up and said, "oh yes please."

TIM: We transferred and evolved our skills and expanded our brand to create several award-winning hit TV shows for basic cable.
[The entire room at once, as if rehearsed goes, "HOY!"]

ERIC: We conquered the world—we appeared on talk shows like *Jimmy Feldman* and *Jimmy Kiss* and toured the world—as well as Australia…
[Eric high-fives Tim and both spin and leapfrog each other. It's something to see!]

TIM: But we were left with a void. Somehow all the fame and glory didn't fill the massive black hole in our heart and soul. It was a dark period full of doubt and pain. I recall one week where I couldn't get out of bed.

ERIC: Ooooh behave!
[The audience laughs for about a full minute.]

TIM: Alright, OK. I get it, very funny.

ERIC: Of course we joke but this is serious stuff.

TIM: Absolutely. Like I said, we were down but we had to keep working. We created a number of popular television shows like *Silly's Good Time Hour*, *Brad Garrett Is Watching You*, and *Tuff Pup*, but for the first time creating art and entertainment felt like a chore, a job. There was no question about it—we were in a rut.

ERIC: Then we met—Ba'hee Nodaramoo Priss Dimmie!
[The crowd chants in unison: "Ba'hee Nodaramoo Priss Dimmie."]

TIM: And everything changed. It's actually a funny story. Eric and I were down in Baja for a cigarette boat competition. The conditions were perfect and my boat had just been serviced so I was eager to take it on the water and see how fast I could go!

ERIC: My boat was not in the best shape, so I was very nervous to race against Tim. I remember kicking myself: "Why didn't you get your boat serviced before the race?!!!"

TIM: Well we raced—just the two of us—and Eric beat my pants off. It was just one of those moments where you can see the paradigm shift happening in real time: how did the unserviced cigarette boat beat the newly serviced one? It's a question that, later over eggs and wine, we couldn't get over—was this a sign? Could we rethink our own way of doing things to the point where we are truly achieving our goals and having fun at the same time?

ERIC: I think we stared at each other silently for over two hours.

TIM: It was weird. And wild! Walking back to the hotel along the shoreline we kept thinking—who are we? What are we doing? What CAN we do? I think at some point I suggested Eric should just become a professional cigarette boat racer—he was THAT good!

ERIC: Vroom!
[Eric simulates the motions of a cigarette boat race, lapping around Tim. The audience remains reverently silent during the 25-minute mime.]

TIM: Just then, as we walked under the full moon, a shape formed about 20 yards out into the ocean. It was a body. It was a man! This man walked out towards us. As he got closer we saw him more clearly... He was very, very small and round, like a turkey. He had no hair and was wearing a black rubber shirt. Once on the sand, he would walk a few steps then roll on the ground, get up and repeat. Eric and I stopped and watched. It was fascinating.

ERIC: This wonderful man stopped about 3 feet in front of us and smiled.

TIM: It was a smile bigger than the sun itself!
[The audience spontaneously erupts in a half-hour-long standing ovation. Tim and Eric take this time to use the bathroom. Tim returns to the stage earlier than Eric (having only gone number 1].

ERIC: Now where were we?

TIM: The smile. This man smiled. It's all he did. It's all he HAD to do. He warmed our hearts with his smile and then gazed into our eyes for what seemed to be an eternity.

ERIC: It was several hours.

TIM: The sun began to come up and finally I managed to clear my throat and try to put some words together:
[The lights dim—GIANT marionettes of Tim, Eric and the turkey man descend from the rafters. Tim and Eric leave the stage.]

TIM (Marionette): Who… Are you?

TURKEY MAN (Marionette): I am Ba'hee Nodaramoo Priss Dimmie!
[The crowd repeats: Ba'hee Nodaramoo Priss Dimmie! The marionettes ascend back up into the rafters. Tim and Eric return to the stage.]

ERIC: Ba'hee Nodaramoo Priss Dimmie.

TIM: Ba'hee Nodaramoo Priss Dimmie.

ERIC: He's why we're all here today.

TIM: That's right. Ba'hee Nodaramoo Priss Dimmie gave us the tools which we used to build *Tim & Eric's* ***ZONE THEORY***™.

ERIC: Over the next several weeks Tim and I spent every waking hour with Ba'hee Nodaramoo Priss Dimmie in his apartment, learning how to access remote centers of inner strength.

TIM: He taught me the simplest lesson possible and it's one simple sentence that, truthfully, bypasses the entire ***ZONE THEORY***™. I like to think it's the secret to life and the secret to happiness: [redacted]

[Not available in this edition]

ERIC: As valuable as that sentence is, we felt like we could expand on it and create a system to live by—a new code. A ZONE THEORY.

TIM: Now let's talk ***ZONE THEORY***™.

ERIC: Everyone open their ***ZONE THEORY***™ book and skip past the introductions and the transcript of this event.

ZONE TIPS AND TRICKS 1:

GIVE THE SIMPLE GIFT OF LAUGHTER TO A STRANGER: APPROACH SOMEONE WAITING FOR A BUS AND DROP TO THE GROUND AND ROLL AROUND CACKLING AND SNORTING. SEE IF YOU CAN GET INTO SOME TRASH.

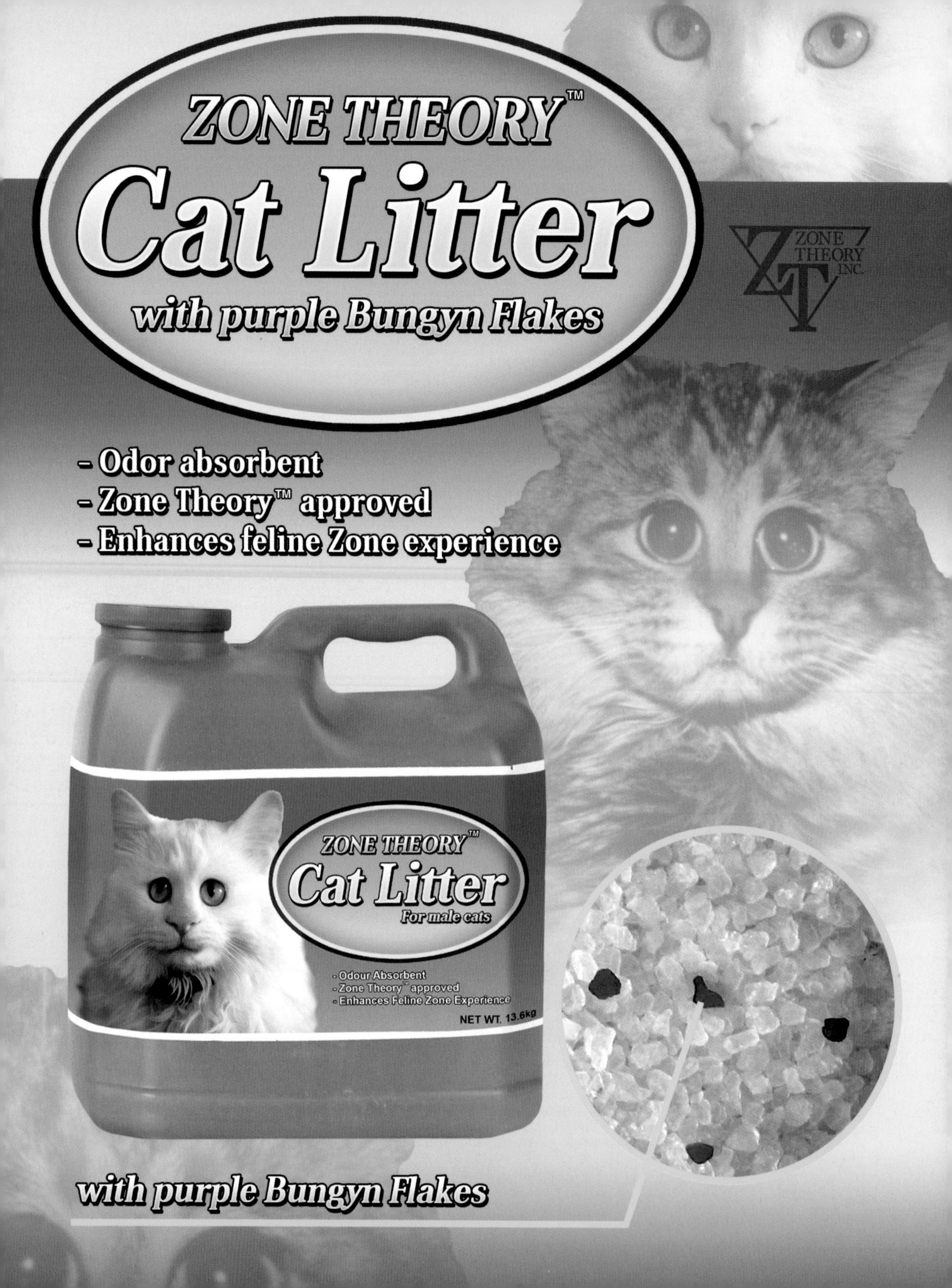
ZONE THEORY™
Cat Litter
with purple Bungyn Flakes
ZONE THEORY INC.
- Odor absorbent
- Zone Theory™ approved
- Enhances feline Zone experience
ZONE THEORY™
Cat Litter
For male cats
- Odour Absorbent
- Zone Theory™ approved
- Enhances Feline Zone Experience
NET WT. 13.6kg
with purple Bungyn Flakes

WHO IS BA'HEE NODARAMOO PRISS DIMMIE?

Nothing is known of Ba'hee Nodaramoo Priss Dimmie aside from the description given by Tim and Eric—as a turkey man. Attempts to locate Ba'hee Nodaramoo Priss Dimmie have failed. There is no further verifiably accurate information at this time.

Zone master Tim Heidecker was recently placed in a trance state and dictated the following potential biography of Ba'hee Nodaramoo Priss Dimmie. This very well may be the true story of Ba'hee Nodaramoo Priss Dimmie. *(as told to Eric Wareheim)*

Zone master Tim Heidecker was recently placed in a Zone Plane 3 trance state—using an official pram guide (aka Eric Wareheim).

[*Eric returns.*]

ERIC: My apologies. I forgot we were doing this.

TIM: You are a bad pram guide.

ERIC: I'm not the best. Where were we?

TIM: I am now speaking with the turkey man and he is telling me about ***ZONE THEORY***™.

ERIC: Good. Now what?

TIM: The turkey man crawled into an oven which had been preheating at 425.

ERIC: OK.

TIM: I take the turkey man out and I baste him and let him set for 30 minutes.

ERIC: He told you to eat him?

TIM: Yes. The turkey man instructed me exactly how to herb and season his body. He even scolded me for not basting properly. But it didn't matter because the time has come for me to bite into that juicy turkey man.

ERIC: Mmm. I'm getting hungry.

TIM: I carved him up and made myself a plate of dark and light meat.

ERIC: The ***ZONE THEORY***™ is inside you.

TIM: Right.

NO FURTHER INFORMATION IS AVAILABLE

THIS LAST YOU WILL

Ba'hee Nodaramoo Priss Dimmie

HE IS NOT ALL THAT! HE JUST INSPIRED THIS WHOLE THING.

NO MORE BA'HEE NODARAMOO PRISS DIMMIE BULLSHIT.

IS THE
TIME
HEAR ABOUT

PART II

THE ZONES

NES
HE ZO

THE YOU ZONE

There is one Zone not listed in the 7 Zone structure.[5]

YOU: WHAAAAAAAAAA?

It's perhaps the most important Zone of them all: The YOU Zone.

[5] There are thousands of Zones that exist beyond and above the 7 listed. We are working hard to identify these Zones and write more self-help books like this one.

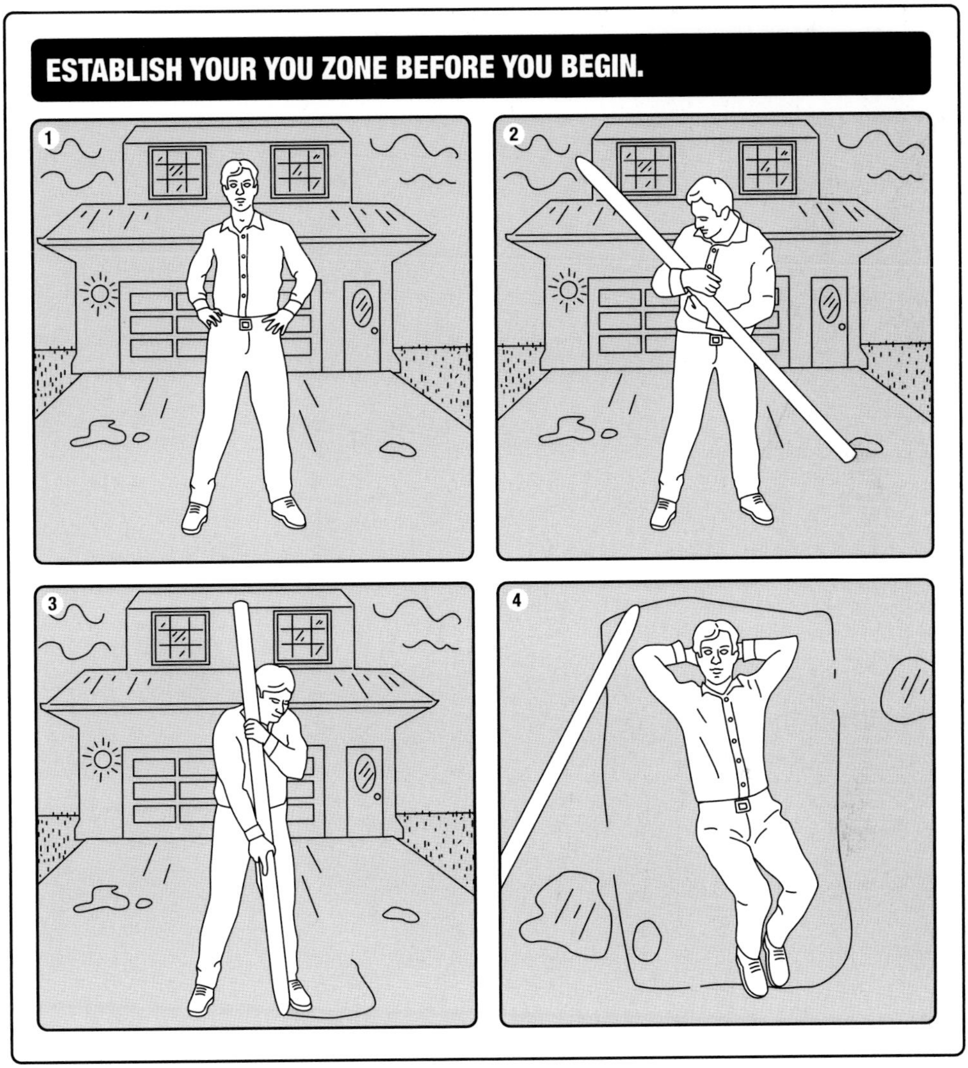

STEP 1. Designate a large area around YOU. (Pavement, driveway or sidewalk is preferable.)

STEP 2. YOU purchase, borrow or obtain a large stick of white chalk.

STEP 3. Draw a box with the chalk around YOU.

STEP 4. CONGRATULATIONS! YOU have just established your YOU Zone!

ACCESSING THE LOW GOD PRIM

Before ascending to Zone Plane 8 YOU must come to terms with the low god Prim. You must access the low god Prim—Accessing the low god Prim can be difficult, painful and sometimes almost impossible. So how can we access the low god Prim?

I know what you're thinking:

YOU FUCKER YOU LIAR YOU PIECE OF SHIT—I DID THE WORK I WANT ZONE PLANE 8 AND NOW YOU TELL ME ABOUT THE LOW GOD PRIM! WHO THE FUCK IS LOW GOD PRIM AND NOW I HAVE TO DEAL WITH HIM??? FUUUUUUUUCK!

READ IN THE MIRROR. UPSIDE DOWN.

[YOU ARE FLIPPING OUT, ROLLING AROUND ON THE GROUND
AND MAKING A SCENE—YOU'VE THROWN THIS BOOK
AGAINST THE WALL AND ARE NOW PISSING ON THE BOOK.]

FUCK YOU!!!

The low god Prim awaits you at the gate before Zone Plane 8!

Honor low god Prim.

Gary Dork

ZONE THEORY™ IS ONLY FOR MEN. SORRY. PLEASE DESTROY BOOK NOW.

ZONE 1
FRIENDSHIP

INT. CHUM'S NUDE RECREATION CENTER

JOE (a heavy, nude man) waits
outside the locker room.
TED (a very short, nude man) approaches.

TED: Are you Joe?

JOE: Yes. Ted?

TED: You got it.

JOE: Great to finally meet you!

TED: You too!

They hug.

JOE: Up for some horseplay?

TED: As long as it's light.
I pulled my back out this morning.

JOE: Ouch! You should get a rubdown.

TED: Yeah—after some
horseplay though.

BEFORE WE ARE EVEN BORN WE HAVE FRIENDS.

"WHAAHAHAHAHAHA?"

THINK ABOUT YOUR FATHER'S SPERM FOR A MOMENT.

Think of his ball sac, swinging in his pants (or shorts). If he is nude and freshly showered, think how the water wets the pubic hair and drips from the red skin. Inside that hairy (now gray?) ball sac, swim thousands of sperms who are in fact (science has proven this) FRIENDS.

One of those sperms was YOU. You actually existed for many, many years before you were born, in the SPERM state—perhaps YOU were known in the sac as Jack—JACK from the sac—Jack loved the sac. It was home. It was where your very best friends lived. You swam together, ate together, loved together and played together. You were a troublemaker with a great sense of humor who didn't exactly follow the rules. Your BEST friends, Brian and Mike, knew you better than anyone and they let you just be you.

It was Heaven in the sac. But one day Brian was swept away when your father, on his way to work, stopped by a gas station and masturbated in the men's room. Did you or Brian know it was coming? The gas station was not an unusual place for Dad to stop—he filled up there once every two weeks. But this was a Tuesday. Why fill up on a Tuesday? Generally Dad filled up on the weekend. Did he pull in to urinate? This didn't make sense as the gas station was only a few minutes from work—couldn't he hold it in? But there he was getting out of the car, heading to the cash register, requesting the key attached to a billy club and heading into the 24th St. Texaco's disgusting men's bathroom. He unzipped his pants and did his business. You and all your friends were just "doing your thing" when suddenly Brian was swept away in a current of semen and other sperm. You shrieked, "Brian! No!" But it was too late. Brian was gone.

EXERCISE - CALL YOUR FATHER NOW AND ASK HIM WHY HE STOPPED BY THAT TEXACO AND MASTURBATED.

Ask him.

And so it's easy to see how important friends have been and continue to be. When we are born, the first people we truly identify with are other babies around us. Our mothers and fathers are frightening to us—doctors and nurses, evil—other aunts, uncles and adults appear to be monsters or aliens from another planet intent on our destruction. Only when babies catch the eye of other babies does some sense of normalcy settle in.

However, later in school, especially in high school, it's natural and normal to have no friends. Often having no friends during that stage can be a sign that you are "ZONE READY" and will take to ***ZONE THEORY***™ faster than someone who had tons of friends in high school and was very popular and well liked.

We are hard at work on ***ZONE THEORY***™ ***FOR CHILDREN***™—which runs in stark contrast to ***ZONE THEORY***™—stop reading now if you are under 10.

Adult friendships are absolutely vital for ***ZONE THEORY***™ to work—it's why we've made friendship Zone 1. It's truly the base which we build everything around.

But do you even know what an adult friendship is? Is it Jason from work? No, probably not. Is it a guy you talk about the sports scores with at the local sports bar? Maybe. Let's explore further and TONE OUR ZONE.

ZONE CERTIFIED "WHAT IS A FRIEND" ACTIVITY QUIZ

You might be saying to yourself right now: "I know a lot of men but who are my friends and who are just men I know?" It's important to identify and categorize those men in your life that qualify as friends. It's also going to be helpful to see who's on the horizon as potential friends. Most of your current friends may be "Discards." It's helpful and advisable to encourage them to become Zone Certified.

Fill out this quiz for every man you know. Ideally you would take this quiz with the person you are testing but in some cases this could be impossible:

IS ______________________________ A FRIEND ?

1) ____________ is Zone Certified. ☐ TRUE ☐ FALSE

2) ____________ is just a man I see on the bus. ☐ TRUE ☐ FALSE

3) ____________ knows all my uncles' names. ☐ TRUE ☐ FALSE

4) ____________ works with me but never ever has made eye contact. ☐ TRUE ☐ FALSE

5) ____________ is not someone I would call if I discovered a rash on my ass. ☐ TRUE ☐ FALSE

6) ____________ is someone I would call if I discovered a rash on my ass. ☐ TRUE ☐ FALSE

7) ____________ is a real friend I can count on during hard times. ☐ TRUE ☐ FALSE

8) ____________ thinks he is all that and doesn't even care if I live or die. ☐ TRUE ☐ FALSE

9) ____________ has a huge CD collection of Rock, Rap and Jazz/Blues. ☐ TRUE ☐ FALSE

10) ____________ likes to party but knows when enough is enough. ☐ TRUE ☐ FALSE

(Did you answer correctly?)

KINDS OF FRIENDS

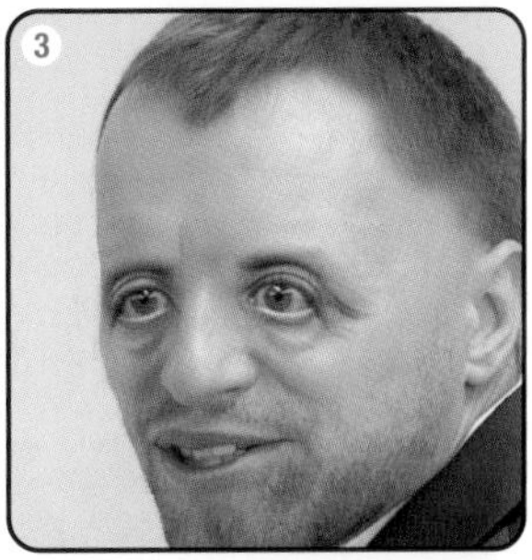

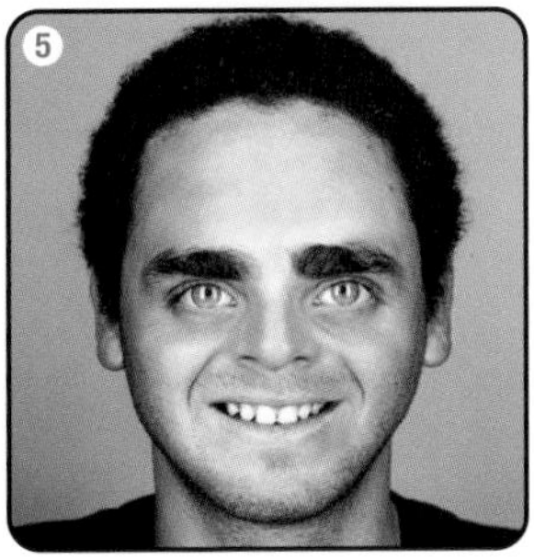

1. Good chum
2. Guy from work
3. Businessman
4. Man from bus
5. Old friend
6. Best friend
7. Internet friend

TIME FOR YOUR BRAIN WEIGHT CHECK-IN!

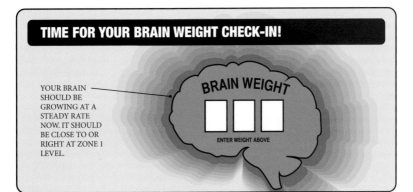

YOUR BRAIN SHOULD BE GROWING AT A STEADY RATE NOW. IT SHOULD BE CLOSE TO OR RIGHT AT ZONE 1 LEVEL.

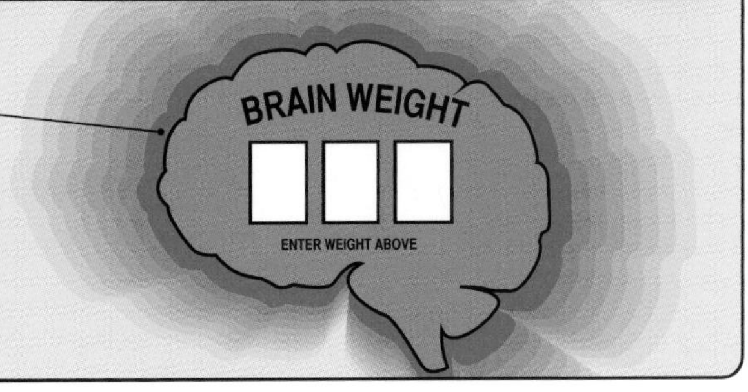

FRIENDSHIP ACTIVITIES

Now that you have identified who your friends are, what the hell are you going to do together? Friendship is not just about having a certificate! The friendship certificate (page 65) is just a piece of paper. It's worthless. It's nothing!

Friendship is about being friends and doing things together that you wouldn't do with anyone else. (Not even your Zone Wife!)

Here are some Zone Certified suggestions and tips for two friends to do together.

ADULT HORSEPLAY

Adult Horseplay is now ranked as the number one friendship activity amongst Zone Plane 8s!

So why aren't you engaging in Adult Horseplay? Adult Horseplay works so well because it is so easy! Anyone can do it! All you have to do is engage in clowning around, shoving, light wrestling, tussling and other roughhousing. What's amazing about Adult Horseplay is that you are in control! There are no rules.

But **WHERE** can two new friends engage in Adult Horseplay? As anyone knows, nude recreation centers have been popping up everywhere! NRCs provide a great meeting place and an ideal place to meet new people who may often become friends![6]

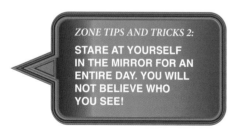

ZONE TIPS AND TRICKS 2:

STARE AT YOURSELF IN THE MIRROR FOR AN ENTIRE DAY. YOU WILL NOT BELIEVE WHO YOU SEE!

[6] Some anonymous nude recreation centers are masked while others are unmasked—however, not all masked nudist centers are anonymous.

EXAMPLES OF HORSEPLAY LEVEL 1

Fist touch

Delicate embrace

Prohibited kick

NUDE RECREATION CENTER
LOCATIONS WORLDWIDE

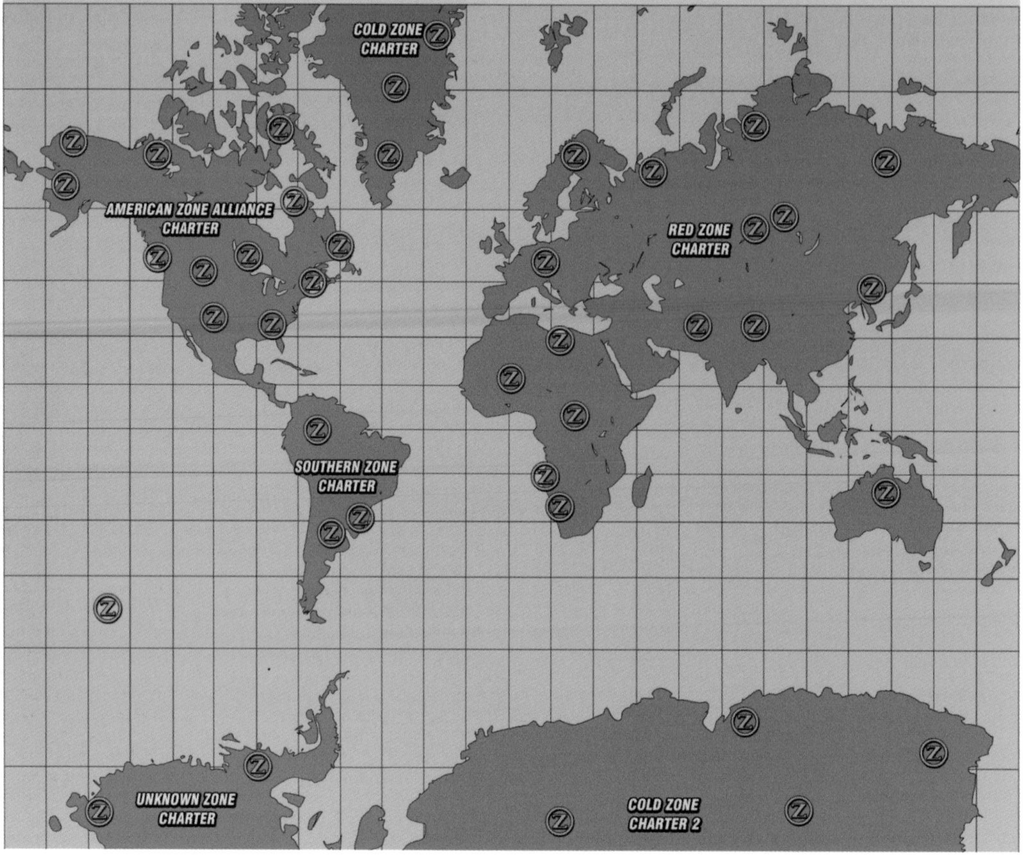

EXERCISE - TAKE OUT A MAP OF YOUR AREA AND IDENTIFY THE CLOSEST NRC TO YOU. AVOID UNLICENSED NRCS—LOOK FOR THE OFFICIAL *ZONE THEORY*™ NRC SEAL BEFORE PROCEEDING.

EXAMPLES OF HORSEPLAY LEVEL 2 *(NUDE/MASKED)*

Light palming

Shoulder tussle

Reverse embrace

E AM
MING
????

WARNING: D[illegible]URN BOOK

UPSIDE DOWN TO READ THIS!

WHER
I CO
FROM

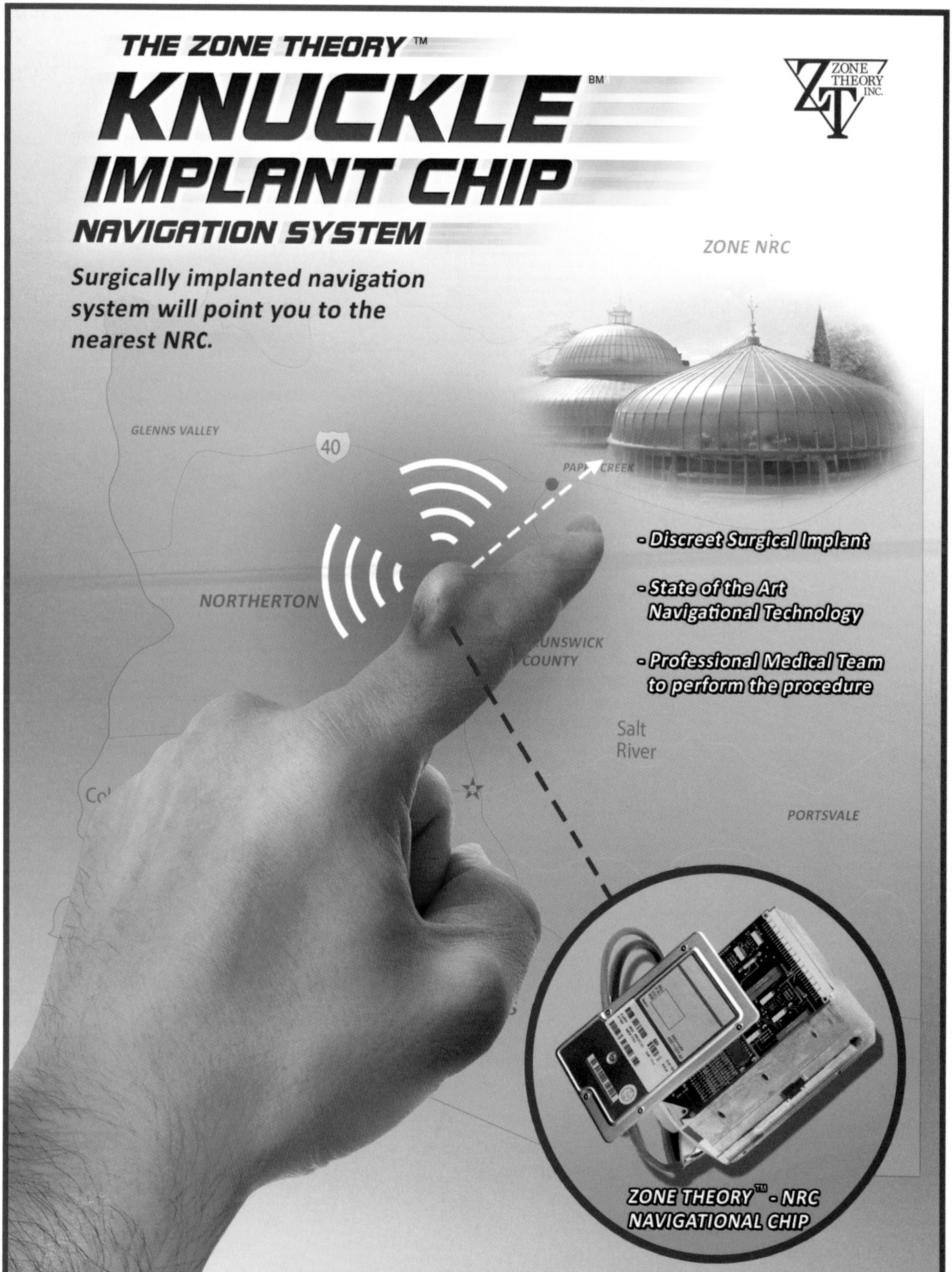
THE ZONE THEORY™
KNUCKLE℠
IMPLANT CHIP
NAVIGATION SYSTEM
ZONE THEORY INC.
Surgically implanted navigation system will point you to the nearest NRC.
ZONE NRC
GLENNS VALLEY
40
NORTHERTON
COUNTY
Salt River
PORTSVALE
- Discreet Surgical Implant
- State of the Art Navigational Technology
- Professional Medical Team to perform the procedure
ZONE THEORY™ - NRC NAVIGATIONAL CHIP

OTHER ACTIVITIES

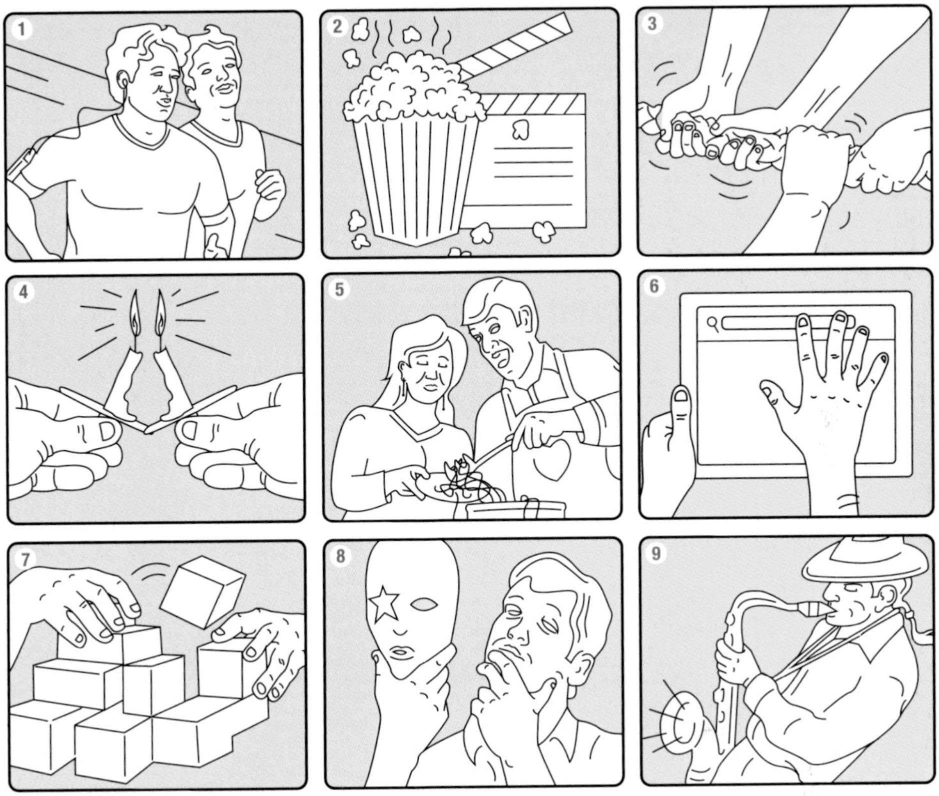

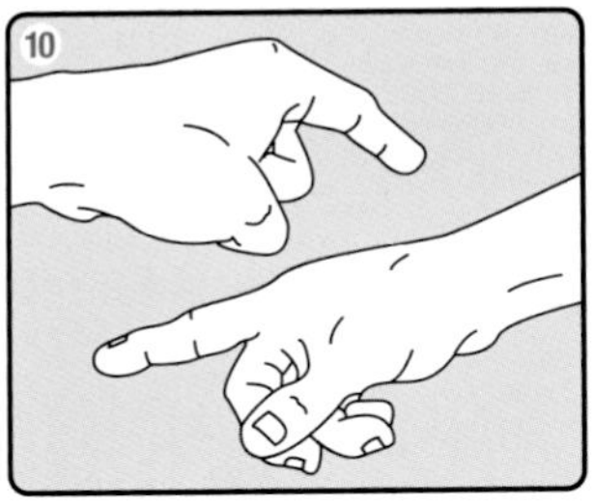

1. Close Jogging
2. Movie Marathons
3. Roping
4. Candling
5. Making Spaghetti
6. Internet Search
7. Blocking
8. Mask Shopping
9. Sax/Trumpet Lessons
10. This and That

Adult Horseplay far and away ranks atop any other friendship activities—but often, due to weather, circumstances and/or nude recreation center closings Adult Horseplay is not practical. The above chart shows some other activities that you can do with a new friend.

MASKED OR NOT MASKED? THE AGE-OLD QUESTION

MASK DECISION

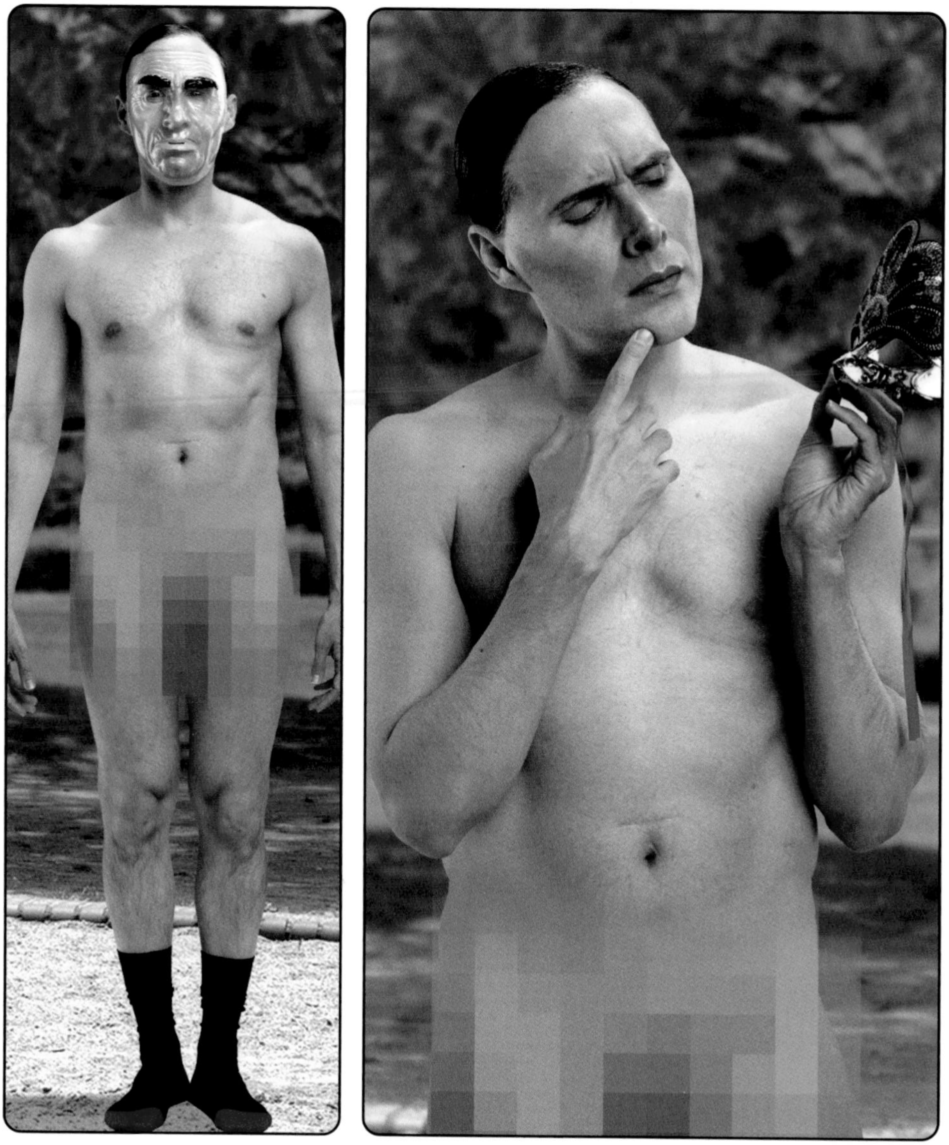

Of course, all people carry and collect masks. They are a great way to disguise ourselves from the people we know, and they are also fun and collecting them can be a rewarding hobby.

But, often, when meeting up with a new friend you might be staring at your mask collection saying: "Do I or do I not wear a mask?" Here's a helpful guide to when it makes sense to wear a mask when meeting up with a new friend:

	YES	NO
Car Wash	☐	☑
Devil Stick Convention	☑	☐
Farmer's Market	☐	☑
Tire Shopping	☑	☐
Ultimate Frisbee	☐	☑
Chip n' Putt	☑	☐
Sun Gazing	☐	☑
Power Surfing (web only)	☑	☐

CUT, FOLD AND PLACE AROUND HOME.

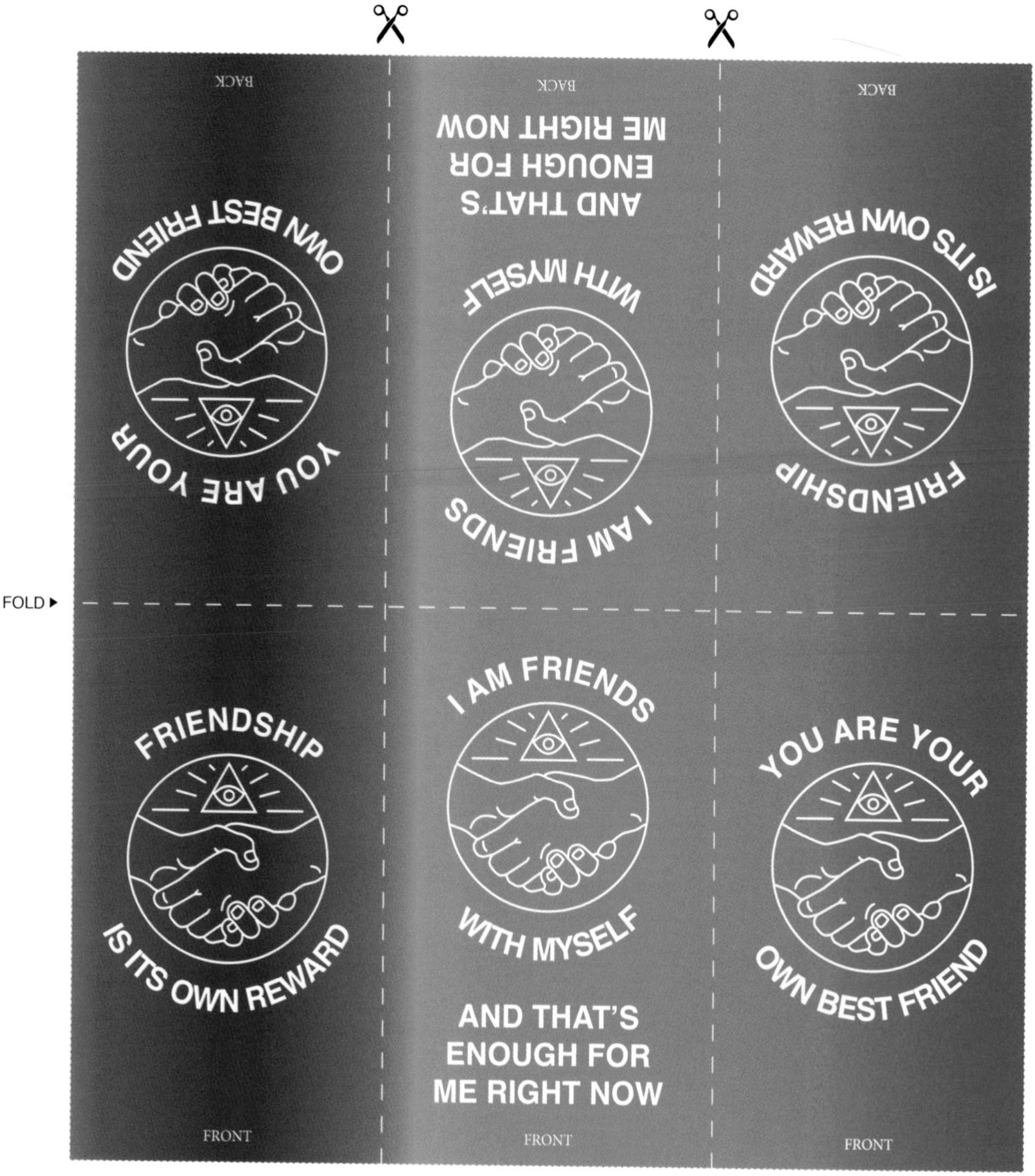

CUT, FOLD AND PLACE AROUND HOME.

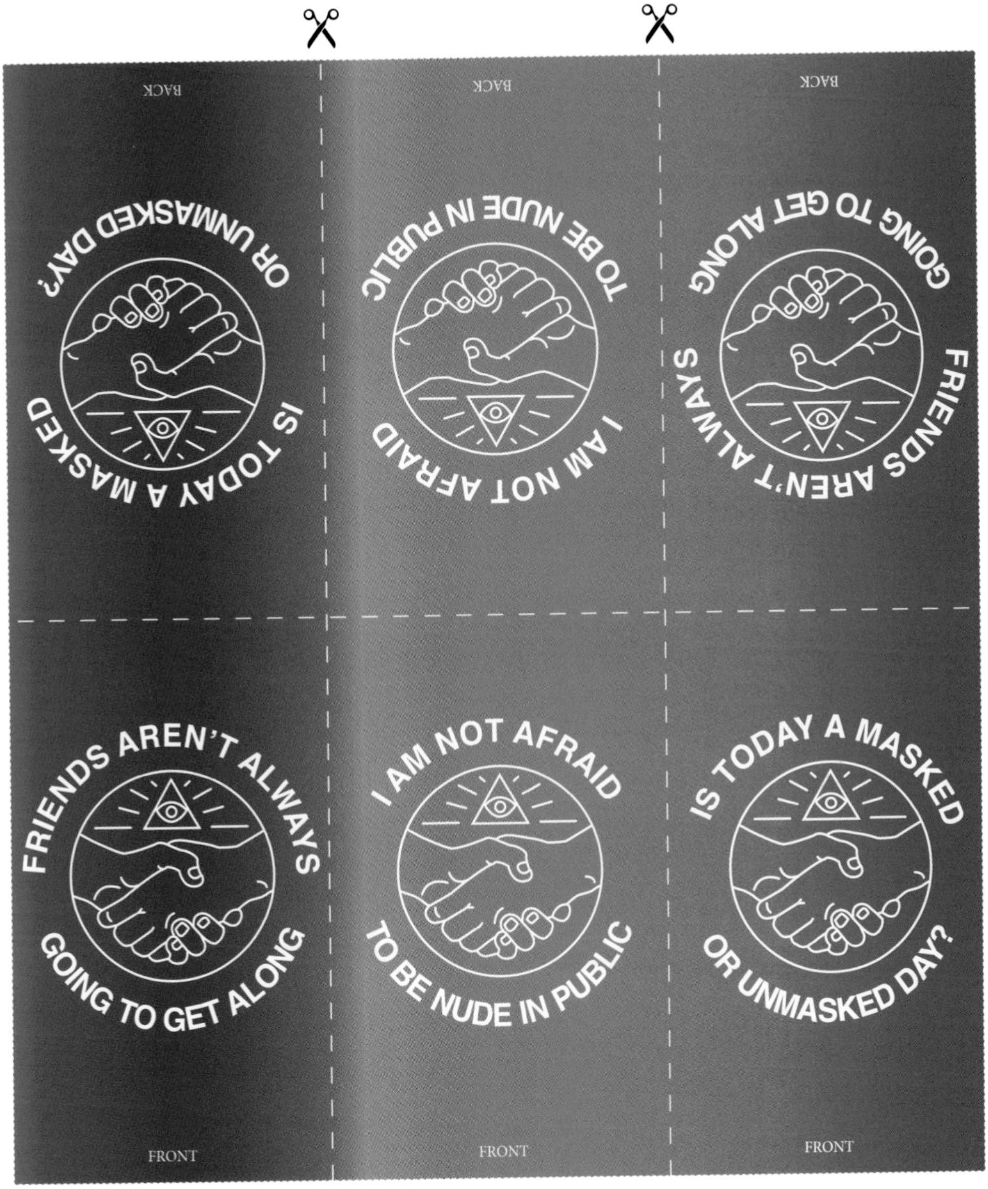

◂FOLD

ENDURING FRIENDSHIPS

There is no friendship bond stronger than the bond between two high-profile people. These friendships in the public eye have proven to be among history's most enduring. Match the well-known person with their lifelong best friend!

A. **MEAT LOAF,** *Rock singer*

B. **BENITO MUSSOLINI,** *Fascist dictator*

C. **CHARLES M. SCHULZ,** *Cartoonist*

D. **TEX WATSON,** *Convicted murderer*

E. **FAMOUS AMOS,** *Cookie impresario*

F. **LIZA MINNELLI,** *Actress/vocalist*

1. **CARLOS SANTANA,** *Rock guitarist*
2. **ADOLF HITLER,** *Fascist dictator*
3. **MICHAEL "KRAMER" RICHARDS,** *Comic legend*
4. **CHARLES MANSON,** *Convicted murderer*
5. **ORVILLE REDENBACHER,** *Popcorn impresario*
6. **DR. CLEAL DEPLUNGGE,** *"Kidney transplant" huckster*

ANSWERS:

A-2 (Loaf/Hitler), B-1 (Mussolini/Santana), C-4 (Schulz/Manson), D-5 (Watson/Redenbacher), E-3 (Amos/Richards), F-6 (Minnelli/DePlungge)

Are you a
ZONE THEORY™ REWARDS
member?
10,000 POINTS Local Judge
6,000 POINTS Policemen
3,200 POINTS Employer
2,600 POINTS Pets
2,500 POINTS Grandparents
2,000 POINTS Cousins
1,500 POINTS Acquaintances
1,000 POINTS Neighbors
Finally a pyramid scheme that works!
Inform your friends and family about
THE ZONE THEORY™
and become a part of the
ZONE THEORY™ REWARDS system.

QUIK QUIZ 2

Which of these 9 men might become **YOUR** friend?

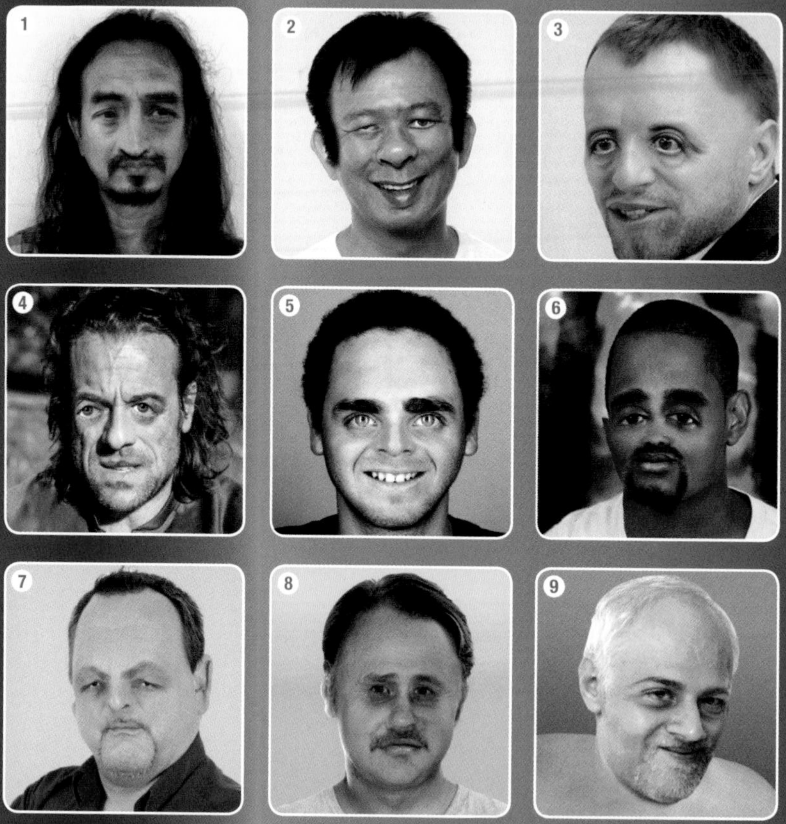

QUIZ 2 ANSWERS: 1, 2, 4, 5, and 6.

CUT HERE AND FRAME FOR DISPLAY

Certificate of Friendship

THE ZONE THEORY™

OFFICE OF NOTARY COMMISSIONS AND AUTHENTICATIONS

THIS IS TO CERTIFY THAT ________________

IS NOW THE OFFICIAL ZONE BEST FRIEND OF ________________

ISSUED ON THE DAY OF ____________

________________________ TIM HEIDECKER, ZONE THEORY™ FOUNDER

________________________ ERIC WAREHEIM, ZONE THEORY™ FOUNDER

THIS DOCUMENT IS INVALID WITHOUT PERSONAL ZONE SIGNATURES OF FOUNDERS TIM HEIDECKER AND ERIC WAREHEIM.

CUT HERE AND FRAME FOR DISPLAY

ZONE THEORY • SEAL OF APPROVAL •

FRIENDSHIP WORKSHEET

(Tear out and make 20 copies—or one for each friend)

Name of Friend: ____

Date of Certification of Friendship: ________________________________

Category of Friend *(circle one)*

Man from Bus   Best Friend   Close Friend   Acquaintance

Not Great   Bus Driver   Guy I Know but Don't Like

Convenience Store Employee   Luke   Hobo   Priest   Mando Man

Activities Completed: ____

____

____

____

Notes:____

____

____

____

CALCULATE YOUR ZONE SCORE NOW

	FRIENDSHIP
X	**FAMILY**
X	**BUSINESS**
X	**LOVE**
X	**HEALTH**
X	**POEMS**
X	**FOOD**
	TOTAL

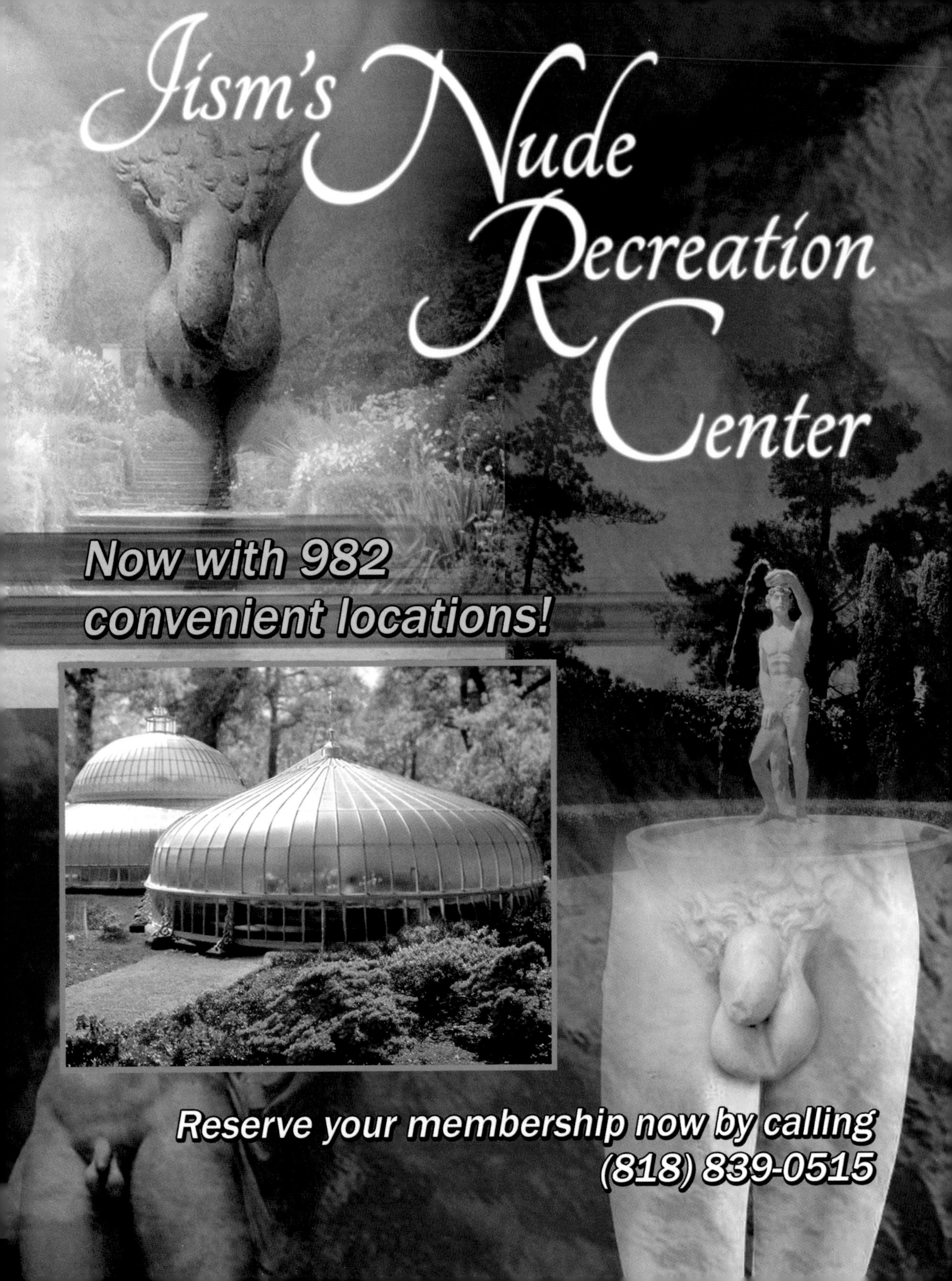
Jism's Nude Recreation Center
Now with 982 convenient locations!
Reserve your membership now by calling
(818) 839-0515

TIM ON FRIENDSHIP

Honestly my best friend is Eric Wareheim. We've known each other for over 20 years! We are very different, always have been, but when push comes to shove I know I can count on Eric. He's always been there for me, during the great times like my first mass marriage to Chinga, Donna, Domaine and Min and the births of my 11 children, to my gold medal weight lifting ceremony where I deadlifted 500 lbs...)

Eric was there.

And during the dark pre–***ZONE THEORY***™ days: days of confusion, sadness, drug abuse, nineteen suicide attempts… The day my mass marriage fell apart:

Eric was there.

Eric was there. He was there through it all. He was right behind me, literally holding me and guiding me—pointing me in the right directions, being a constant source of inspiration. He is a holy, holy man full of grace, commitment, poise and fortitude. He is my rock, my shining knight on the hill.

We spend our time together in a variety of ways: horseplay, watching movies, taking long drives and talking about "The World." We share CDs, go for horsey rides and collect trains together. There's almost nothing we DON'T do together. Sometimes I think my Zone Wife J'hasi gets jealous of the close bond Eric and I have.

Last year Eric and I did something very special together. We named a star together through the national star registry. Good old NSHF-359358 is now officially "Tim and Eric are Best Friends." Think about that the next time you are looking up into the heavens. ;)

ERIC ON FRIENDSHIP

Josh is number one on my speed dial. I just hold down the number one on my handset and it calls Josh like magic. I call Josh just about every night and we talk and talk. Sometimes my ear hurts from talking with Josh for so long. Once we talked all night and watched the sunrise together. As a ***ZONE THEORY***™ advance exercise (not available in this edition) I made a list of the friends I value most. What's interesting about this exercise is you can include people more than once if they are really important to you. Here's a sneak peek at that very list:

1. Josh
2. Josh
3. Josh
4. Josh
5. Josh
6. Josh
7. Josh
8. Tim Heidecker
9. Abe Klingman

But Josh wasn't ALWAYS my best friend: When I first met Josh I thought he was a filthy young hobo. I said, "Get away from me you disgusting begger boy." And I kicked some dirt and trash on him. He said, "I'm not a beggar boy. I'm just a man waiting for the bus. Get away from me." Just because he was a small man didn't make him a dirty beggar boy. I learned a very important life lesson that day and also made a best friend. I lifted him up into my arms, twirled him around and apologized. I said, "I am a Zone master. You are safe now." He replied with, "I'm Josh."

ZONE 2
FAMILY

INT. BACKYARD

Some fat and sad bald blob burns burgers on a small charcoal grill. A boy bounces a ball against a wooden fence.

BLOB: HEY, STOP THAT! You'll ruin the fence!

BOY: I was only trying to have fun.

BLOB: I'm your father and you listen to what I say.

BOY: Yes, Father.

BLOB: Now come over here and sit at this dirty picnic table.

The boy sits down and the blob throws down a blackened hamburger in front of the boy.

BOY: This is burnt.

BLOB: Meat is meat. Now shut up and eat!

THERE IS NOTHING MORE IMPORTANT than family, therefore it's the most important Zone and that's why it is listed second. Who are your family? Where did your family come from? Most families came from Europe and landed in America on steam ships that sailed into Ellis Island. They settled here in America but brought over their time-tested recipes for classic meals like a nice stromboli and pasta fagioli—ooh it's a pooosta marainaria. Ooh that's a nice sauce for the sphaghootie you gotta add a lil gravy to the noodle. Oooh....

Many people relate to the experience of growing up in a family of faceless strangers. You look at the cast of jokers around you: "Uncle Robert, Cousin Roy, Aunt Nancy..." Who are these rats, these thieves? Not related to me, I hope. Maybe I was adopted, maybe I was sent down the river like Moses, a Jew boy, and taken in by the Pharaohs?

Remember family vacations? What was the point? 12 people crammed into a station wagon with NO air-conditioning—drive 48 hours just to show up and camp at some dirty, overcrowded, polluted lake? And then what? Rent a canoe and sit out in the baking sun and get a sunburn and later get sick from your mother's spoiled potato salad? You'd rather be locked in a closet with bees!

What about the holidays? Oh, what am I gonna get from Aunt Joan? Another fucking sweater? I didn't like the sweater you got me last year so why the FUCK should I expect to like it THIS YEAR??? And Grandma's DRY turkey—about as dry as her vagina. Hey, Grandma—how about a fucking ladle of gravy for God's sake?! What is this, the Mojave Desert?

Alternately, some have the experience of growing up in a loving, supportive environment where their parents legitimately seem to care for them. These people are rare and are not suitable for ***ZONE THEORY***™. Everything always works out for them anyways.

Your family is most likely a gigantic weight that you carry around your neck—an anchor that keeps you back from being YOURSELF! Your family is nothing but a collection of "Discards" who are a waste—they DRAIN YOU!!!! ***ZONE THEORY***™ believes in separating and disassociating from your family and building a NEW family. A ZONE FAMILY.

But first you must identify who your family is—and we need to look deeper into how you became a part of your family. ***LET'S...***

TONE THE ZONE.

What do we do with Discards? What can be done with Discards under the law? Your family belongs in plastic garbage bags, don't they? Look at them, don't you wish they were dead? Can you murder them "under the law"? Yes. But not at the Zone Plane you are at right now. Patience. Murder is coming.

(Fuck them)

ZONE THEORY™ CONCEPTION REENACTMENT EXERCISE (C.R.E.)

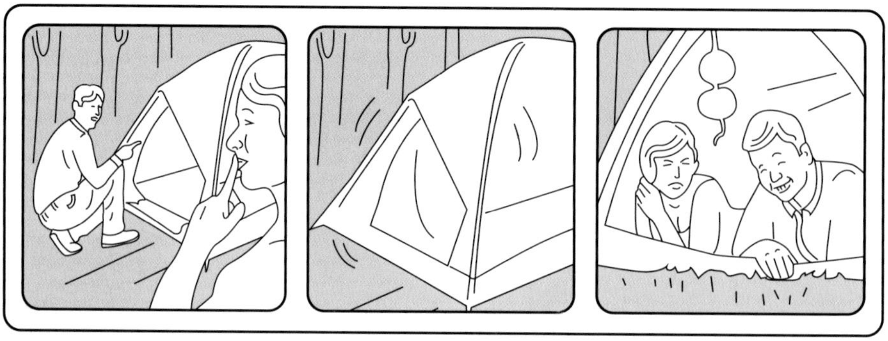

Before you can investigate and understand who your family is you have to go back to the source of it all and learn about your own conception. It's a fun and easy exercise which we will guide you through now:

STEP ONE: Find out who conceived you. Most likely it is your mother and father—but there is a very, very, very small chance that you are either:

a) Adopted

b) A bastard

c) A test-tube baby

If you identify with either A, B or C, unfortunately ***ZONE THEORY***™ is not designed for you. Please destroy this book now.

STEP TWO: Extract as much information from your mother and father about the details of the conception as you can. Ask them where the sex act took place. What time of day was it? What music or sounds were playing in the background? Ask them to sketch a cartoon of the event.

STEP THREE: Gather and organize the details of the conception and build a screenplay[7] from your research. Be sure to make it rich in detail—don't just throw something together—make it a rich reading experience.

STEP FOUR: Time to crew up! Now that you have a working screenplay you'll need to find and hire a crew of talented people to bring your script to life. Key positions are:

a) Cinematographer (Director of Photography)
b) Production Designer
c) Costume Designer
d) Hair and Makeup
e) Location Manager
f) Casting Director
g) Various Other Crew Departments

Your crew will help you find a stage or location, cast with actors, light and film the scene, and finally edit together and arrange for a screening. Your crew will work hard and they should be paid and fed well. This isn't a charity exercise for them.

STEP FIVE: Work with your Zone Certified casting director to find the perfect actors to play Mom and Dad. They must look exactly like your parents. Many actors are comfortable performing sex acts on camera so finding the right match should be easy.

STEP SIX: Showtime! It's your directorial debut! It's your script. It's your story. It's the story of YOU and how you came to BE! Work hard and stay focused but enjoy it. Directing your Conception Reenactment is a once in a lifetime experience and you should really try to be IN the moment.

STEP SEVEN: Now that you've edited, color corrected and sound mixed your Conception Reenactment, it's time to screen it! But your Conception Reenactment is only for you! Throw a small premiere party in your den or basement. Guest list: One. You.

Now simply watch your Conception Reenactment video seven times a day for seven weeks. And the Conception Reenactment Exercise will be complete.

FAQ

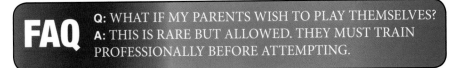

Q: WHAT IF MY PARENTS WISH TO PLAY THEMSELVES?
A: THIS IS RARE BUT ALLOWED. THEY MUST TRAIN PROFESSIONALLY BEFORE ATTEMPTING.

---

[7] ***ZONE THEORY***™ highly recommends taking a screen writing class before beginning. It's important to know and understand story structure and screenplay formatting before attempting to write a screenplay. Many community colleges offer these sorts of courses—you can also investigate taking an "online" course.

IDENTIFYING YOUR E.B.F.s (EXTENDED BIOLOGICAL FAMILY)

Your family is not just Mom and Dad. Did you think that was all your family was? Return to your ***ZONE THEORY***™ Mirror and honestly answer that question. If you answered "yes" you must perform a Level 2 G'hor Hoo procedure on yourself.

YES =

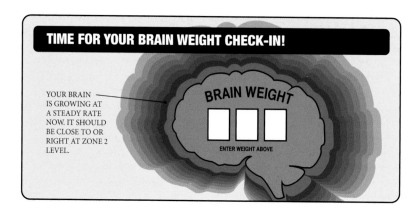

TIME FOR YOUR BRAIN WEIGHT CHECK-IN!

YOUR BRAIN IS GROWING AT A STEADY RATE NOW. IT SHOULD BE CLOSE TO OR RIGHT AT ZONE 2 LEVEL.

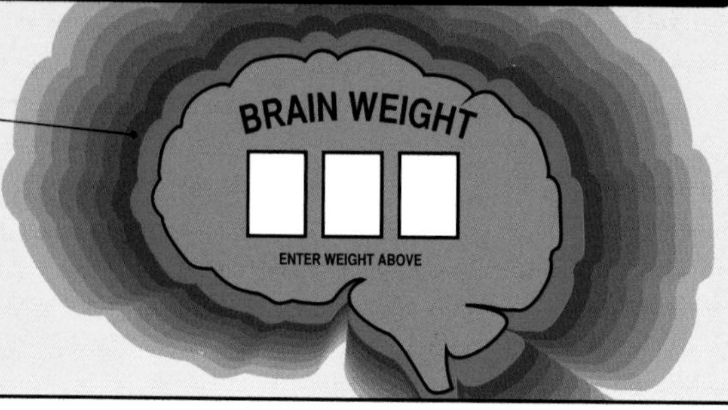

LEVEL 2 G'HOR HOO

STEP 1. Awake at sunrise, stare into your **ZONE THEORY™** Mirror and fully shave your body from head to toe.

STEP 2. Fill bathtub with shards of glass from broken bottles or windowpanes.

STEP 3. Carefully sit down into tub.

STEP 4. Repeat following phrase: "I am a trash boy" until sundown or until you lose consciousness.

You must identify your E.B.F.s—collect them in one place as to identify them correctly. There is only one Zone Approved way to do this:

THE ZONE CERTIFIED FAMILY REUNION SCAM

A family reunion is the perfect way to deceive your extended family into having them all meet up at one place. They'll expect you will provide food and drinks and games to play. They'll have no idea they are stepping right into your trap.

Secure a location for the family reunion (fire hall, convention center, park) and have your mom gather all the email addresses of your grandparents, aunts, uncles, brothers and sisters. Now send a group email using your email software. The email should read something like this:

FAMILY REUNION!

You Jones
to: family

Hello. You are invited to the JONES Family Reunion. I will provide food drinks and games to play. You are required to attend this family reunion.

JONES FAMILY REUNION
2-3 PM
ANYTOWN FIRE HALL
1234 Main St. USA

Signed,

You Jones

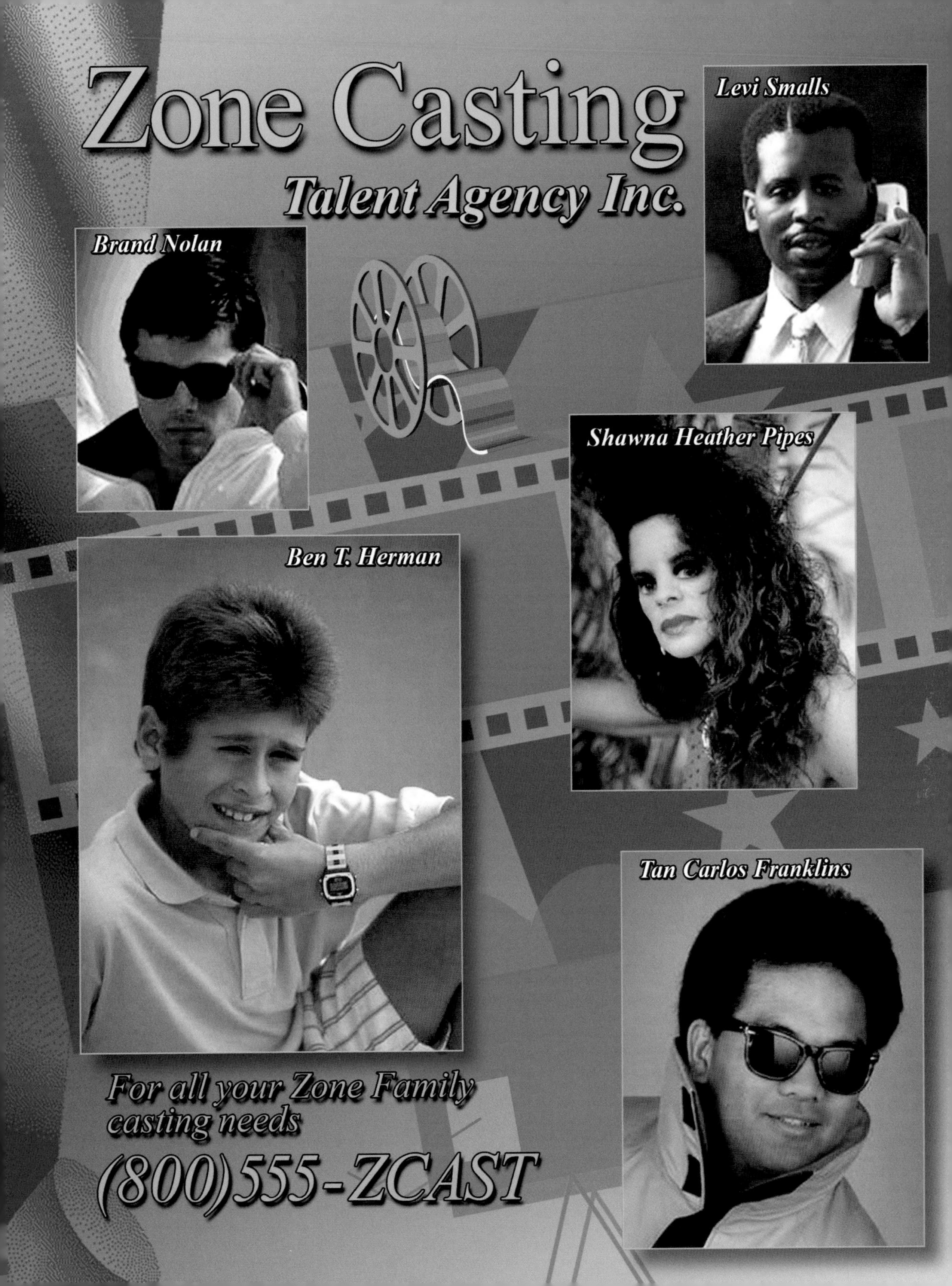
Zone Casting
Talent Agency Inc.
Levi Smalls
Brand Nolan
Shawna Heather Pipes
Ben T. Herman
Tan Carlos Franklins
For all your Zone Family casting needs
(800)555-ZCAST

THE BIG DAY IS HERE. FAMILY REUNION DAY.

When people enter the fire hall the first thing you need to do is insist they fill out the following form.

NAME: ______________________________

ZONE CERTIFIED? ☐ **YES** ☐ **NO**

BLOOD TYPE: ______________________________

EMAIL ADDRESS: ______________________________

MAILING ADDRESS: ______________________________

HOURS OF THE DAY WHEN
YOU ARE GENERALLY NOT HOME: ______________________________

(Send in these completed cards to your nearest Zone Center.)

This will be helpful in determining who are "Discards" and who are "Zone Certified." Anyone who fills out "Zone Certified" should know what's coming and will quietly hang back and watch as the madness unfolds.

FOOD AND DRINKS

Don't worry about actually getting food and drinks… Certainly when people arrive at the family reunion they will be asking: "Where are the food and drinks?" Tell them:

"There was a terrible traffic accident; there are many dead and the driver with the food and drinks may be responsible for the accident. He is talking to highway investigators as we speak and is reporting back to me. Seems like he could be tied up for the rest of the afternoon though."

Your family will understand and will feel guilty for even asking.

GAMES

Now you can skip right to the games. You offer to go first in suggesting games. You suggest "Talent Show" and offer to perform first. Go up to the stage with your acoustic guitar[8] and perform the following song:

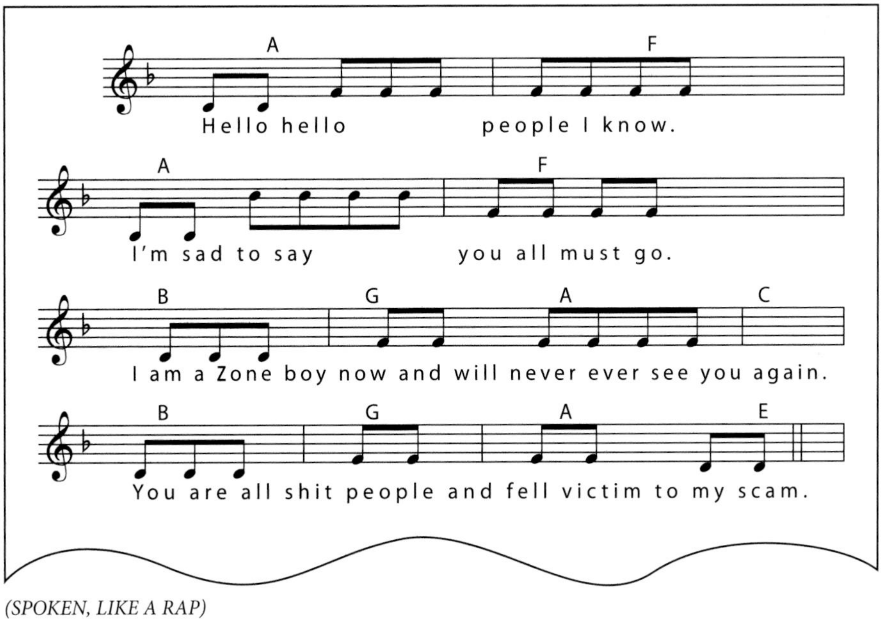

(SPOKEN, LIKE A RAP)

IF YOU ARE A MAN AND WANT TO BE ZONE CERTIFIED PLEASE STICK AROUND AND I CAN TELL YOU ABOUT ORDERING THE *ZONE THEORY*™ BOOK.

Wait until you see them all drop their jaws! Whoooo! They will scurry for the exit, cursing your name, but who cares, you delivered the message: Message received, family. Bye, bye! Disconnected for good. Bye!

[8] Can't play guitar? Destroy book now.

C O N G R A T U

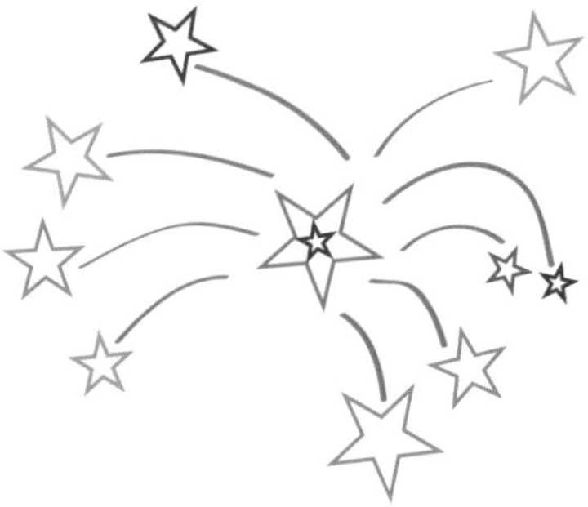

L
A
T
I
O
N
S
!

YOU DID IT! YOU ARE NO LONGER CONNECTED IN ANY WAY TO YOUR BIOS (BIOLOGICAL FAMILY) OR YOUR E.B.F.!

YOU ARE THE CHAMPION!

YOU REALLY ROCK.

WE WISH WE COULD GIVE YOU A HIGH FIVE.

YEA!

DOESN'T IT FEEL GREAT!?

HOW TO TALK TO YOUR DAD ABOUT THE *ZONE THEORY*™

Now that you have completely disassociated yourself from your family it's time to break the news to your dad:

Here is a sample of how the call to your father on the phone might go:

SON: Hi, Dad?
DAD: Go ahead, son.
SON: I am part of the ***ZONE THEORY***™.
DAD: Fine.
SON: Which means we are no longer related. I must find my Zone Father. He will be my True Dad.
DAD: Fine. Here's Mom.

END

HOW DO YOU FEEL? ______________________________
____
____
____

Hopefully you feel freed of the weight of family! That anchor around your neck is gone!

YOU ARE FREE!!

Now it's time to:

BUILD YOUR ZONE FAMILY FROM SCRATCH
A typical Zone Family tree should look something like this:

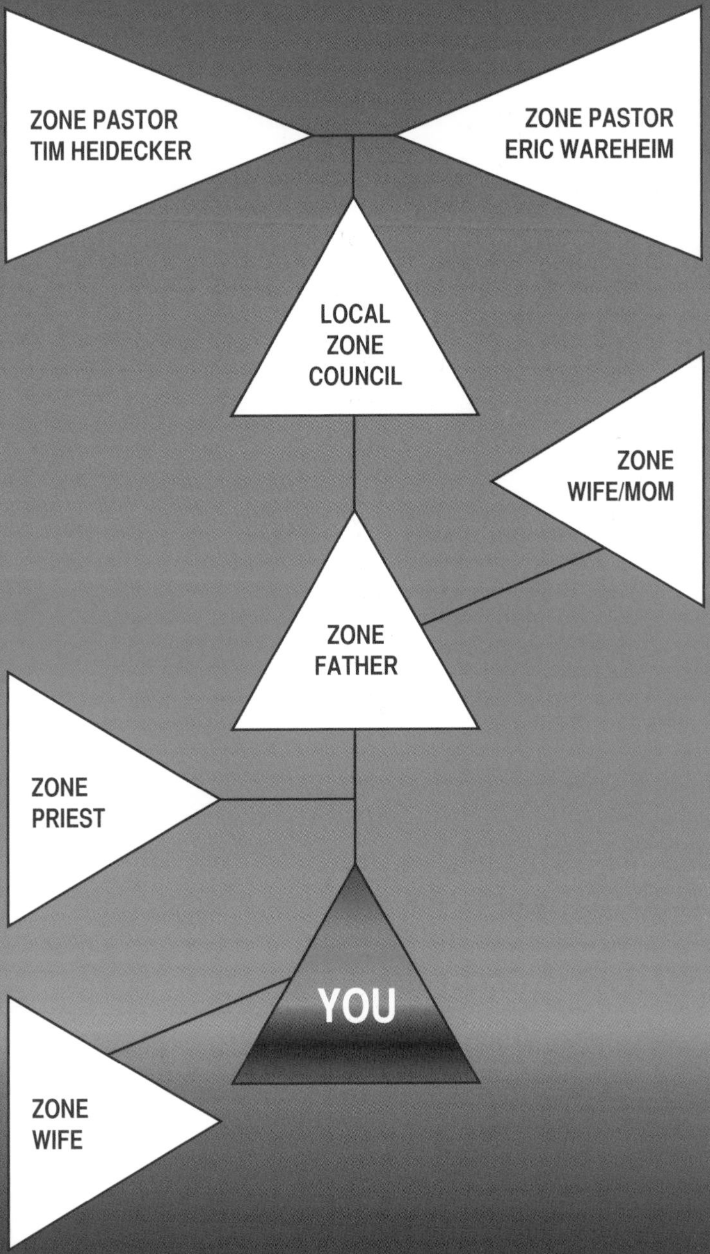

Locate your closest *ZONE CENTER*[9] to begin building your Zone Family. If you do not live within 3 miles of an official *ZONE CENTER*—**PLEASE DESTROY BOOK AND STOP PURSUING *ZONE THEORY*™.**

[9] No Zone Centers have been established yet.

FINDING YOUR ZONE FATHER

Your Zone Father will become the most important person in your life. It's a complicated relationship that often disguises itself as a friendship or business partnership. But for the sake of simplicity and Zone clarity, ***ZONE THEORY***™ identifies this man in your life as your Zone Father.

What is a Zone Father and how can you find the Zone Father that's right for you?

A Zone Father is a man between the ages of 50 and 90 who MUST have white hair! He will guide you through the most difficult moments in your life with a calm, guiding wisdom that enriches your life experiences and helps you understand the world around you. He is a full-time replacement for your now discarded biological dad so he will be present for all holidays, Zone Family get-togethers… He may even get to attend your funeral!

Imagine watching the big game with your Z.F.! You're both rooting for the same team so the thrill when Batter X hits the go ahead run? There's nothing on Earth like it. You turn to him and embrace him. "I love you, Zone Father." He looks at you and kisses you on the lips. "I love you, Zone Son." What a strange and beautiful moment and this is only the first time you've spent time with your Z.F.! Imagine how excited you'll be to see him the next time!

So how do you find the Zone Father that's right for you?

The easiest way to find your Z.F. is to mail or email a Zone Father request form to a local Zone Center. A Z.F. will be in touch after 6 to 8 weeks of processing.

A more hands-on approach would be to show up at an old age home and look for some old man who's bored, playing checkers alone in the corner somewhere, with drool coming down his chin. Just go up to him and say, "Hello, old man—I am a Zone Boy in search of a Zone Father. Do you think you'd be my Zone Father?" Hopefully he says yes and now you have your new Zone Father.

ZONE TIPS AND TRICKS 3:

KEEP CANS OF CORN IN CORNERS OF YOUR HOUSE. IT'S FUN TO TELL HOUSEGUESTS YOU HAVE CORN IN YOUR CORNERS.

CONNECTING YOUR ZONE FATHER

Once you have established who your Zone Father is, you need to officially connect him to you and your life. This is the easiest step. We call it the Head Touch Simple Connect Process (H.T.S.C.P.).

Simply touch foreheads together and hold this position for an hour. It's important this step happens within the first 5 minutes of meeting your Zone Father.

5 THINGS TO THINK ABOUT DURING A NORMAL H.T.S.C.P.

1. Rain
2. Sharm (Raisins)
3. Leather Straps
4. Concert Tickets
5. Lagoo Poon (The Female Parts)

5 THINGS TO AVOID THINKING ABOUT DURING NORMAL H.T.S.C.P.

1. Dust
2. F'lisp Roo (Toes, Fingers)
3. Software
4. Tonamona (Six-String Bass Guitar)
5. Bio Dad

QUIK QUIZ 3

Which one of these men would be ideal for your Zone Father?

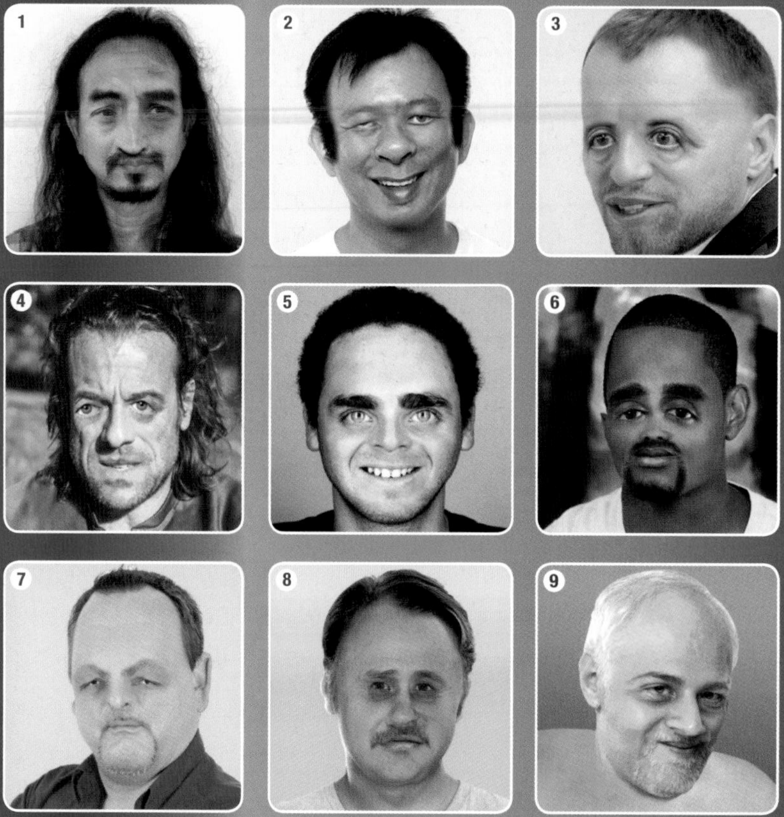

QUIZ 3 ANSWERS: 1, 2, 4, 5, and 6.

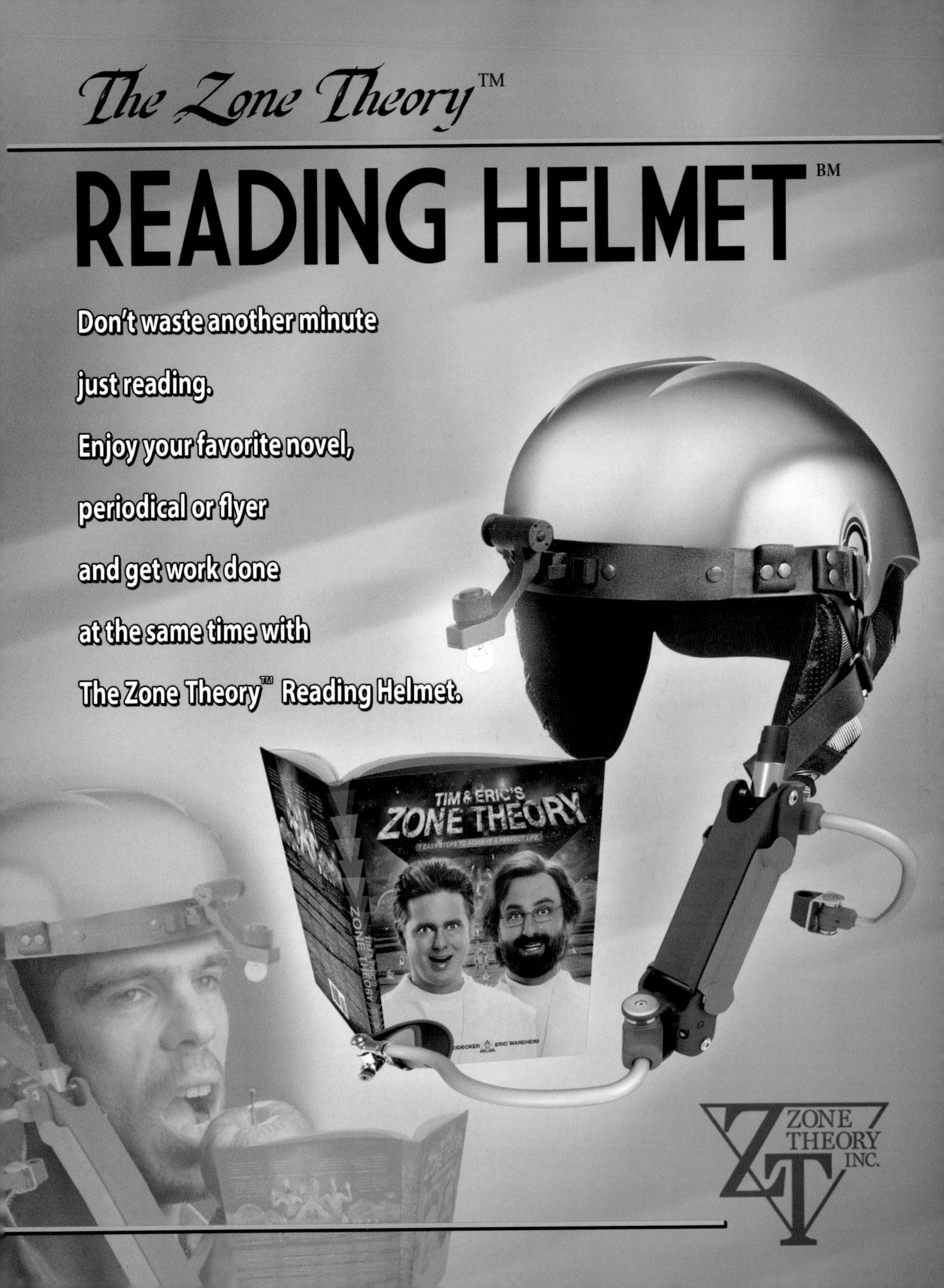
The Zone Theory™
READING HELMET℠
Don't waste another minute
just reading.
Enjoy your favorite novel,
periodical or flyer
and get work done
at the same time with
The Zone Theory™ Reading Helmet.
TIM & ERIC'S
ZONE THEORY
7 EASY STEPS TO ACHIEVE A PERFECT LIFE
ERIC WAREHEIM
ZONE THEORY INC.

DIVORCING YOUR ZONE FATHER

It's important to note at this point that:

THE ZONE FATHER IS STILL IN THE BETA STAGE OF TESTING AND HAS A VERY LOW RATE OF SUCCESS. THE CHANCE OF DIVORCE IS VERY HIGH.

It's sad, isn't it? You think you're hitting it off with your Z.F. You're spending great, valuable time together and it's working for a while. Yeah, "for a while." Then something changes. He's not who he used to be. Or is it you that's changed? You try to talk about it but it just gets weirder and weirder. Or maybe he's hurt you—physically or emotionally. Has he struck you? Has he? It's time to divorce your Zone Father.

Unfortunately divorcing your Zone Father requires special authorization from your local Zone Council. It's not something the Zone Council is going to take lightly and most Zone divorces are rejected. Why? Because the focus needs to be on making the Zone Father / Zone Son relationship work! ***ZONE THEORY***™ is working to make the Zone Father divorce process easier. Please bear with us during this time.

TIM AND ERIC DIVORCING THEIR ZONE FATHERS

"Sorry, Dad."—Eric Wareheim

"I wish you the best."—Tim Heidecker

DIVORCING YOUR ZONE FATHER REALLY WORKS!

STEPS TO DETERMINE IF YOU SHOULD DIVORCE YOUR ZONE FATHER

Here is a helpful early warning checklist you can use to determine if it's time to divorce your Zone Father. If you have checked 3 or more of these warnings begin Zone Father divorce proceedings immediately.

- ☐ Z.F. appears at your doorstep without calling ahead.
- ☐ Z.F. marches in circles in your lawn. (Normal in some cases)
- ☐ Z.F. makes repeated and unusually phrased requests such as "Is there spaghetti nearby for me?" or "Will it be easy for me to get to the area where there is spaghetti now or later?"
- ☐ Z.F. becomes silent for long periods of time (10 to 20 weeks).
- ☐ Z.F. moans all the time.
- ☐ Z.F. goes, "You don't love your Zone Father anymore, you're just a big old bitch for your Zone Wife. Why don't we toss the ball like in the old days?" (This is a clear sign it's time to dump the Z.F.)
- ☐ Z.F. gets sneezy around cats.
- ☐ Z.F. forgets to charge his phone and when he comes over needs to plug into your units.
- ☐ Goes around calling himself "Zoney Baronie: The Daaaad."

WARN

PREPAR

DIVORC

!!!!!!

ING!!!

E FOR

E NOW

!!!!!!

QUIK QUIZ 4

Identify The Zone Family vs. The “real” family?

QUIZ 4 ANSWERS: ZONE FAMILY: 2. “REAL” FAMILY: 1.

EVEN WE QUESTION ZONE THEORY™!

A personal testimony from Tim Heidecker

Here's a mind bender—I don't know if I believe in the **ZONE THEORY™**.

WHAAAAAAAAAAAAAAAAAAAAAAAAAAAT?

I know, can you wrap your head around that one? It's called doubt and we all have it. We've had it since the sperm state. We developed the **ZONE THEORY™** *very quickly and under a great deal of stress—so there was very little time or will to go back, do the work, CHECK the work, test the work and thus, see if any of it works, or makes sense or if the spelling was correct etc. etc… I even fought with the publishers over releasing this book. My lawyers told me that I had signed a contract to write this book and I had spent every single dime of the advance. I was trapped. The book was coming out and it was a pile of shit. It didn't make any sense.*

I am shit.

It was a phrase I've heard me say to myself before.

But maybe this time it was true.

I am shit.

Is that a true statement? It's really hard to know.

But I'm so EXCITED by the possibility that it ISN'T true.

Maybe **ZONE THEORY™** *DOES work! It's got a chance and that's why I BELIEVE in* **ZONE THEORY™**.

It is shit.

Thanks,
Tim Heidecker

NOW IS A GREAT TIME TO WRITE A CHECK FOR $999.99 AND SEND TO ZONE THEORY, INC.

CALCULATE YOUR ZONE SCORE NOW

☐	FRIENDSHIP
☐	FAMILY
☒	BUSINESS
☒	LOVE
☒	HEALTH
☒	POEMS
☒	FOOD
☐	TOTAL

TAKE A BREAK AND PLAY A GAME!

WORD CHALLENGE

(Using Zone Words)

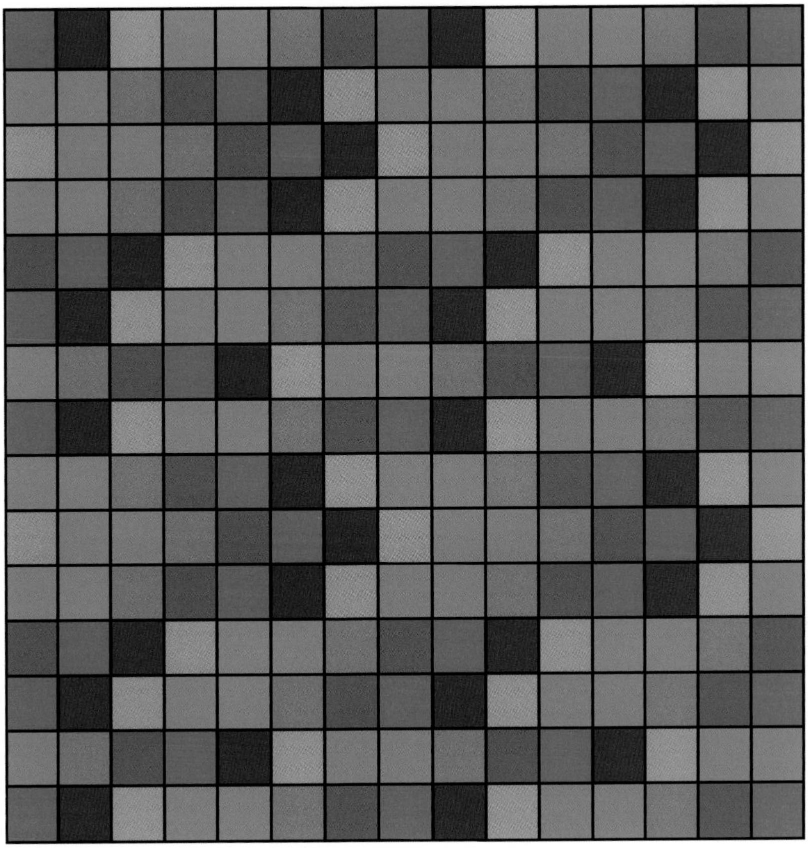

Fill in the squares with the letters of the words below but **DON'T** use the green squares. **DO NOT** overlap or cross words.

Zone Boy, Bungyn, Mask, ***ZONE THEORY***™, Ba'hee, Torsch, Josh, G'hor Hoo, Lagoo Poon

Can you complete the puzzle?

TIM ON FAMILY

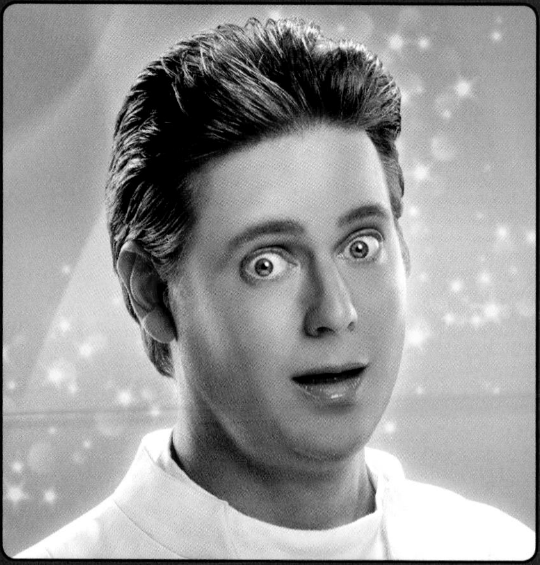

The other morning I took out the old family scrapbook and studied it closely. Who were those Bios? I hardly recognized them anymore. I wondered why I had kept the scrapbook for so long. Of what use did it provide me? I took the book out to my backyard where I keep a constant roaring fire burning and ripped each page out one by one and threw them into the flame. I almost heard my useless, Discard Bios screaming in pain from the hot heat. I secretly wished I could truly set them afire and watch their skin bubble and burst; their eyes pop out of their skull like two little condoms, stuffed and filled to the brim with hot, wet semen… The thought of semen got ME hot and I unloaded a fresh torrent of real semen into the hot flames—momentarily spiritually draining my body of the essence of Sham Twee (advanced Z.P. 8—don't ask). By the end of it all, the last remaining memories of my original family were now simply ashes and dust. They were gone for good and that made me so glad I jacked it again. ;)

ERIC ON FAMILY

The loss of your Bios is a very hard thing. Just a few hours ago they were your loving parents. Now they are just shit Discards.

But think about some of the benefits:

- Far less gifts for birthdays and life events.
- Never having to listen to Uncle Dale's stories about "The War."
- No more calls to Grandma saying "How are you."

I think of my Bios and E.B.F.s as a disease. That's how I get through it. I say this to myself in the morning.

"Thank goodness I don't have that disgusting disease."

Then I'm skipping through my house happy as can be.

ZONE 3
BUSINESS

EXT. OFFICE—DAY

EMPLOYEE: Hey, Boss.

EMPLOYER: What's up?

EMPLOYEE: I quit. Starting my own business based on ***ZONE THEORY***™. I am a Zone Boy now—well on my way to Zone Plane 8.

EMPLOYER: OK.

EMPLOYEE: Go fuck yourself and the two weeks' notice I agreed to. I am not your slave.

EMPLOYER: Whatever.

(He is shit and doesn't care.)

THERE'S A MAGICAL LINE in the film *Jerry Maguire*, "Show me the money!" If you haven't seen it don't bother, you are better off. It is shit. Just read the above line again:

SHOW ME THE MONEY! At the end of the day it really is all about the money. You gotta get it all and you gotta get it now. Fuck the other Zones, "zone in" on $$$$$$$ and

YOU
WILL
WIN
LIFE
PERIOD,
SON.

But why is money so important and how can you get all of it and where can you keep it?

The first step is getting into business! I'm talking about serious business not some bullshit chickenshit Arby's franchise diarrhea company, I'm talking about stocks and bonds, Wall Street, climbing the corporate ladder and saying, "Fuck you, I can buy and sell you as if you were a stock. Clear?"

Get your ass in the CEO's chair—I'm talking about chairman of the fucking board and then you can get yachts and private beach houses and then you're in charge. Get it?

"Oh but I'm too tired. I just want to play my skin flute all day and watch video games," you say. Then I'm afraid this has been a giant waste of your time. Destroy this book now.

But before you do, consult the FORGETTING THIS BOOK exercises in the appendix.

If the above has inspired you then I'd like to say, "Welcome to the players club, Jack!"

ZONE THEORY™ BUSINESS EXEMPTIONS

***ZONE THEORY*™** is not for everyone—if you are any of the following please destroy this book immediately:

- Mechanic
- Repairman
- Janitor (1) (horrible)
- Worker
- Steel mill employee
- Car salesman
- Work at a store (2)
- Teacher
- Work at the airport (3)
- Drive a bus
- Blue collar type
- Gas station jackass (4)

SOME VISUAL EXAMPLES OF BUSINESS EXEMPTIONS

WHAT MATTERS MOST

- STOCKS
- BONDS
- MONEY
- HARD CASH
- REAL ESTATE
- GETTING PAID!

ZONE THEORY™
AUTHORIZED
BUNGYN
BULK SALE!
BULK SALE!
BULK SALE!
BULK SALE!
BULK SALE!
Best PRICE
1 OUNCE WEIGHS 1 TON!
Warning: Bungyn is hot to touch. Handle with caution.
SAVE

EASY WAYS TO MAKE IT RICH! QUICK!!!!

You must be asking yourself:
"But I want to be a big-time player! I want to rule the roost with tons of cash money, living big and playing bigger."

How are you supposed to be big in business, make tons of money and live the rich and famous lifestyle when you've got nothing? ***ZONE THEORY***™ has a process which will CHANGE YOUR LIFE! And it's so simple literally anyone can do it. First you have to understand the basic laws of economics:

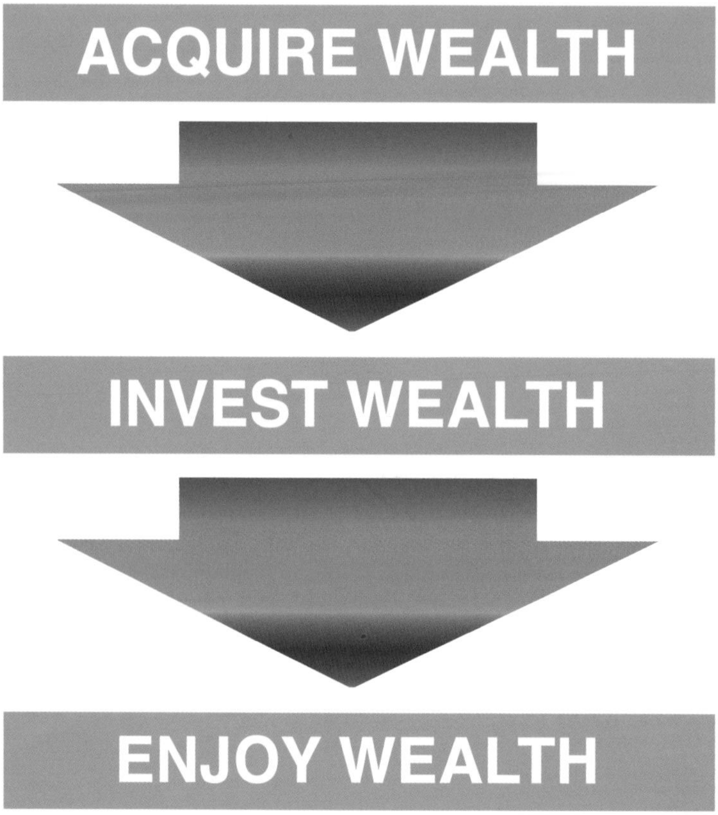

Simply put, you got to get the money, then you got to get that money to work for you and finally you got to spend the money so you can feel good about YOURSELF!

LET'S TACKLE THE FIRST STEP NOW WITH THE *ZONE THEORY*™ GET-RICH-QUICK PLAN!

ACQUIRE WEALTH

ZONE THEORY™ has identified 3 EZ ways to acquire tons of fast cash without a whole lot of work. Let's review:

WINNING AT SLOTS

Slots (a mechanical game of chance found in casinos) are the easiest and fastest way to strike it rich. Head over to your closest casino and sit down in front of the slot machine that appeals to you. Most slot machines feature flashing lights, music and some even have a brand tie-in to popular movies, TV shows like *Gilligan's Island*, *Happy Days*, *The Brady Bunch* or bands like Kiss or Aerosmith. Next you'll place cash ($1, $5, $10 or $20) in the machine and start pulling. You are looking to combine the symbols in front of you on the screen. For example if you hit 3 sevens in a row you've hit the big time—you can cash out and live forever as a VERY rich man.

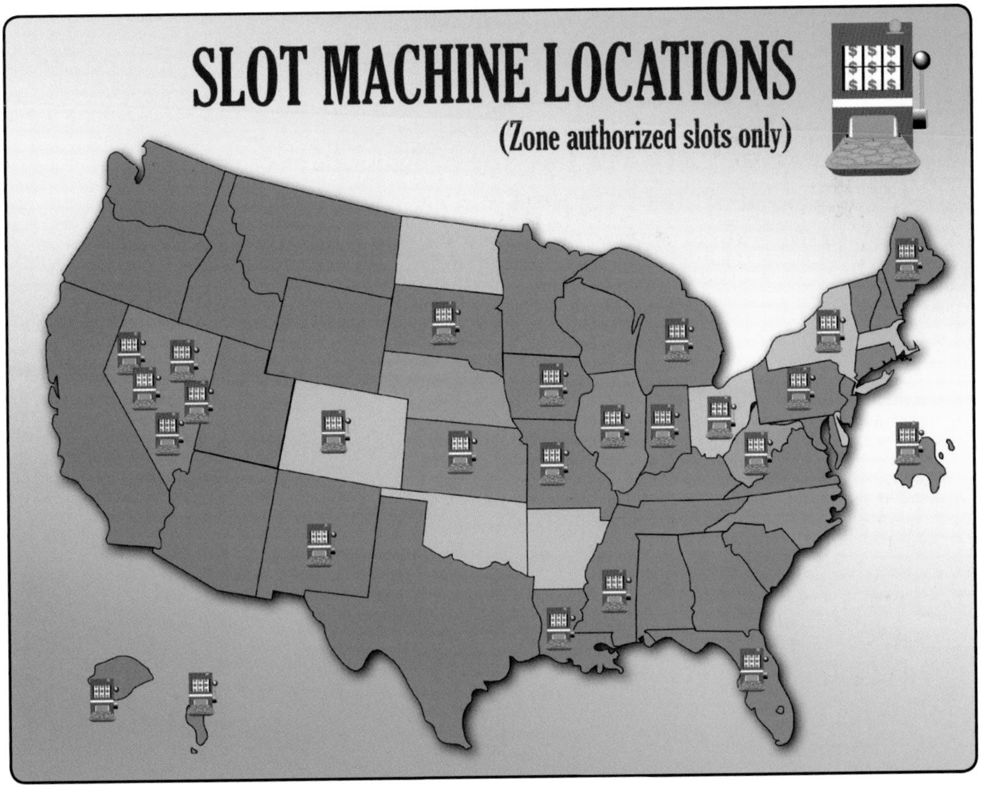

THE LOTTERY—Simply scratch and win? It's THAT easy!

Let's face facts, when you play the lottery the chances aren't **great**. But they are VERY good. You can pretty much guarantee you will win SOMETHING—and often it's MILLIONS of dollars.

Do you have a penny? Then you can win. Here's how it works.

GO down to the local shop and purchase 10 or 20 scratch-and-win tickets—they often have entertaining themes like "A Pirate's Hidden Treasure" or "Leprechaun's Pot o' Gold"—take the time to appreciate and enjoy the theme—you can even use the theme to create a little story based on the "loot." Do this in your mind.

TAKE the 10 to 20 tickets into a fully soundproofed room in your house—lock the door and take the penny as mentioned above and begin scratching.

READ the instructions on the back of the ticket to determine what you are looking to see when you scratch away. Often, you are looking to match 3 or 4 items in a row. Be patient, you might not strike a match on the first few. Oh well, we never said it was going to be THAT easy!

When you find the match you know you've won—wondering why we made sure you were in a locked soundproof room? Because at this point you must celebrate your big win! In a very high-pitched scream you will now vocalize:

YOU: *YIP YIP YIP YIP YIP YIP HEEEEEEE YIP YIP YIP YIP YIP YIPHEEEEEEEE!!!!*

Don't be afraid to really belt this out. Remember you are in a soundproof room and there is now NO danger in disturbing the neighbors… Aren't you glad we insisted on the soundproof room?

Repeat this exaltation until you are hoarse *(aka Sore Throat).*

Now check the back of the ticket again and either:

- Determine the amount promised based on the match.
- Return to the place you purchased the ticket and receive your money. If the amount is over 1 million dollars (which it almost always is) you may have to receive a cashier's check, which is annoying because you have to then go to the fucking bank and wait in line but hey we never said it was going to be THAT easy!

You should also see about getting reimbursed for the ticket that didn't pay out. You have a case: Those tickets were bullshit and you should be paid back for them.

ZONE TIPS AND TRICKS 4:

CREATE AN INVENTORY OF ELECTRONIC CABLES IN YOUR HOME—UNCOIL AND RECOIL USB CABLES. REMEMBER THESE CABLES.

ZONE LOAN

A perfectly acceptable third option is the Zone Certified Zone Loan System. If playing the odds (which again, are very good) through slots gambling or scratch lottery doesn't appeal to you, you might be the perfect candidate for a Zone Loan.

Z.L.s are a great way to create an initial infusion of quick cash: cash which you will use in the second phase of the ***ZONE THEORY***™ GRQP.

Zone Loans are flexible and can be designed to meet your specific needs. Interest rates are typically very low[10], depending on your metrics (DOB, SS#, height, weight, etc.).

Apply for a Zone Loan TODAY and get your cash fast so you can start your new...

RICH

& FAMOUS

LIFE

NOW!!!

[10] Average rates are >40%

ZONE LOAN FORM 1-A

I______________________ agree to a loan term of 16-58 mo.s starting dependent on quarter year values and an interest rate of fluctuation points determined by Zone Theory, dependent on prime rates plus a certain factor to be determined by loan zone, inc and the surrounding bodies as templates towards fulfillment of goals and values as they pertain to Zone Theory and Zone Loan, Inc.

Loan certification determined through credit history factors including age, race, age distinction, gender, criminal background, culpability and demographic background.

Age determination regardless of age, position becomes factor (x) when converting interest into percentage based factors. Subsequent consumer reports may be requested and used in connection with an update, renewal or extension of credit.
By submitting this Loan application, I/we acknowledge that I/we have read the legal information and the privacy policy. I/we authorize Zone Theory to receive and exchange information and investigate the references and data collected pertinent to my/our creditworthiness. I/We represent that the information I/we have given Zone Theory regarding my/our financial condition is complete and correct and that I/we have no present intention to file for bankruptcy. I/We will notify One Main Financial of any material adverse change in my/our financial condition.

I/We expressly grant Zone Theory the authority to call and/or e-mail me/us with questions related to this application and share information about other products & services available.

If you are applying for a joint account, you and the co-applicant acknowledge it is your intent to apply for a joint account at your loan closing.

Age determination regardless of age, position becomes factor (x) when converting interest into percentage based factors. Subsequent consumer reports may be requested and used in connection with an update, renewal or extension of credit.

Upon request, you and the co-applicant, if applicable, will be informed whether a consumer report was requested and of the name and address of the credit reporting agency furnishing any such report. Subsequent consumer reports may be requested and used in connection with an update, renewal or extension of credit.
A consumer report is usually obtained and reviewed in the evaluation of an application. Upon request, you and the co-applicant, if applicable, will be informed whether a consumer report was requested and of the name and address of the credit reporting agency furnishing any such report.
Subsequent consumer reports may be requested and used in connection with an update, renewal or extension of credit.

IMPORTANT INFORMATION ABOUT PROCEDURES FOR OPENING A NEW ACCOUNT AT Zone Theory Age determination regardless of age, position becomes factor (x) when converting interest into percentage based factors. Subsequent consumer reports may be requested and used in connection with an update, renewal or extension of credit.
To help the United States Government fight terrorism and money laundering, Federal law requires us to obtain, verify, and record information that identifies each person that opens an account.
A consumer report is usually obtained and reviewed in the evaluation of an application. Upon request, you and the co-applicant, if applicable, will be informed whether a consumer report was requested and of the name and address of the credit reporting agency furnishing any such report. Subsequent consumer reports may be requested and used in connection with an update, renewal or extension of credit.
What this means for you: when you open an account, we will ask for your name, a street address, date of birth, and an identification number, such as a Social Security number, that Federal law requires us to obtain. We may also ask to see your driver's license or other identifying documents that will allow us to identify you. We appreciate your cooperation.
If you are applying for a joint account, you and the co-applicant acknowledge it is your intent to apply for a joint account at your loan closing.
Age determination regardless of age, position becomes factor (x) when converting interest into percentage based factors. Subsequent consumer reports may be requested and used in connection with an update, renewal or extension of credit.
Upon request, you and the co-applicant, if applicable, will be informed whether a consumer report was requested and of the name and address of the credit reporting agency furnishing any such report. Subsequent consumer reports may be requested and used in connection with an update, renewal or extension of credit.
A consumer report is usually obtained and reviewed in the evaluation of an application. Upon request, you and the co-applicant, if applicable, will be informed whether a consumer report was requested and of the name and address of the credit reporting agency furnishing any such report. Subsequent consumer reports may be requested and used in connection with an update, renewal or extension of credit.
IMPORTANT INFORMATION ABOUT PROCEDURES FOR OPENING A NEW ACCOUNT AT Zone Theory Age determination regardless of age, position becomes factor (x) when converting interest into percentage based factors. Subsequent consumer reports may be requested and used in connection with an update, renewal or extension of credit.
To help the United States Government fight terrorism and money laundering, Federal law requires us to obtain, verify, and record information that identifies each person that opens an account.
A consumer report is usually obtained and reviewed in the evaluation of an application. Upon request, you and the co-applicant, if applicable, will be informed whether a consumer Rev. 5-29-14To help the United States Government fight terrorism and money laundering, Federal law requires us to obtain, verify, and record information that identifies each person that opens an account.A consumer report is usually obtained and reviewed in the evaluation of an application. Upon request, you and the co-applicant, if applicable, will be informed whether a consumer report was requested and of the name and address of the credit reporting agency furnishing any such report. Subsequent consumer reports may be requested and used in connection with an update, renewal or A consumer report is usually obtained and reviewed in the evaluation of an application. Upon request, you and the co-applicant, if applicable, will be informed whether a consumer rRev. 5-29-14 ies each person that opens an account.A consumer report is usually obtained and reviewed in the evaluation of an application. Upon request, you and the co-applicant, if applicable, will be informed whether a consumer Rev. 5-29-14To help the United States Government fight terrorism and money laundering, Federal law requires us to obtain, verify, and record information that identifies each person that opens an account.A consumer report is usually obtained and reviewed in the evaluation of an application. Upon request, you and the co-applicant, if applicable, will be informed whether a consumer report was requested and of the name and address of the credit reporting agency furnishing any such report. Subsequent consumer reports may be requested and used in connection with an update, renewal or A consumer report is usually obtained and reviewed in the evaluation of an application. Upon request, you and the co-applicant, if applicable, will be informed whether a consumer rRev. 5-29-14 ies each person that opens an account.A consumer report is usually obtained and reviewed in the evaluation of an application. Upon request, you and the co-applicant, if applicable, will be informed whether a consumer Rev. 5-29-14To help the United States Government fight terrorism and money laundering, Federal law requires us to obtain, verify, and record information that identifies each person that opens an account.A consumer report is usually obtained and reviewed in the evaluation of an application. Upon request, you and the co-applicant, if applicable, will be informed whether a consumer report was requested and of the name and address of the credit reporting agency furnishing any such report. Subsequent consumer reports may be requested and used in connection with an update, renewal or
What this means for you: when you open an account, we will ask for your name, a street address, date of birth, and an identification number, such as a Social Security number, that Federal law requires us to obtain. We may also ask to see your driver's license or other identifying documents that will allow us to identify you. We appreciate your cooperation.
Zone Theory, Inc. (DE) - AL, AZ, CO, DE: One Main Financial, Inc. is licensed by the Delaware State Bank Commissioner to engage in business in Delaware under license numbers: 011786, 011787, 011788, 011789, 011790, 011791. Expiration 12/31. FL, GA, ID, IL, IN, IA, KS, KY, LA, ME, MD, MS, MO, MT, NE, NH, NJ, NM, NY, NC, ND, OH, OK, PA, SC, SD, TX, UT, VA, WY.
Zone Theory, Inc. (HI) - CA: Loans made or arranged pursuant to Department of Business Oversight California Finance Lenders License, OR, WA.
Zone Theory, Inc. (MN) - KY, MI, MN, NC, WI.

[illegible]

Signed____ Date______________

Introducing
THE ZONE
B-BAG
DELUXE BUSINESS BAG
No more fuddy, duddy briefcase!
AVAILABLE FOR 10,000 ZP
- Comfort - Practicality - Elegance -
Maximum weight capacity of Zone Business Bag is 1.34 lbs

ZONE THEORY™ has identified 3 unique and Exciting Investment Opportunities.

(E.I.O.s)

That based on derivative investments of small cap percentages has, due to fluid markets and yield growth in second-term markets based on annual percentage rates determined by value set against earnings is guaranteed.

INVEST WEALTH

Take a quick break from reading this book and look at your bank account.

IT'S HUGE!!!!

Tons of cash just sitting in there wasting away. Why don't you put that money to work so you can lie back and ENJOY your life instead of working like a slave.

TIME FOR YOUR BRAIN WEIGHT CHECK-IN!

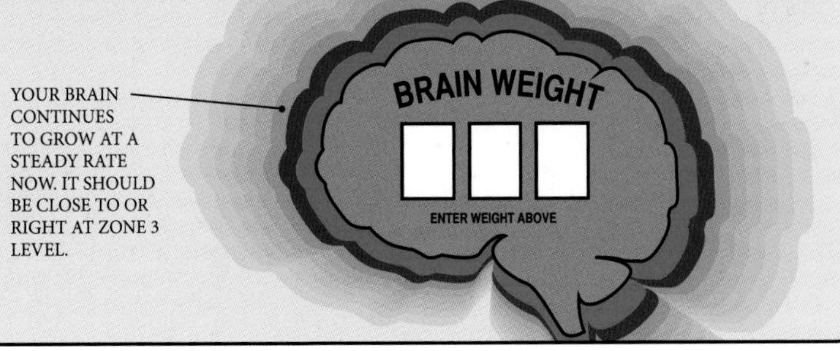

YOUR BRAIN CONTINUES TO GROW AT A STEADY RATE NOW. IT SHOULD BE CLOSE TO OR RIGHT AT ZONE 3 LEVEL.
BRAIN WEIGHT
ENTER WEIGHT ABOVE

E.I.O. #1: REAL ESTATE

We've all heard the expression:

BUY LOW, SELL HIGH

But what does that mean? It means when investing it's important to buy something at a very low price and then, later, sell it when the price is high so you make extra money. It's that simple. Making money is simple and it's even easier when you've got a lot of money to spend.

One EZ way to invest that cash is in **REAL ESTATE**. Real estate is literally real "estate"—or LAND.

People buy and sell land, homes, properties, boats, canned goods, trees, parks, camping equipment, etc. all the time. This is called real estate.

You can buy a tract of land for nothing and then sell it to builders who will then sell it to families to live in homes that the builders built. That's just one way real estate works. Another cool job is to be a real estate agent. These people show up and help families buy houses—they have an inside track on what houses are for sale and for rent.

TIP: Hire a real estate agent now.

Zone Theory, Inc. holds a large variety of "starter properties." Most of these "marsh style" lands are affordable, flexible and ready to convert to livable acreage. Call a Zone Certified Realtor today to inquire about a ***ZONE THEORY***™ starter property and pick a parcel that speaks to you.

DEAN PROOSH

ZONE CERTIFIED REALTOR

(800)555-2423

- FAST AND FRIENDLY SERVICE
- OVER 5 YEARS OF EXPERIENCE
- SPECIALIZING IN ZONE APPROVED PROPERTIES

E.I.O. #2: FRANCHISE OPPORTUNITIES

One of the easiest and most satisfying ways to invest your money is to own a franchise. Franchising is a time-tested, guaranteed way to establish a business that's already proven to be successful—the most popular kind of franchise available is the "Fast Food" category. Think about it: Everyone loves to chow down and no one has the time to sit down and have a long eight-course meal. Food has to be quick and it has to be good.

ZONE THEORY™ has partnered with Zone O's "O"-shaped sandwiches to create a franchise opportunity like none other. Zone O's sandwich shop has all the "ingredients" to be "successful."

- Strange-shaped food creates confusion and generates impulse buying.
- Conveniently priced food products keep customers coming in for more.

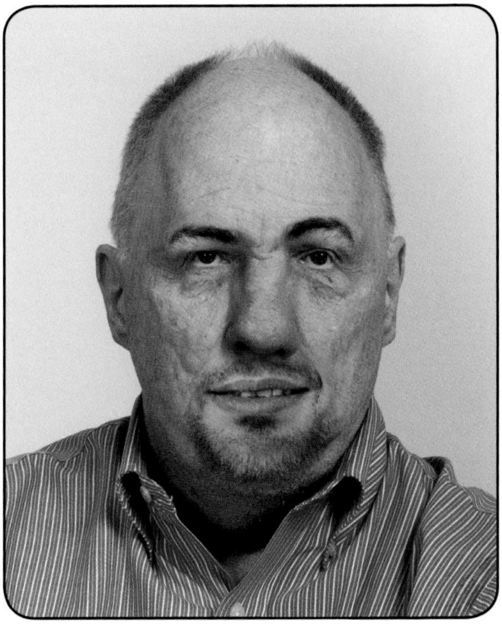

George O'Boyo

George O'Boyo is the founder and CEO of Zone O's and a Zone Plane 8 Vice Minister. He has been active and supportive of the ***ZONE THEORY***™ system for over 15 years.

Q: Thank you for taking the time to talk with us; you must be a very busy boy.

A: I am, thank you for acknowledging that. We now have 430 Zone O's in 12 countries and I am overseeing and managing every aspect of each restaurant.

Q: Wow! That must be a lot of work. You must be very busy!

A: I am.

Q: If you have time…

A: [politely interrupting] I always have time for ***ZONE THEORY***™...

Q: Right, well this is sort of what I was going to ask you—can you talk a bit about how ***ZONE THEORY***™ works for you and your business?

A: I really don't have time to get into the specifics but I can promise you that it's literally shaped who I am as a man and has created a management style and system for my business that's made me a very successful business boy. Hoy Broon Hee Takem! (Zone Plane 8 chant)

Q: Quickly, do you see Investment Opportunities in Zone O's (I.O.Z.O.) as a potentially groundbreaking and successful strategy for NEW ***ZONE THEORY***™ practitioners?

A: Absolutely.

Q: Thank you for your time.

E.I.O. #3: REFURBISHING BATTERIES

Perhaps not as sexy and cool as being a real estate baron or fast-food king, but buying, refurbishing and then selling used batteries to developing markets can be a lucrative way to invest your money.

Simply contact your local municipality and speak with their waste management supervisor. Most likely they have a recycled battery program. Inform him/her that you intend to purchase the batteries from their waste… Then set up a third-party distributor in an emerging market and sit back and watch the money roll in.

For more information on refurbishing batteries read Zone Pastor Chub Throad's excellent book *Refurbishing and Reselling Batteries to Poor People.*

Now please take a moment to review the following pages of motivational posters.

ZONE THEORY INC.
FOCUS!
"Intense concentration at all times increases brain size"
- Tim & Eric -

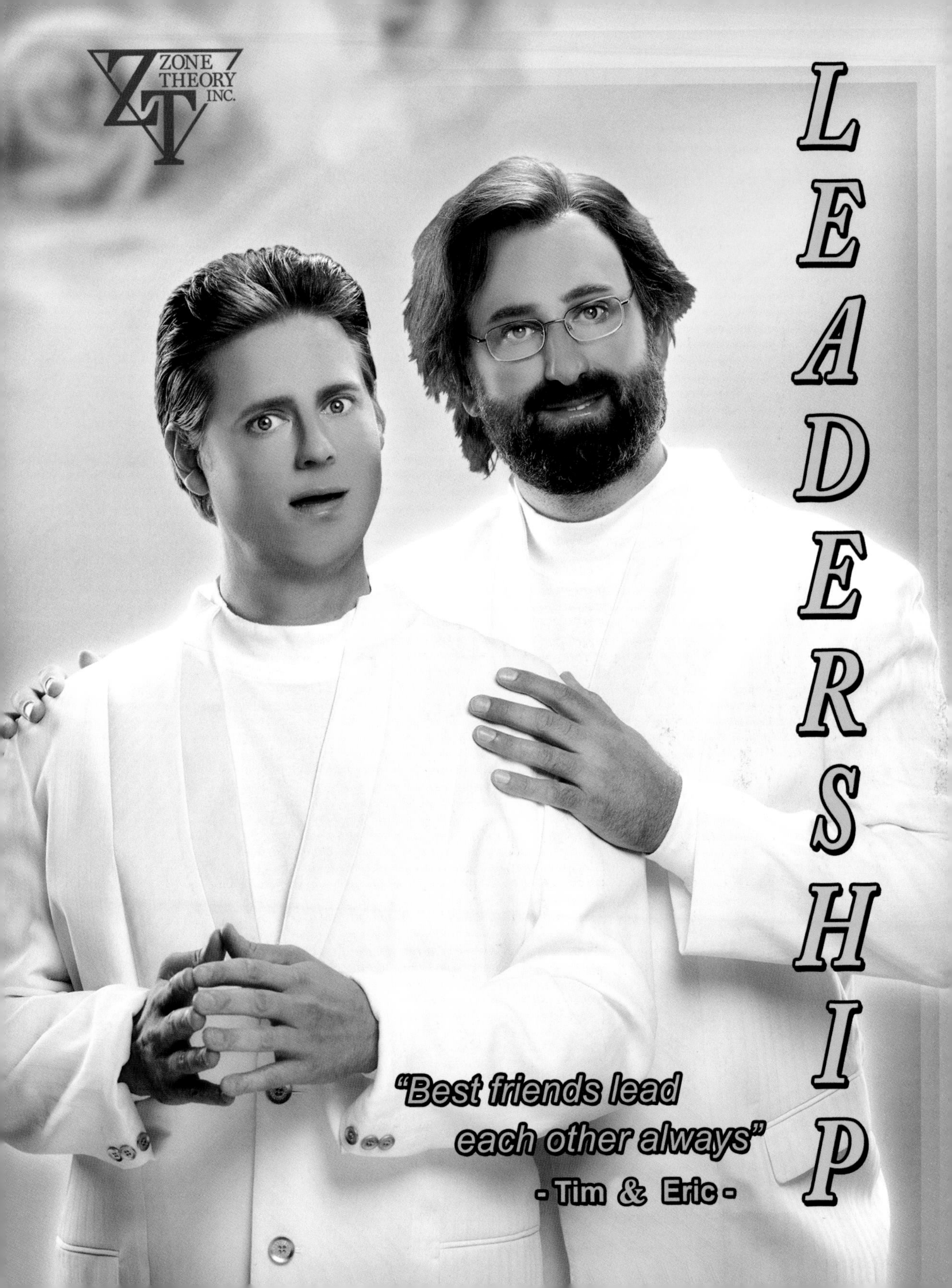
ZONE THEORY INC.
LEADERSHIP
"Best friends lead each other always"
- Tim & Eric -

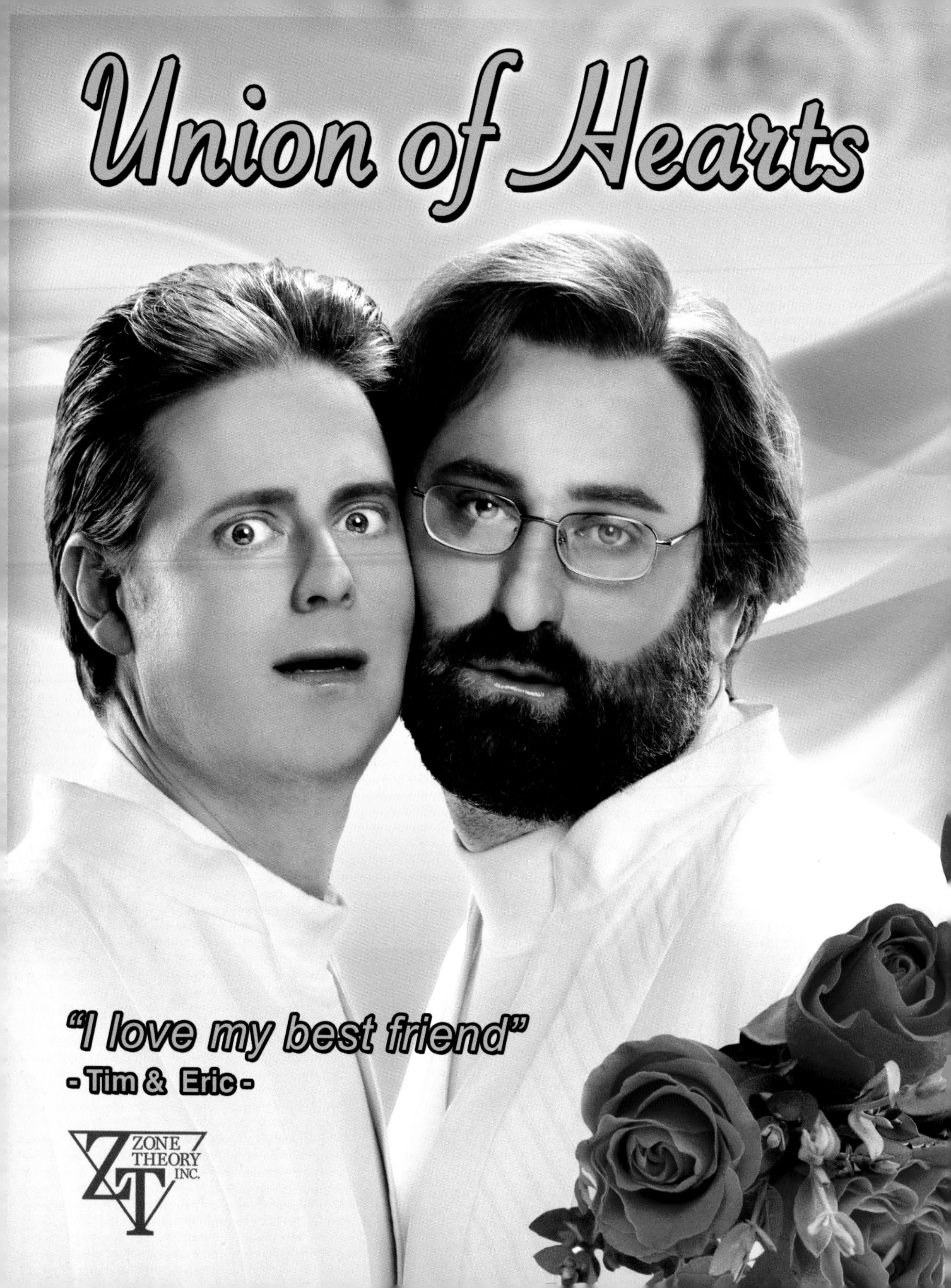
Union of Hearts
"I love my best friend"
- Tim & Eric -
ZONE THEORY INC.

ZONE THEORY INC.
TEAMWORK
"Working together guarantees success"
- Tim & Eric -

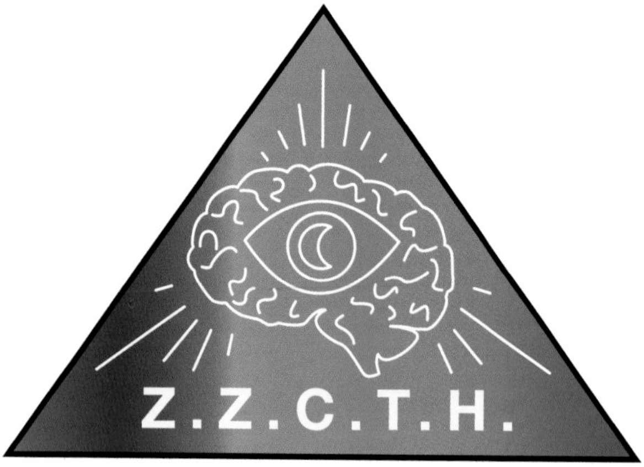

THE ZONE-ZONE COMMUNAL THOUGHT-HOUSE

Prior to the publication of this book we purchased one million acres in the tiny desert hamlet of Lou Gramm, Oregon. Every purchaser of this book has automatically purchased one square inch of land at our compound—it is included in the price of the book. Congratulations, you are now a landowner! If there is a perforated proof-of-purchase stamp still in the book (thieves usually remove them), you can exchange it for your deed and claim your right to "move right in." If you would like to expand your living quarters and/or use them as a toilet, that is possible too, but you will need to argue your case before a tribunal to earn the right to squat down and shit on your new land. Additionally, you will need to pay a yearly Landowners Maintenance Fee of $100 (non-negotiable) assessed beginning on January 1, 1990, and adjusted for inflation, WE WILL SEND A MESSENGER TO COLLECT THIS MONEY. Please do not argue with our messengers; they do not set policy, they only enforce it. These are hardened men with dark backgrounds and low IQs who will not hesitate to use violence, though we have, on occasion, asked them not to use it.

Z.Z.C.T.H. is the central building and communal meeting spot for Zone Theory'ers. Z.Z.C.T.H. operates a 24-hour nude dining sauna; a 24-hour, 2-mile-long Brokk-style bowling laneway; and a 24-hour freon supermarket, where you can purchase jugs of freon as well as our own full-color 164-page calendar featuring the photography of Mr. Pardural Bie. Make no mistake about it, our land is Heaven on Earth and we will fight to the death anyone who does anything to change that.

Z.Z.C.T.H. FAQ

Q: I am thinking of moving to Oregon and being a part of your ***ZONE THEORY***™ community. Is this land habitable?
A: No, unfortunately, it is not.

Q: Is there water there?
A: Human beings are 35% water; the rest is dust. Squeeze any excess water out of your midriff into the provided metal bowl, and drink it, or carbonate it to make soda pop. You will need a tortilla press if you choose to extract water from your ankles and feet.

Q: Does the bus go there?
A: Not anymore.

Q: Where can I store my money that I bring?
A: We have a "one-way vault" that is open to the public for depositing valuables.

Q: What about nude Adult Horseplay?
A: What about it? As you know, it is our norm. Nude means nude. No condoms should ever be worn during this 1000% non-sexual, non-consensual horseplay.

Q: How do I know this isn't some sort of pyramid scheme?
A: It IS. We use a pyramid. So did the ancient Egyptians—they invented the pyramid, and they presided over the most successful era that humankind has ever known. Do you have a problem with that?

Q: Is this affiliated with Hilton Resorts?
A: The Z.Z.C.T.H. and affiliated properties are independently owned and operated, and are not owned or operated by the owner of the Hilton brand. Certain names, trademarks, and trademarked phrases, including "Zone-Zone," "Zonus," "Penis Night Buffet," and "Dandy!!! This Is Just Dandy!!!" (collectively, the "Zone Theory Trademarks") are licensed for use on the property by T.E. Lou Scamms LLC ("T.E.L.S.L.") to Zone-Zone Communal Thought-House Inc. ("Z.Z.C.T.H.") and its affiliates. Members of the Hilton Honors program and purchasers of timeshare interests in Hilton Club Vacation Resorts have no interest in the license granted to T.E.L.S.L., Z.Z.C.T.H., S.Y.X.Y.R., or their affiliates and have no right of any kind to the use of the property, as there is no connection now, or ever, between Hilton Hotels and our patented mind-control/kidney-failure system.

QUIK QUIZ 5—Aptitude & Cognition

1. How many pages are in this book?

2. How many pages are in this book?

3. When can you read this book?

4. How many pages are in this book?

QUIZ 5 ANSWERS: 1. 324 2. 324
3. From 5AM to 8AM and 11PM to midnight. 4. 324

CALCULATE YOUR ZONE SCORE NOW

☐	**FRIENDSHIP**
☐	**FAMILY**
☐	**BUSINESS**
☒	**LOVE**
☒	**HEALTH**
☒	**POEMS**
☒	**FOOD**
☐	**TOTAL**

FAQ

Q: Do your teachings go against the teachings of Jesus?
A: No, it's mostly the same. You are free to join!

Q: What is the best reason to spend all this money? I'm skeptical.
A: ***ZONE THEORY***™ gives you a clarity of thought that you could never have gotten the other way.

Q: I collect soda pop bottle caps from the turn of the century onward. I have a museum-quality collection of over 25,000 caps from all eras. Recently my collection has begun to dominate my life and has almost cost me my marriage. Can ***ZONE THEORY***™ get me on the right track to turning my life around?
A: You are free to drink any beverage you choose while undergoing our process.

Q: Why should I trust TV actors with my life?
A: Because your family and friends have failed you.

Q: Some of these things seem sketchy, and a little extreme to me.
A: They aren't. Your life is shitty and it's getting worse, even while you read this. Stop whining at the only people who care enough to help you, you fucking asshole.

Q: I have tried it all, from Jesus to Buddha to Manson. I have experimented with hard drugs, and am now in my third year of sobriety. I am completely disillusioned after a bad experience with a bum guru. What you say makes sense to me, but how do I know it is my true calling?
A: You sound annoying. I don't think we'd want you to be involved in this thing.

Q: I am on a low-sodium diet. Do you have modified versions of the ***ZONE THEORY***™ Fast that can accommodate me? I can't eat a one-pound block of salt each day as you recommend.
A: You can't just pick and choose aspects of this that you like. The salt blocks are important and you must eat them. If you can't or won't do it, you will remain retarded, and you've only your own cowardice to blame.

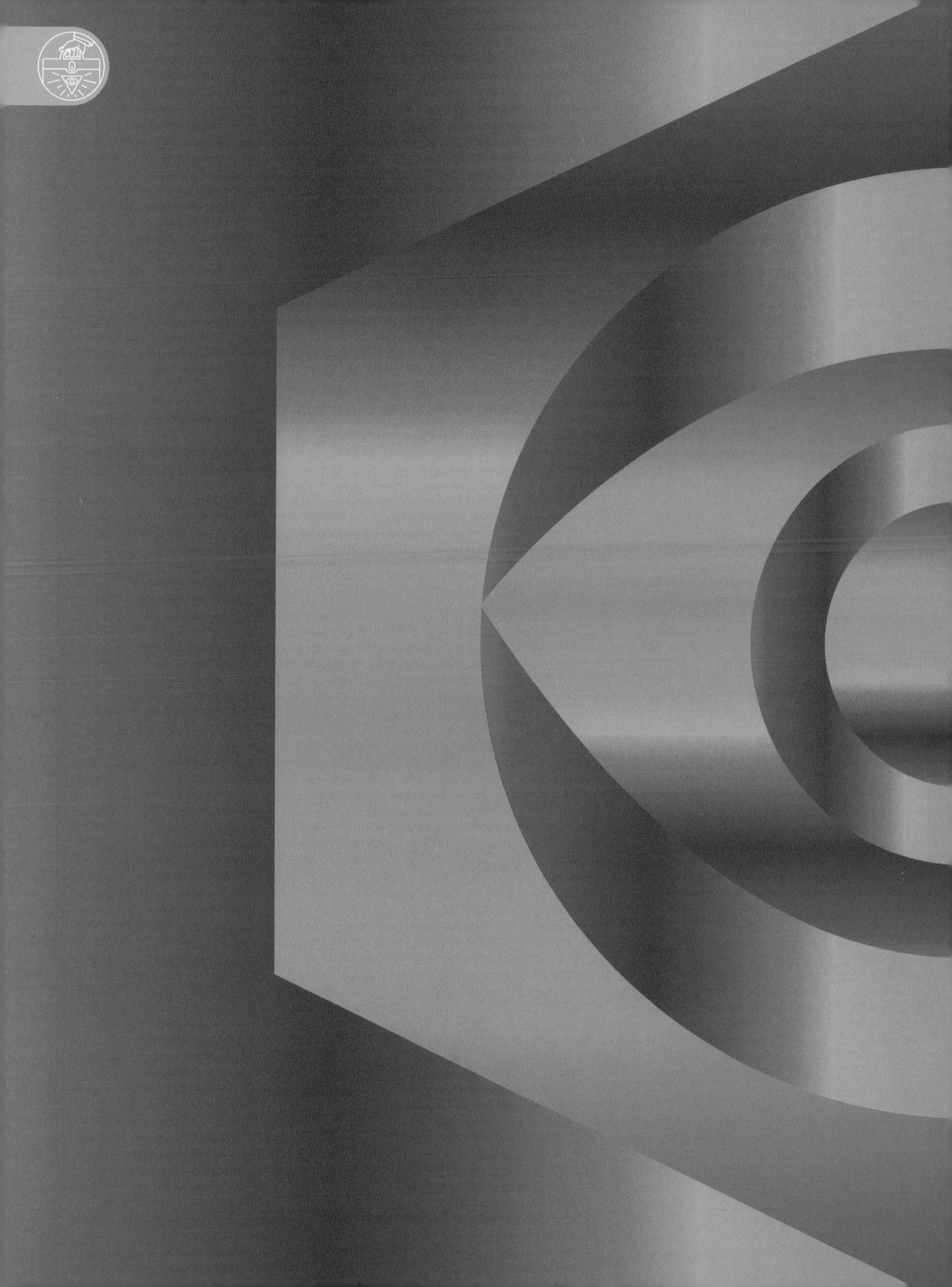

TIM ON WEALTH

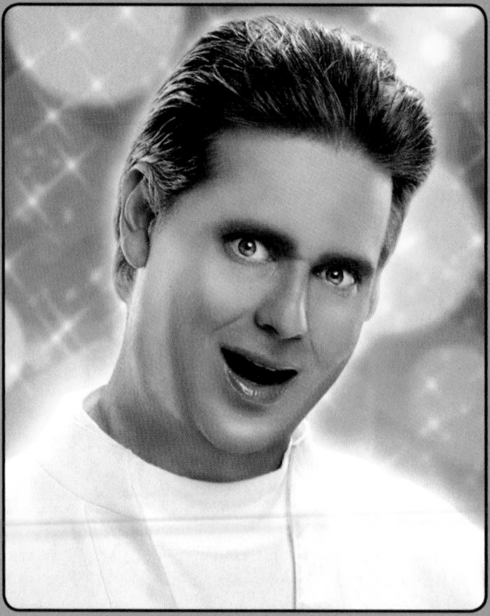

Did you know I'm worth several billion dollars?

I am.

I own several homes, boats, cars, ranches, motor homes, motorcycles, sailboats, farms, vineyards, roads, etc… My wealth is not only measured in dollars and cents but in the things I own! I'm so proud of my wealth and my ability to acquire wealth, property, items and happiness. I recently donated over 100 million dollars to the Heidecker Fund, which is a set of annuities and mutual funds that help my wealth grow and expand.

My wealth is what makes me who I am—whether I'm riding on my $750,000.00 horse named SpiderBoy or cruising through the Gulf of Diaz (not mapped) on *Cha-Ching*, my 1.5-million-dollar speedboat, I know that I'm rich and rich is who I am and who I should be. I got the money. I really do. It's in me. It's running through my damn blood and if you cut me, I'll bleed, but it'll be gold-colored blood from all the coins in my system.

Gold coins.

How did I amass such incredible wealth? Simple:

ZONE THEORY™.

Z.T. works, ya dope. It just works. Apply it, use it, study it and if you don't make a MINT then you must be working with half a deck. You would be considered a Grade A dumb bunny in my book. I'm not even joking around about that.

So get started, get into it! Put this book down and get on with it! You don't need a book to tell you what you need to do! You just need to go out there and grab that low-hanging fruit! Use the ***ZONE THEORY***™! It's working for me, why shouldn't it work for you??????

TIM ON WEALTH

Did you know I'm worth several billion dollars?

I am.

I own several homes, boats, cars, ranches, motor homes, motorcycles, sailboats, farms, vineyards, roads, etc… My wealth is not only measured in dollars and cents but in the things I own! I'm so proud of my wealth and my ability to acquire wealth, property, items and happiness. I recently donated over 100 million dollars to the Heidecker Fund, which is a set of annuities and mutual funds that help my wealth grow and expand.

My wealth is what makes me who I am—whether I'm riding on my $750,000.00 horse named SpiderBoy or cruising through the Gulf of Diaz (not mapped) on *Cha-Ching*, my 1.5-million-dollar speedboat, I know that I'm rich and rich is who I am and who I should be. I got the money. I really do. It's in me. It's running through my damn blood and if you cut me, I'll bleed, but it'll be gold-colored blood from all the coins in my system.

Gold coins.

How did I amass such incredible wealth? Simple:

ZONE THEORY™.

Z.T. works, ya dope. It just works. Apply it, use it, study it and if you don't make a MINT then you must be working with half a deck. You would be considered a Grade A dumb bunny in my book. I'm not even joking around about that.

So get started, get into it! Put this book down and get on with it! You don't need a book to tell you what you need to do! You just need to go out there and grab that low-hanging fruit! Use the ***ZONE THEORY™***! It's working for me, why shouldn't it work for you??????

ERIC ON WEALTH

Getting rich the Wareheim way. Friends are replaceable.

Money is not.

An "ex"-friend is just a friend who has made you "ex"-tremely rich. Do not worry about using these unfortunate sad sacks as literal stepping-stones in order to pursue your dream.

To rise to the top of a pyramid, you will need to step on many outstretched hands…please break them all!

I lost many, many friends along the way to becoming one of the wealthiest people in District 10. To bilk a gullible friend of his family's fortune is one of the most spiritual things you can do, according to the holy text. Bilk with beauty! Praise the results!

Money is like water—it evaporates into thin air and then reappears in a pool in my backyard! Money is everything…Try and buy a Rolex watch, or a sexual surrogate, by reaching into your pocket and showing off your walletful of "hot air." It ain't gonna happen, man. (Straight talk.)

I once had a friend with a big heart, who died. His money is now in my account, and his big, stupid heart is forgotten forever.

Tim disagrees with certain aspects of my methodology. When we first envisioned this book I believed we would go 50/50 on our ideas. But Tim won't allow me to share with you some of my greatest tricks and tips for getting rich. I own 20 platinum coffins, which I store in a secret location. Tim has lied. I can't help but wonder if he would like to take up residence in one of my expensive coffins?

TIP: READ THIS CHAPTER AGAIN

ZONE 4
LOVE

EXT. PARK—DAY

A woman jogs in the park.
You run up beside her.

YOU: Excuse me. I am looking to marry a Zone Wife. Could you be her?

WOMAN: Perhaps.

YOU: Great. But let's see how things go. I'll court you now.

WOMAN: OK.

YOU: "EWWWWW! Girls are gross."

WHAT IS LOVE?

Where would we be without love? Love keeps us healthy, happy, horny and sane. It's what makes the world go round, it's the most important Zone and I love that.

Love. Cherish it. Love being in love and MAKE love while you can.

How can we focus our love, use it properly and connect it with our other Zones? How can we turn on our Love Zone and make it work for us, not leave us brokenhearted and in the dumps?

This chapter is on that. :)

Of course there are different kinds of love but the love we are talking here is the love you will foster and grow with your ZONE WIFE. Zone Plane 6 Ministers know this love as "Zhahl Sufficient A-3" but for beginners like you, the term "love" can be used.

Finding, courting, marrying and procreating with your Zone Wife is the most important step in the ***ZONE THEORY***™ System[11]. That's why we're including it here.

---

[11] Amassing 100,000 Z.A.F.s through the Zone Rewards System, you can bypass Zone Wife entirely!

But **HOW** do you find your Zone Wife?

And **HOW** do you court her?

And **WHERE** will you marry her?

And **HOW** do you procreate with her?

This chapter is about that.

FINDING YOUR ZONE WIFE

Finding your Zone Wife is an important first step—you can't just walk out onto the street and randomly grab a woman off the street and command her to make you her Zone Husband.[12]

There are several ways to meet women: You can try talking to some of them at work, at a singles' bar, at a friend's party, on the internet in chat circles, online, during general internet meeting hours… You can even try walking around a public park and confront women who are alone—ask them to date you. Some have even had success randomly but gently grabbing a woman right off the street. Be up front. Don't hide the fact that you are looking for a Zone Wife. Women love honesty and there's no point in deceiving them right off the bat.

Ideal qualities to look for in a Zone Wife:

- Is blond with big cans.
- Can make her own masks and masks for you.
- Owns her own spaghetti set (pot, strainer and tongs).
- Can lift over 300 lbs.
- Gets you.

[12] Technically there is no such thing as a "Zone Husband." You are simply "Zone Certified Jake" or "Zone Certified Mark"—more on changing your name in the "Changing Your Name" chapter in the Appendix (not available).

COURTING YOUR ZONE WIFE

Once you have settled on who your Zone Wife will be, you need to dedicate a specific amount of time to courting her before you can Zone marry her. Courting is a scam—an elaborate ruse to create the illusion that you sincerely care and appreciate your future Zone Wife. It's best to just follow these Zone Approved courting steps—they are guaranteed to work and you don't have to mess around with your own ideas.

COURTING STEP 1

Invite her over for a spaghetti dinner. (Don't have a spaghetti set? Then you should throw away this book right away because you didn't follow the rules. See: Shopping List, page 22. Do you think we included that as a joke?)

Prepare the spaghetti dinner an hour before she arrives. Make sure your apartment is clean (but not too clean) and there is toilet paper. Decorate your place with tons of fake rose petals—go to a party store and get a bunch of Valentine's Day junk (hopefully it's March and there's a clearance sale on that stuff).

Serve the spaghetti on fine china or anything that's not paper plates. Talk about how you are so very much in love with her while at the same time making sure she's also enjoying the spaghetti. Make sure to have crushed red pepper and parmesan cheese on the table. Offer her parmesan cheese after each bite. If she refuses after the third bite you can lay off asking.

After you both have finished eating, jokingly suggest you will do the dishes. This will send her the message that the least she could do is clean up. You will notice that once she gets into cleaning up she'll do a general clean of the whole kitchen. She'll get it cleaner than it's been for years!

Also have red wine with the dinner.

COURTING STEP 2

Take her to several movies and plays. Engage in heavy wet kissing and fondling during movies and plays—touch her big round cans until the nipples get hard. Put your fingers in her vagina. Let her play around with your penis and balls.

COURTING STEP 3

After a session of heavy wet kissing and fondling at your apartment, take out your acoustic guitar[13] and perform for her the following song:

PREPARING AND EXECUTING YOUR ZONE MARRIAGE

Well the big day is approaching! From the moment you first spoke to her, she's been waiting for you to bring it up. It's time to get Z.M.'ed![14]

It's a simple question you should ask her now:

YOU: Gina, it's been 3 weeks and I have appropriately courted you according to the ***ZONE THEORY***™ system. Shall we get Z.M.'ed?

GINA: Yes.

See? It's EZ!

[13] Don't have an acoustic guitar? Don't know how to play? Get one and learn. Don't want to? Then destroy this book now.

[14] Zone Married.

Ideally, you will get married at midnight by a Zone Priest at a Zone Center[15] but this may be impossible. It's best to make the experience quick, affordable and EZ. There is no point to having a huge party for getting Z.M.'ed. It's just another step. You wouldn't throw a big bash just for completing your Shopping List (page 22), would you? Don't be dumb here. Get Z.M.'ed and get it done quick.

HOW TO EXPRESS YOUR LOVE

Learn this song and perform it for your Zone Wife daily for up to eight weeks. During the ninth week you can begin the sex act…

By Zone Council

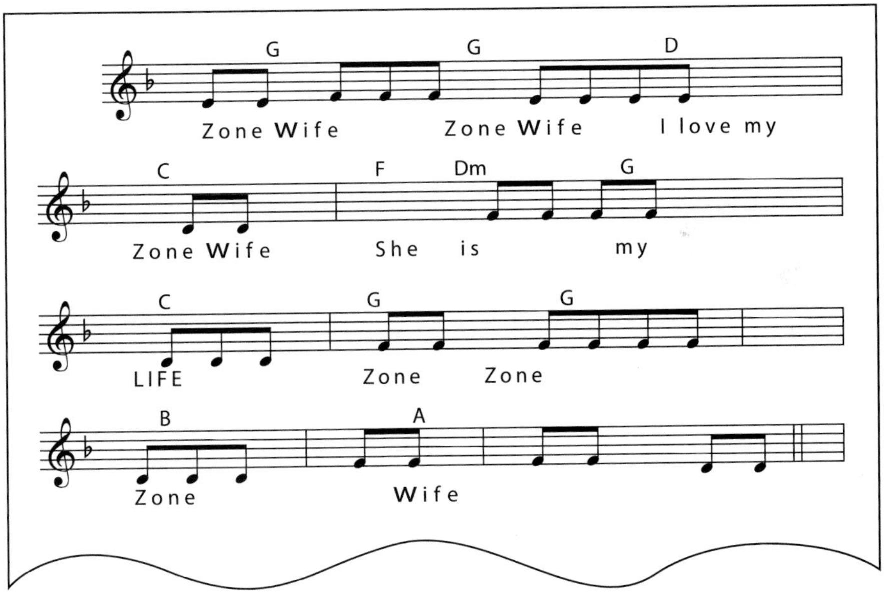

Repeat

---

[15] Zone Centers have not been established as of this printing.

BOTTLING AND STORING PROBO (SEMEN)

WARNING: Probo (semen) should not be exchanged during the act of love within the first several months of courtship.

At first this procedure can be quite embarrassing. You will learn to aim properly so no Probo is left unbottled. After 4 XL mason jars are filled to the brim, your Zone partner will be able to accept your seed. Discarded Probo can be donated to the community for several different uses. You should be able to fill up mason jar 2 within a weeks' time.

All pre-Zone dirt Probo must be cleared before your Zone Wife accepts the pure Probo.

After all jars are filled, go to a Zone Center, drop off your sample. If you are cleared you can inseminate your Zone Wife.

BOTTLING AND STORING PROBO

What is Probo? Probo is human semen from a man. It's a white jam-like substance that can be sticky like glue—Probo contains the seeds of life and several forms of Jagh-Haroo particles (*these particles form the 27 corners on the United Scale*).

OFFICIAL CLEARANCE LETTER

Mark's Probo (Semen)

has been cleared for use
with his Zone Wife

Mark is free to use his Probo for the sex act as instructed by his Zone Councilor. Mark's Probo is to be used only with his Zone Wife.

Print and distribute to friends and neighbors immediately.

CON-
GRAT-
ULA-
TIONS!

BEFORE MOVING ON:
CHANT THE FOLLOWING FOR A DAY:

MY PROBO IS READY TO BE USED FOR PROCREATION

BUT FIRST IT'S IMPORTANT TO UNDERSTAND MORE ABOUT YOUR PENIS.
WHAT KIND OF PENIS DO YOU HAVE?

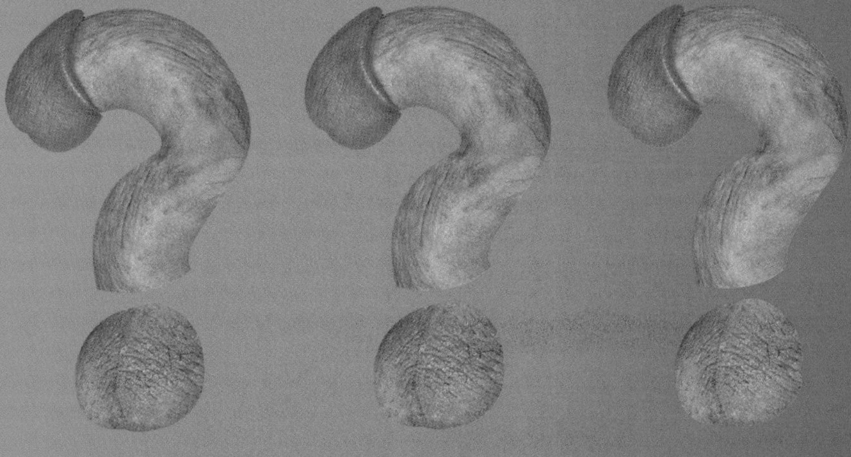

PENISES

1. **LARGE**—Over 3 inches in length and 4 inches in girth.
2. **SMALL**—Under 3 inches in length and 4 inches in girth.
3. **MICRO**—Under 1 inch. Barely visible from 3 feet away.
4. **BIG BALLS**—Circumference over 10 inches. Some traditionalists consider not flattering but actually very healthy and considered perfect in the Zone System.
5. **BIG BALLS/MICRO**—Testicles with a circumference over 10 inches and a shaft under 1 inch. Disgusting.
6. **BIG HEAD**—Thin shaft with mushroom tip. Also referred to as Rose Cock.
7. **NO BALLS**—An average shaft with no testicles. Testicle skin is tight near the body, no sign of balls anywhere.
8. **INNY**—Similar to a bird's nest. Flesh bulges in a circle but actual shaft is inside of body.
9. **DOUBLE**—Two identical penises from one body. Two balls only.
10. **BUSH**—A micro penis when the pubic hair is abnormally large.

LIST "A" – PENIS TYPE

①

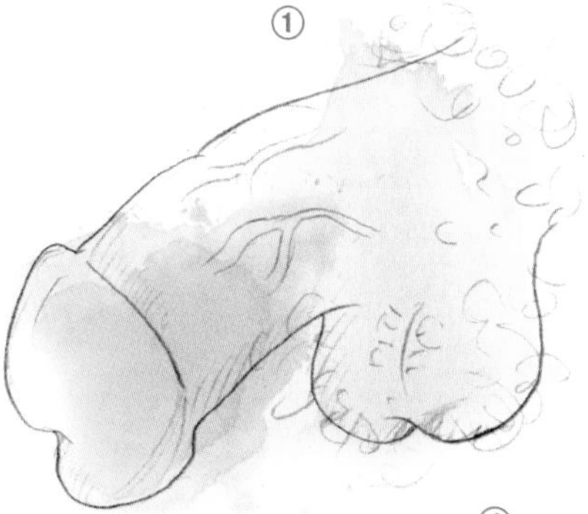

②

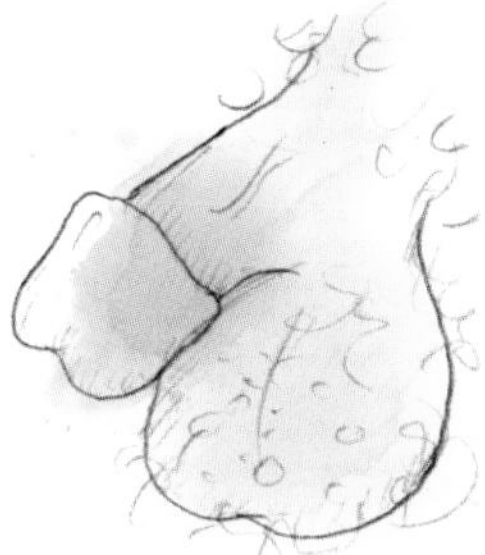

③

④

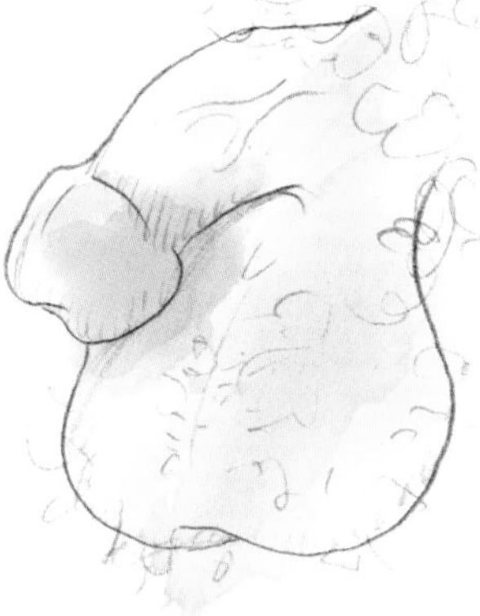

⑤

⑥

⑦

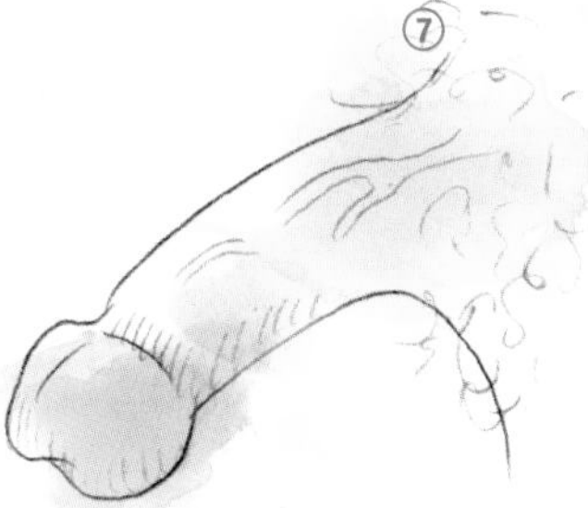

⑧

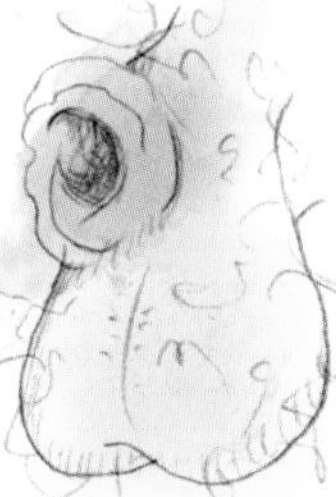

⑨

⑩

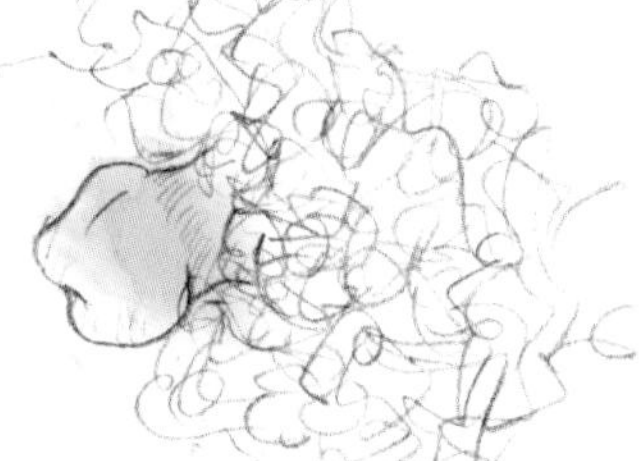

PENIS SAFETY

Calculate and Learn Your CUMulative PenisIQ Number

In order to avoid unnecessary and unattractive penile amputation, it is important to determine and learn your "CUMulative PenisIQ Number." Look at the types of penises from list "A" (the penis types list on page 145 of the book), and choose the number that best suits yours. Next, select the number from list "B" that best describes your penis stench. Add these numbers together and then divide by the number of minutes you can leave a thermometer in your urethra before you begin to cry. The resulting number is your CUMulative PenisIQ Number. You will need to order a special bracelet with this number, and wear it around your scrotum at all times. In the event of an emergency, the doctor will use this number to decide how many times to milk your penis each hour to retrieve any precious minerals (gold, silver) present in your semen. The number is also useful for determining foreskin-scald temperatures.

LIST "B" – PENIS STENCH

These are the five most common penis stenches, present in 99.9% of P.P. (Penis People).

1. **CANNED SAUERKRAUT**—"The smell of ol' '33"—a sour, pungent, overcooked smell, reminiscent of a misused (people have pissed in it) hippie food in a composting bin on a hot summer day.

2. **FERMENTED HERRING**—"A salted stink bomb"—a gruesome smell of fish that has been embalmed in brine in a tin can for a quarter century. Rank and overpowering.

3. **EGG CUM**—"Double deviled Probo (semen)"—the dried-up and caked-on Probo from a fat man who eats half a dozen eggs a day and then masturbates onto his belly without washing his hands or cleaning up afterwards. There are bits of egg directly on his penis, and entrenched in his Probo as well, with the resultant smell accurately described as "homemade mayonnaise from a discredited recipe."

4. **ARTIFICIAL FRUIT PUNCH**—"Hawaiian cock"—a strong chemical smell and taste that frequently can be found in the crotches of homeless men who douse their crotches with cheap cough syrup in a vain attempt to kill pubic lice.

5. **FRONTAL ANUS**—"Who let the hogs out?"—it will smell as if your penis is an anus that has recently evacuated its bowels—strong defecation doo-doo smell. Circus performers, trampoline artists, or anyone who stands on their head for hours as part of their job, and who suffers from Loose Bowel Syndrome, will often find that the unwanted shit has migrated into their penile area, forming solid cakes which are not easily removed. These cakes emit a telltale "crap" smell that can smell similar to feces, if not removed.

SEXUAL POSITIONS TO ENSURE A BABY BOY

The following sexual positions have been approved by the Zone Council and are ideal for ensuring you produce a large-headed baby boy with very few health problems.

BUDDY TABLE—All of your male friends form a table with their bodies. The wife lies on top in missionary while the husband stands. The male friends chant: Soy Ha! Soy Ha! Soy Yup!!!

STEP WIDE—In a small room (guest bathroom ideal) lay your partner out over a closed toilet. Have her spread legs as wide as possible. Mount her and step wide, so your legs are also spread as far wide as possible. Place hand on toilet flusher and place erect penis near vagina hole and ejaculate while flushing toilet over and over.

BROWN ISLAND—Take discarded Halloween candy or used chocolate bars and pile them up in the center of your bed. Take a wax candle or heating element and melt the chocolate so it stains the sheets and creates a brown island. Now both you and your partner stand above the brown island and perform the sex act with your erect penis now entering the vagina hole and ejaculating. Never take eyes off the brown island during the sex act.

KLUNKY BALLS—Tie wooden blocks to your balls. Jump up and around so the blocks klunk into each other—repeat the sex chant "H'wooo Hun Chall" until your lover is wet and wanting the sex act. Remove wooden blocks and have your partner hold the blocks while you enter her with your erect penis.

OLD DONUT—Allow a store-bought donut to age and harden to the exact hardness of your erect penis (roughly 6 to 8 weeks). Place your penis in the hard donut so it dangles on the edge of the tip. Invite your partner to watch as you dangle donut on the edge of your penis tip. Allow the donut to dangle for several minutes. Remove donut and place penis in vagina hole and ejaculate.

LIMP STICK—Maintain a flaccid penis for 48 hours. Next, cram flaccid penis into vagina hole and let it rest there for several minutes. If erection develops, remove, reset (48 hours) and attempt again.

BUM OBSERVER—Locate a homeless man and invite him to your sex room. Perform vaginal sex with your erect penis while the homeless man watches.

STARTING YOUR OWN ZONE FAMILY

ZONE APPROVED BABY NAMES	BOYS' APPROVED NAMES	GIRLS' APPROVED NAMES
	DERM TOOS VORE-EAR NORWALK	PEEN MISVRAD RHAMB OOK

CALCULATE YOUR ZONE SCORE NOW

☐	FRIENDSHIP
☐	FAMILY
☐	BUSINESS
☐	LOVE
☒	HEALTH
☒	POEMS
☒	FOOD
☐	**TOTAL**

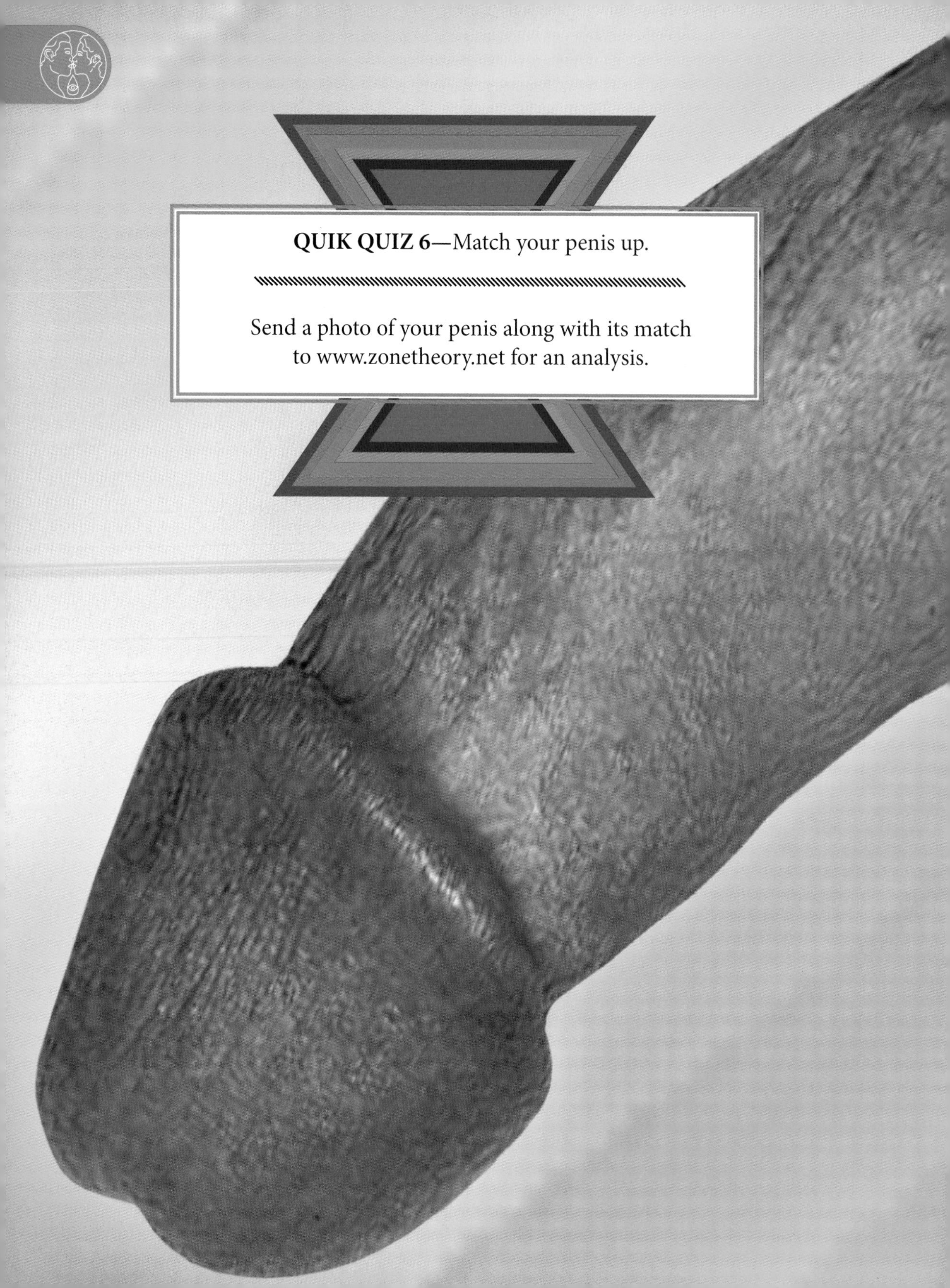

QUIK QUIZ 6—Match your penis up.

Send a photo of your penis along with its match to www.zonetheory.net for an analysis.

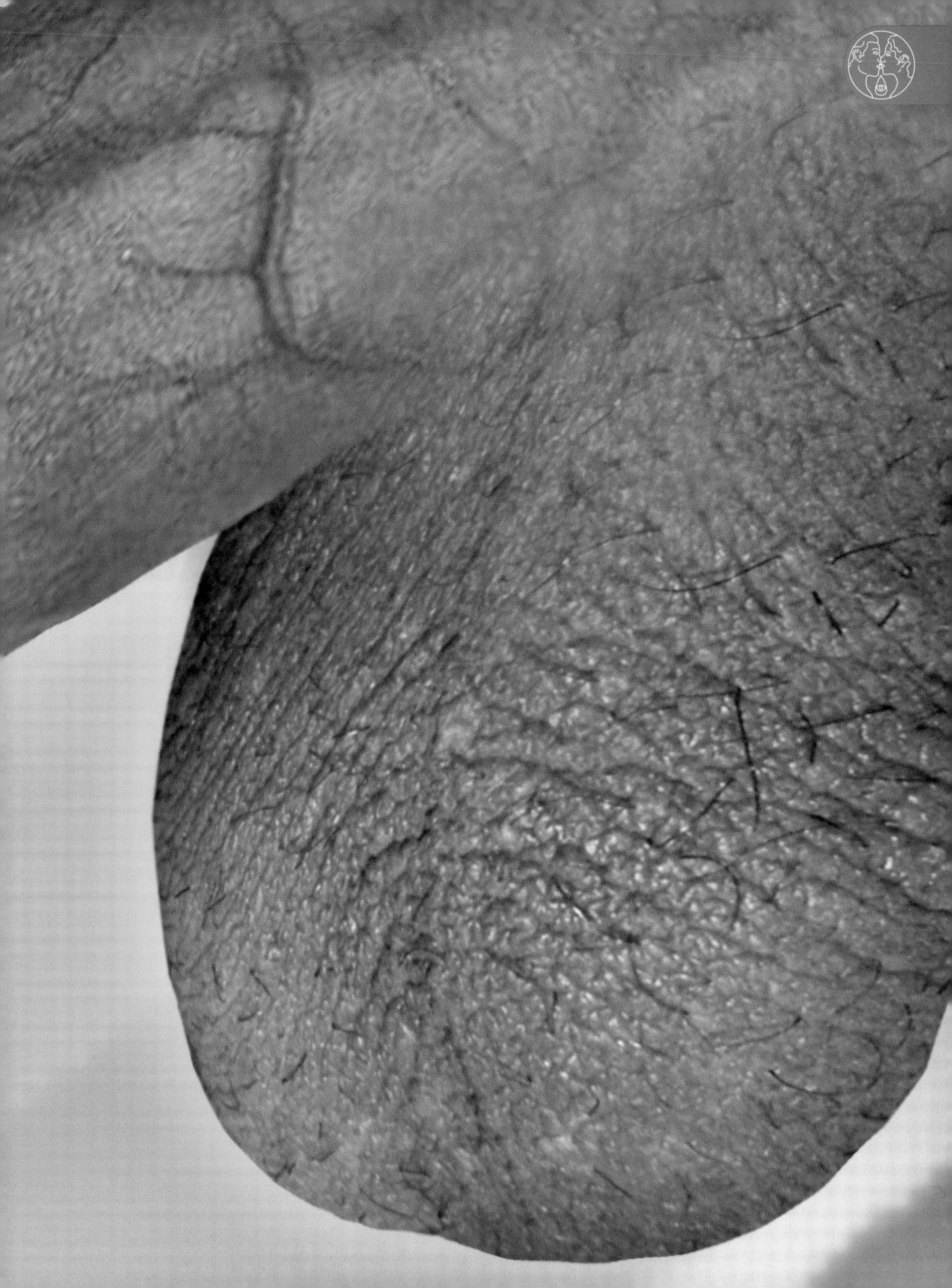

TIM ON LOVE

I have a penis that is several yards long. It's a blessing and a curse. Oftentimes I lose feeling in the tip because it takes so long for the blood to reach the end! When it is fully erect I can direct it towards the floor, lean on it and rise up like a pole-vaulter. I balance myself on the tip of the penis and assume the "Superman" position and pretend to fly through the air, fist out, cape and hair rustling in the wind (provided by fan pointed at me on high setting). There is a downside though; it is impossible for me to use my penis for vaginal sex and I have not yet deposited my Probo into my Zone Wife! It's just another example of the mystery of the ***ZONE THEORY***™ in action. Even as a Zone Plane 8 Zone Minister and High Priest I hope and pray I will one day have the courage to take a sword to my prick and get him down to normal size. My case is rare and will not apply to any current readers of ***ZONE THEORY***™ *2nd Edition.*

ERIC ON LOVE

It came as quite a surprise to my Zone Wife Karen when we started the Probo extraction process. She was ready with her jars and a positive attitude. I told her, "I have something important to tell you." And in unison with me dropping my pants to the ground I gently whispered, "I have no penis." Karen dropped a Probo collection jar and it smashed on the kitchen tiles. My crotch area looks like a mannequin man with a tiny red hole for my urine to drip out. Karen tried to remain positive and enthusiastic but I could tell she had never dealt with a little red man hole like this before. I instructed her to "make a pointing gesture like you see a beautiful Japanese maple tree." Then I grabbed her finger and slammed it into my hole over and over. Eventually I could feel my Probo building up and ready for an explosion. "Stand back, Karen, and hold out your jar." She did as I commanded. I gave her a countdown from 10, then I squirted out 2 tear-sized globs of Probo and landed them in the jar perfectly.

ZONE 5
HEALTH

INT. HOME—DAY

A mother scrubs the kitchen floor. Sweat beads form on her forehead and drip onto the wet Formica. She wipes her brow and gets back to work. She scrubs harder and harder. The grime in between the tiles seems impenetrable. In the background we hear a loud liquid hissing sound. Her son Jason runs in from the other room.

JASON: Mommy, what is that sound? Is it a snake?

MOMMY: No, that's Daddy making diarrhea into the spaghetti pot.

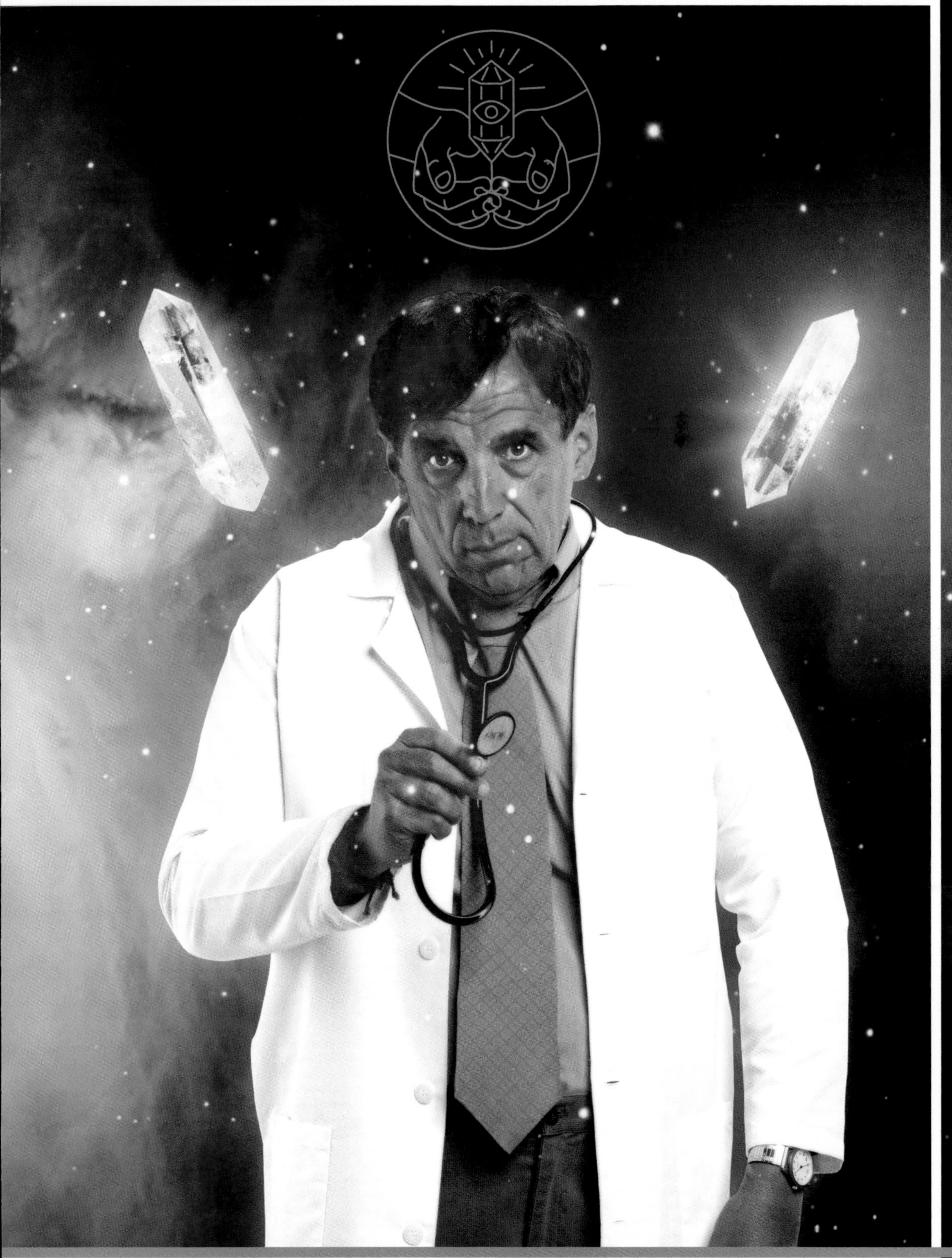

WHAT IS HEALTH?

Health is how we treat our body. Our body is our temple. Our "Zone Temple," and it's important to understand how our body works and how we can use HEALTH to ensure that our body is in optimum health so our body can SERVE us. Health is obviously the most important Zone because without it we'd be dead meat.

Some jackomos don't care about their own health.

In this chapter we will learn how to IDENTIFY our Fhlow (body type), REMOVE the dangerous tubes that pollute our body and UNDERSTAND the mysteries and wonder of our own diarrhea.

REGIONS OF THE BODY

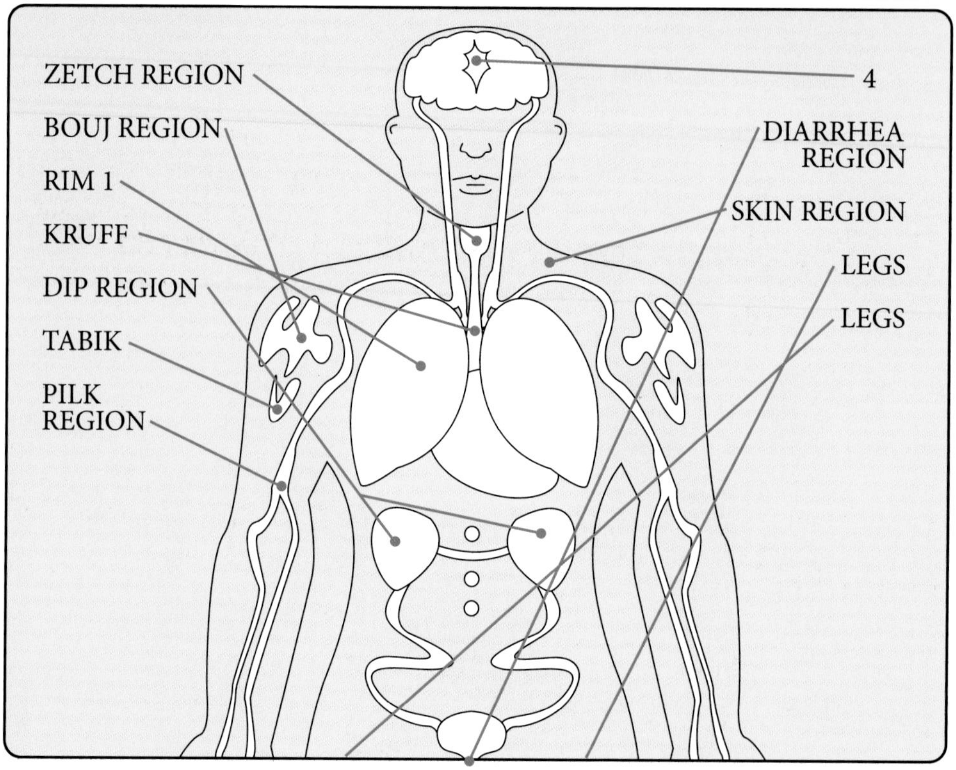

FAQ

Q: HOW DO I INDUCE DIARRHEA?
A: MANY COMMON FOODS CREATE INSTANT DIARRHEA. HERE ARE BUT A FEW THAT CAN GUARANTEE YOU GET INSTANT, WET, SLOPPY DIARRHEA: CORN, FLAX, CHOCOLATE, SOY CULTURES, CHICKEN, LAMB, CEREAL GRAINS, RICE, PECANS, ALMONDS, HOT APPLES.

WHAT IS DIARRHEA?

Diarrhea is the brown liquid mess that shoots out of our ass like a fire hydrant. It's painful, uncomfortable, unpredictable and EMBARRASSING when it happens in public. Healthy men and women experience diarrhea rarely, only about once or twice a week—unhealthy people can experience diarrhea so often that it becomes the normal process of defecation.

But what if we told you that your diarrhea is a COMMUNICATION device your body uses to speak to you!

WHAAAAAAAAAA?????

My body talks to me through my diarrhea?

Of course it does!

WHAAAAAAAAAAA???????

When your body makes diarrhea it's sending you a message. Hidden in the thickness, viscosity, depth, color and volume are unique messages. Don't you want to hear what your body has to say to you?

Decoding your diarrhea is messy business and involves some general understanding of number coding to really get it, but ***ZONE THEORY***™ has cracked the code into 25 discrete and unique messages your diarrhea is potentially sending you. Zone scientists are working hard to identify more messages and one day we hope to discover a codex that will open up an entire "diarrheaese" language and who knows, perhaps one day the diarrhea will be able to understand us!

TIME FOR YOUR BRAIN WEIGHT CHECK-IN!

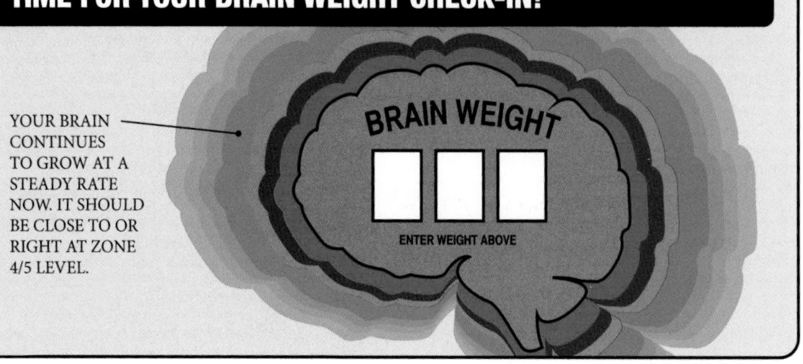

YOUR BRAIN CONTINUES TO GROW AT A STEADY RATE NOW. IT SHOULD BE CLOSE TO OR RIGHT AT ZONE 4/5 LEVEL.
BRAIN WEIGHT
ENTER WEIGHT ABOVE

IDENTIFYING YOUR BODY TYPE

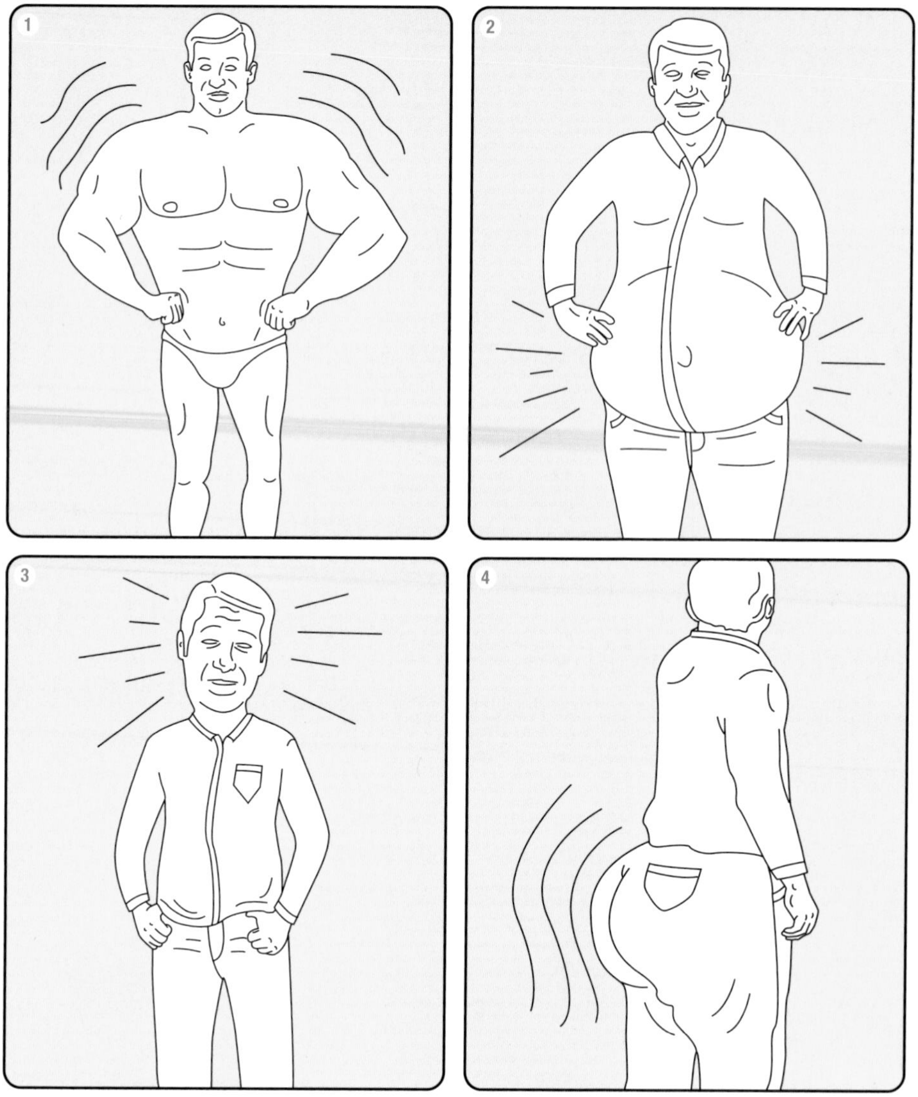

1. MUFFIN MAN: Large torso and head. Small legs.

2. ALL GUT: Tire waist.

3. TOP BOY: Extremely large head.

4. BOTTOM BOY: Huge ass, regular body.

BODY TYPE *(Continued)*

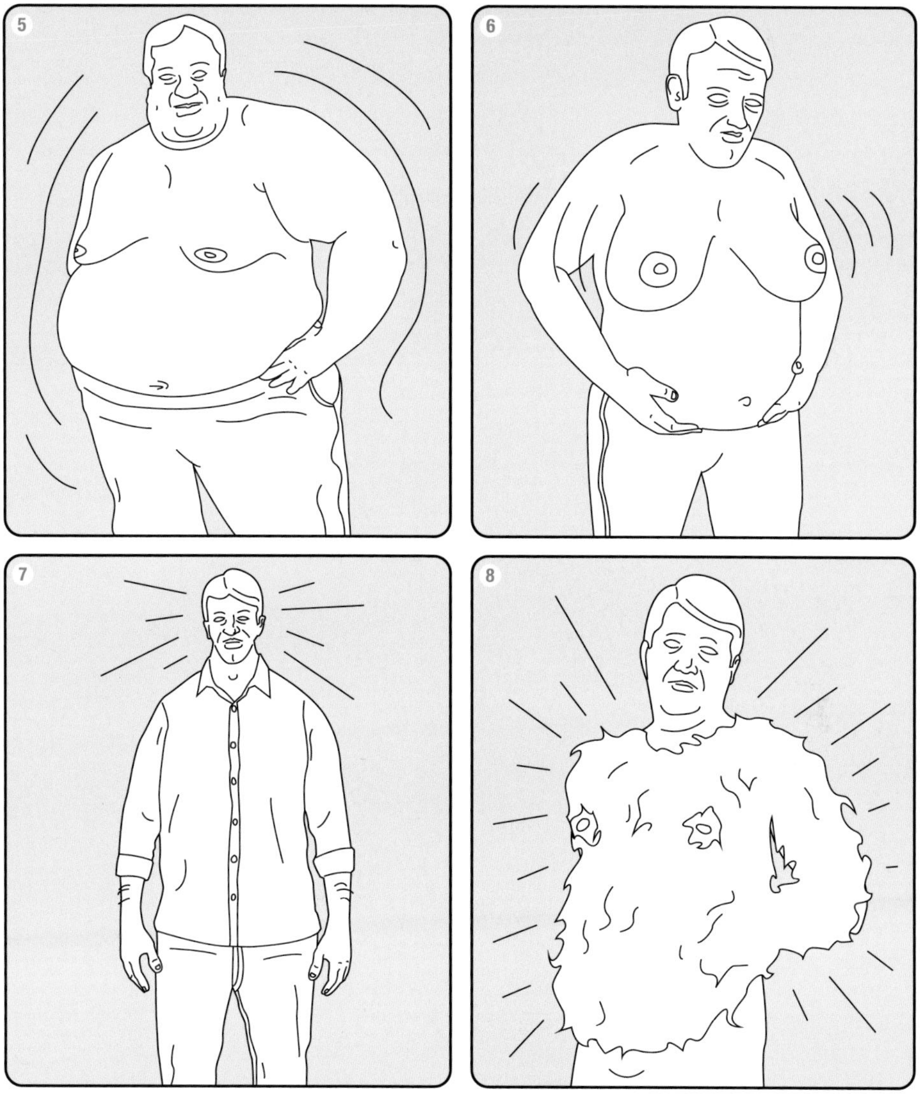

5. GLOBE: Very fat person.

6. BOOB BOY: Large female breasts.

7. PIN BOY: Tiny head.

8. HAIRY MAN: Extreme amount of body hair making you look fat.

REMOVING YOUR TUBES

The human body contains miles of useless tubes. These aren't helpful tubes that deliver or process food and waste, they are meaningless, wasteful tubes that doctors agree have no business being inside our bodies. Not only are these tubes useless, they actually have a negative effect on our body. Our body believes the tubes need to exist so it keeps the tubes alive and that takes energy. Energy that could be better spent on other parts of the body. We removed our tubes about 3 years ago and our energy levels went through the roof. We feel better, and we look better.

The good news is: Your pointless, wasteful tubes can be removed permanently BY YOU! RIGHT NOW! Just follow the easy steps below:

TEN EASY STEPS TO REMOVE YOUR TUBES

1

2

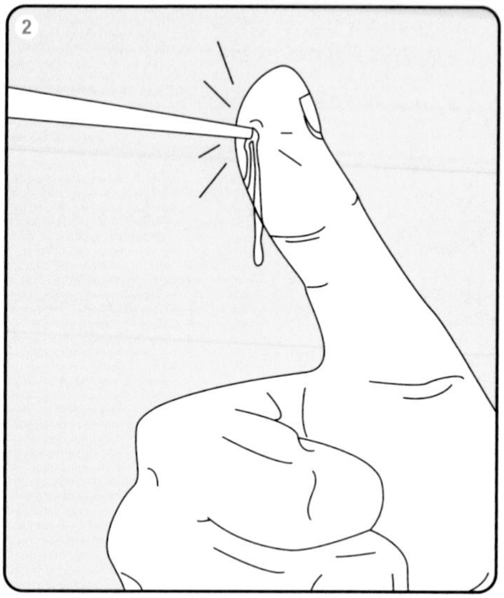

1. Soak in a tub—your body needs to be moist for this procedure to work—combine hot water with scrubbing solution and line tub with a non-stick adhesive to allow some tension.

2. Using a barber's needle puncture the top tip of your opposing thumb.

REMOVING YOUR TUBES *(Continued)*

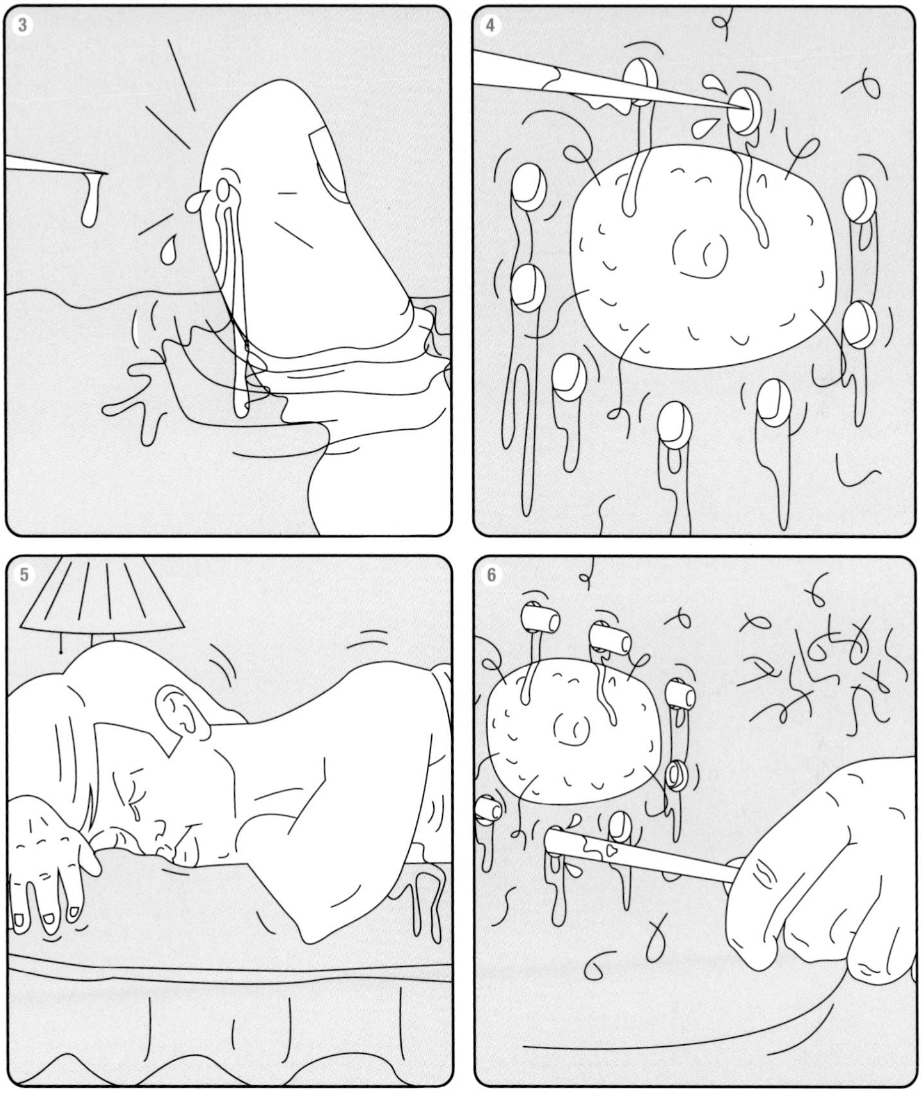

3. Let hole submerge slowly.

4. Using barber's needle puncture several holes creating circles around both nipples.

5. Drain tub—dry and rest.

6. Using a mirror, examine punctures around nipple closely—after several minutes you will be begin to notice small white strings popping out of holes. These are the tubes—tug gently on the tubes until you have about 4 feet of tube free.

REMOVING YOUR TUBES *(Continued)*

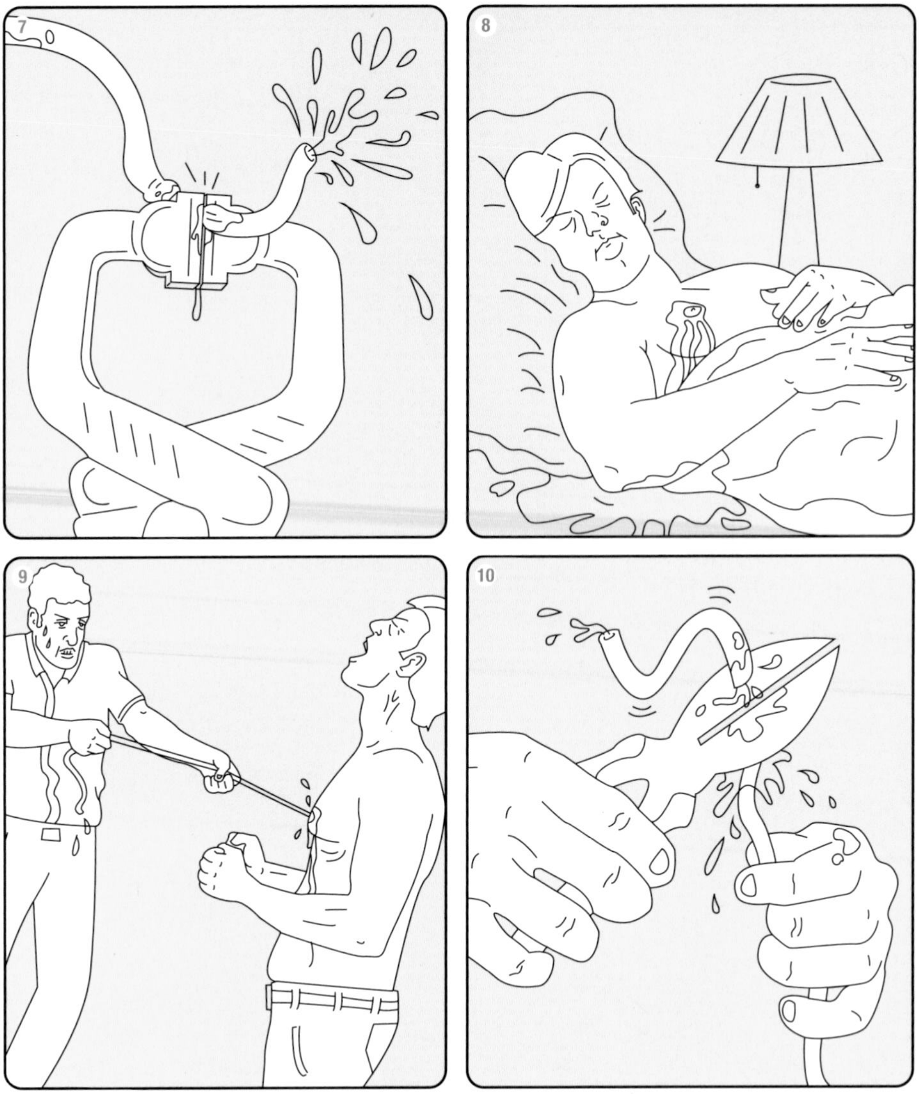

7. Snip tube leaving one foot of slack (this will be very painful and produce a large amount of blood)—clamp tube with barber's clamp or wedge clamp.

8. Bedrest.

9. Employing two or more friends, locate a large open area. Stand leaning back at a 45-degree angle—one friend grabs hold of the tube and walks away from you—the tube will resist for first 10 to 20 feet but after that the tube will move freely.

10. Your second friend should clip the tube every 100 yards or so. Then repeat step 9.

REMOVING YOUR TUBES *(Continued)*

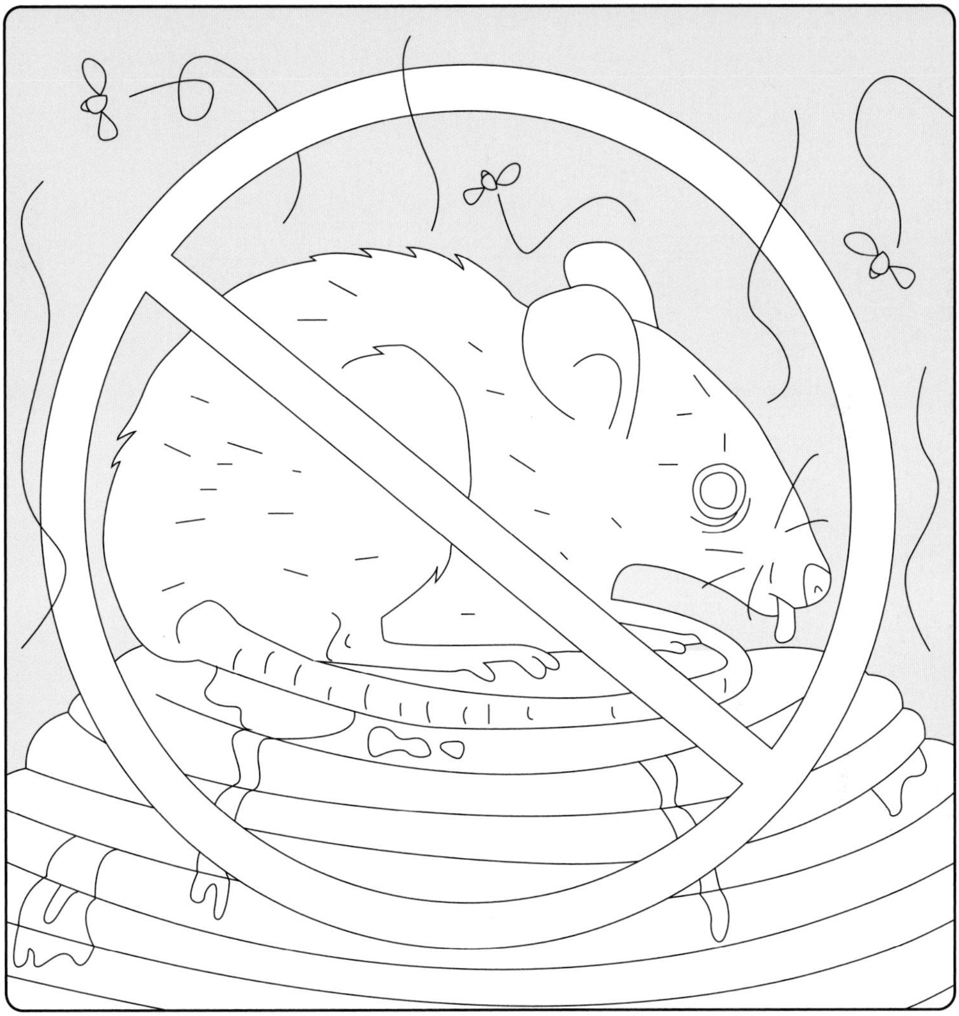

Your massive pile of tubing is likely to attract birds, dogs and rodents. The smell will draw all kinds of pests to the scene. It's recommended to perform this procedure in a rodent-free Zone. If there is no rodent-free Zone near you, simply incinerate tube pile as soon as you can.

Now you are tube free! Are you ready to live a life free of tubes? The first several years will be challenging as your body adapts; after all, you and your body have gotten used to those tubes. But once you adjust you will never ever be able to wipe the smile off your face. You will be permanently happy. In fact you could ignore every other single element of this book and just focus on this one procedure and that would solve everything. But please continue reading.

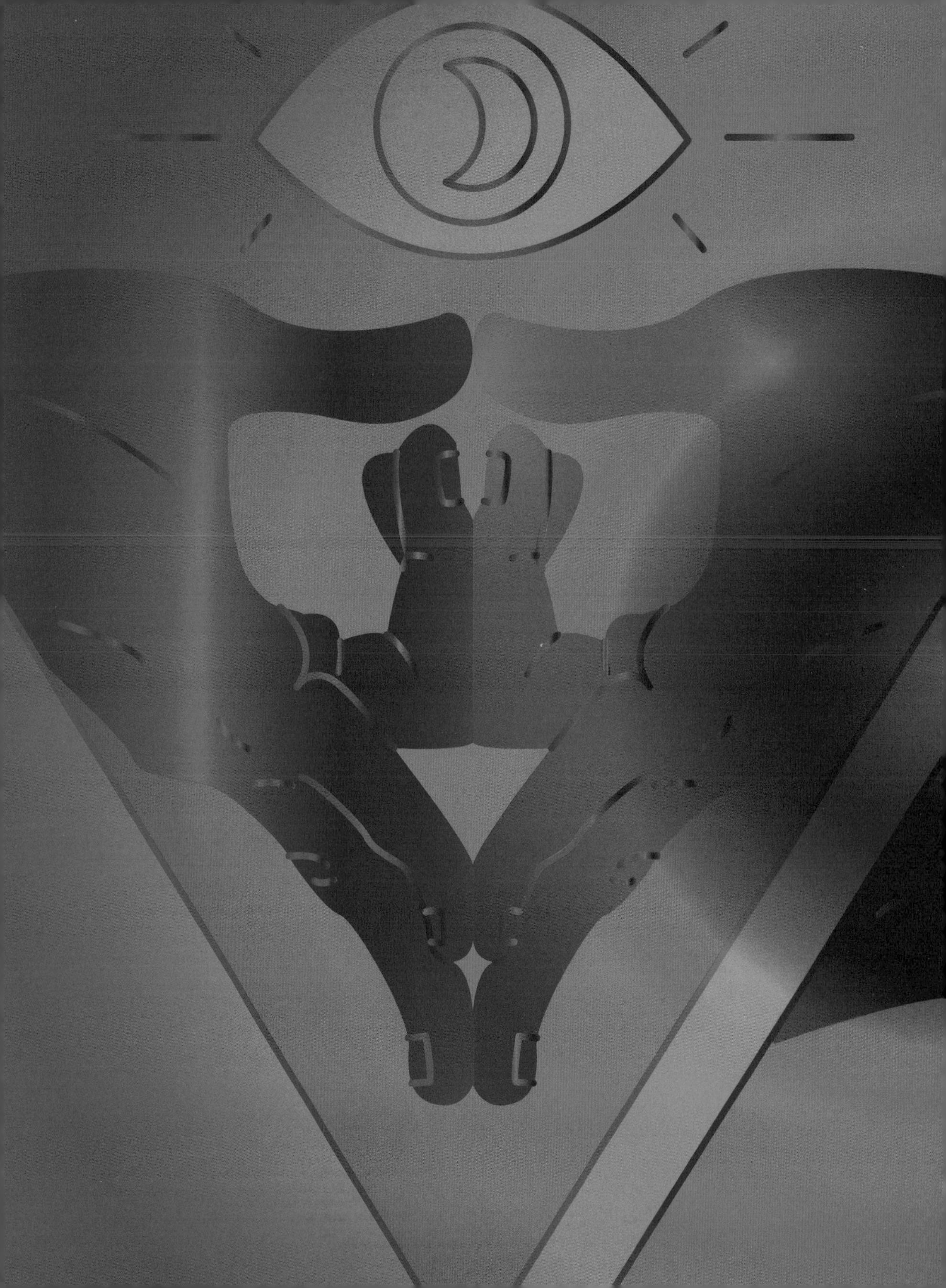

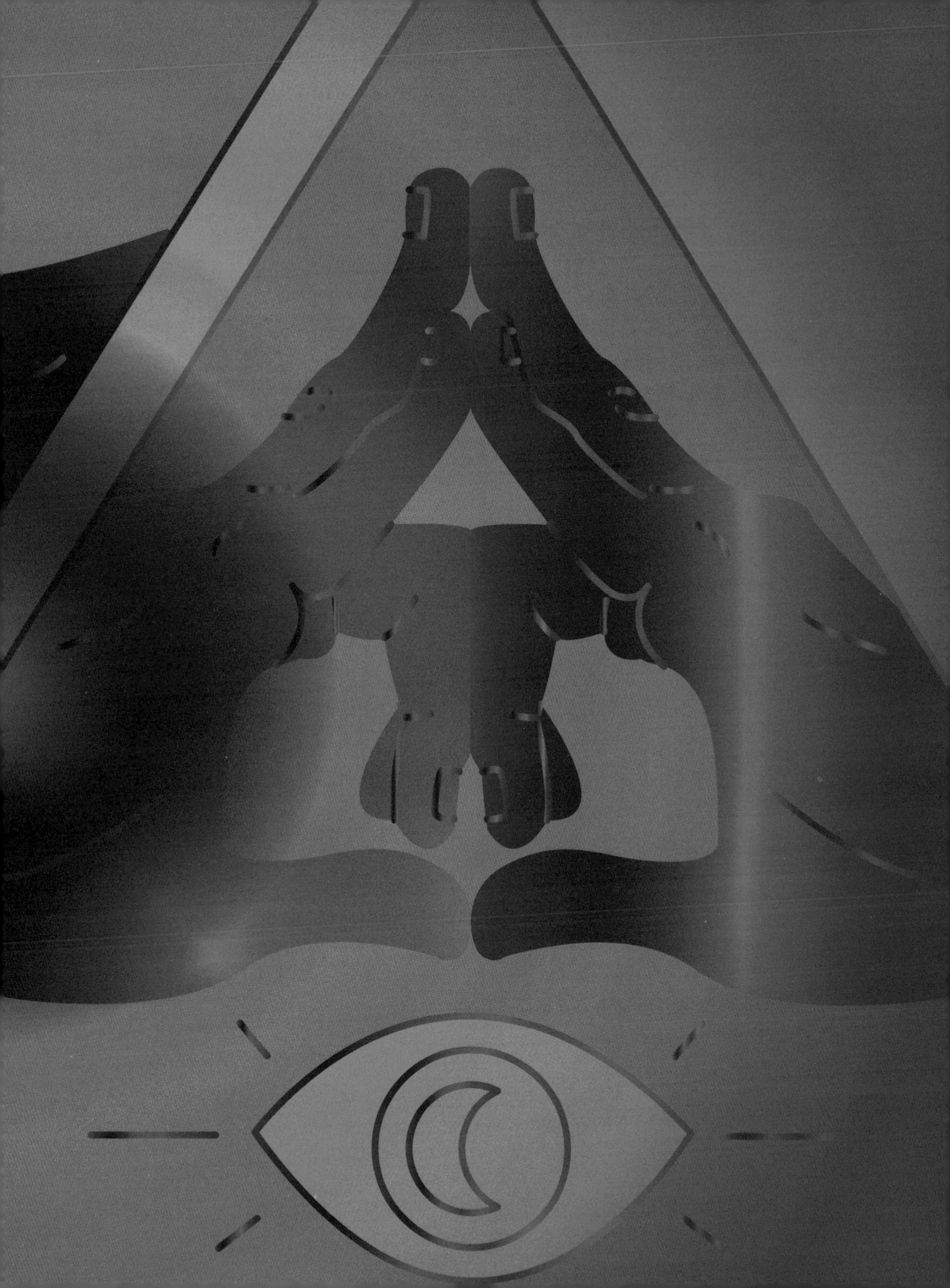

HOW DO I GET MY DIARRHEA TALKING?

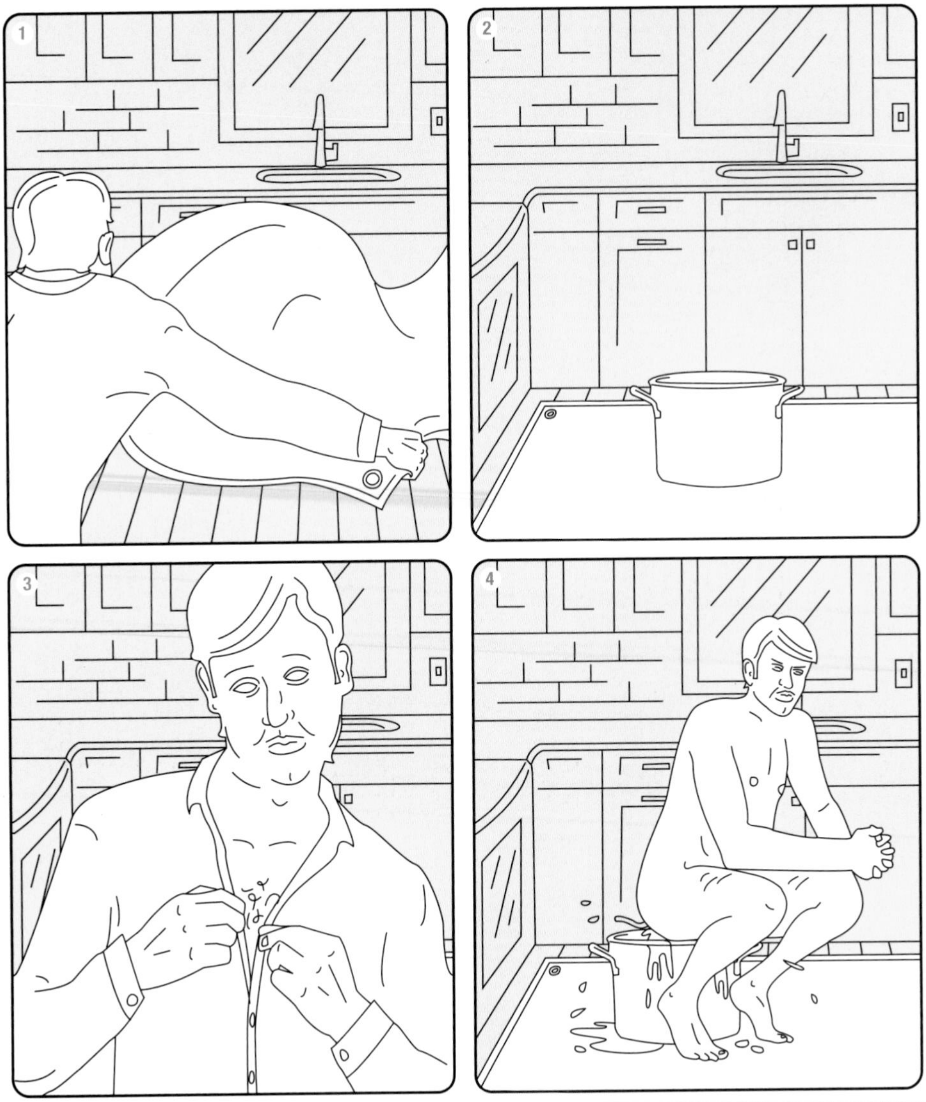

STEP 1. Place a large **ZONE THEORY**™ tarp over your kitchen floor (or basement).

STEP 2. Place clean spaghetti pot on tarp.

STEP 3. Become fully nude.

STEP 4. Squat over spaghetti pot and spray diarrhea. Don't worry if you miss—that's what the tarp is for!

DIARRHEA TALK *(Continued)*

STEP 5. Position your body over the spaghetti pot (on all fours) and urinate[16] into the pot.

STEP 6. Allow urine and diarrhea to marinate together for 48 hours out in the open.

STEP 7. Return to diarrhea pot and place Diarrhea Dipstick in the pot for 90 seconds.

STEP 8. Place Diarrhea Dipstick in the Diarrhea Dipstick machine and wait for your message to play.

[16] Urine provides the perfect amount of alkaline to activate the diarrhea and get it talking.

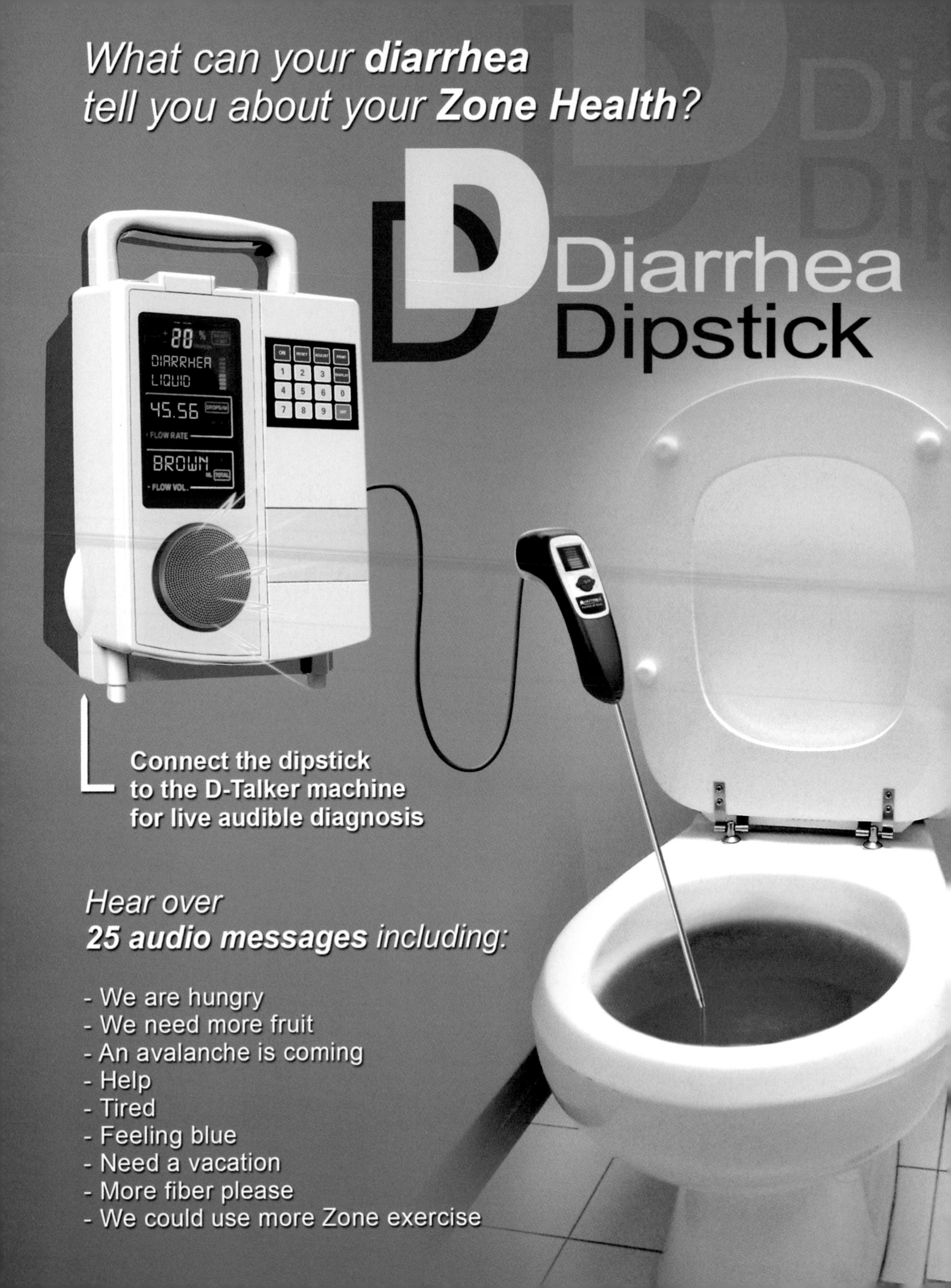
What can your diarrhea
tell you about your Zone Health?
Diarrhea
Dipstick
DIARRHEA
LIQUID
45.56
FLOW RATE
BROWN
FLOW VOL.
Connect the dipstick
to the D-Talker machine
for live audible diagnosis
Hear over
25 audio messages including:
- We are hungry
- We need more fruit
- An avalanche is coming
- Help
- Tired
- Feeling blue
- Need a vacation
- More fiber please
- We could use more Zone exercise

FITNESS / MAINTENANCE EXERCISES

These exercises have been tested to work. Dress in a loose-fitting "bread shirt" made of white flour and sugar. When the shirt becomes yellowed from sweat and body odor, it can be donated to the poor, to eat.

1. "Zone Cross": Place a thumbtack on the floor and stand on it with one foot. Clench the anus tightly to hold feces in. Stretch your arms out in a welcoming manner and wear a beatific expression on your face so as not to scare off potential kidney donors.

2. "Praise Priss Dimmie": We no longer praise Priss Dimmie. Stand in the position popular with Venusians during Seed Week. Hold an imaginary flute. The head of your penis should be exposed. Let semen dribble down your leg until there is enough on the floor that the wooden floorboards begin to buckle.

3. "Testicle Stretch": Pretend that you are holding a 500-lb. book of sexual photography and information. The book is very, very heavy. The photos are imaginary, yet very provocative and stimulating. Allow your penis to grow until it reaches the ceiling.

4. "Friendship Pose": Learn the latest codes used by Nude Recreation Center disciples to signify that it's time to go into the bathroom. Face another **ZONE THEORY™** *disciple and remain standing completely still for 7 days. On the eighth minute of the eighth hour of the eighth day, you both throw up your hands in the position of one of the codes. If the codes match, you must drink lye.*

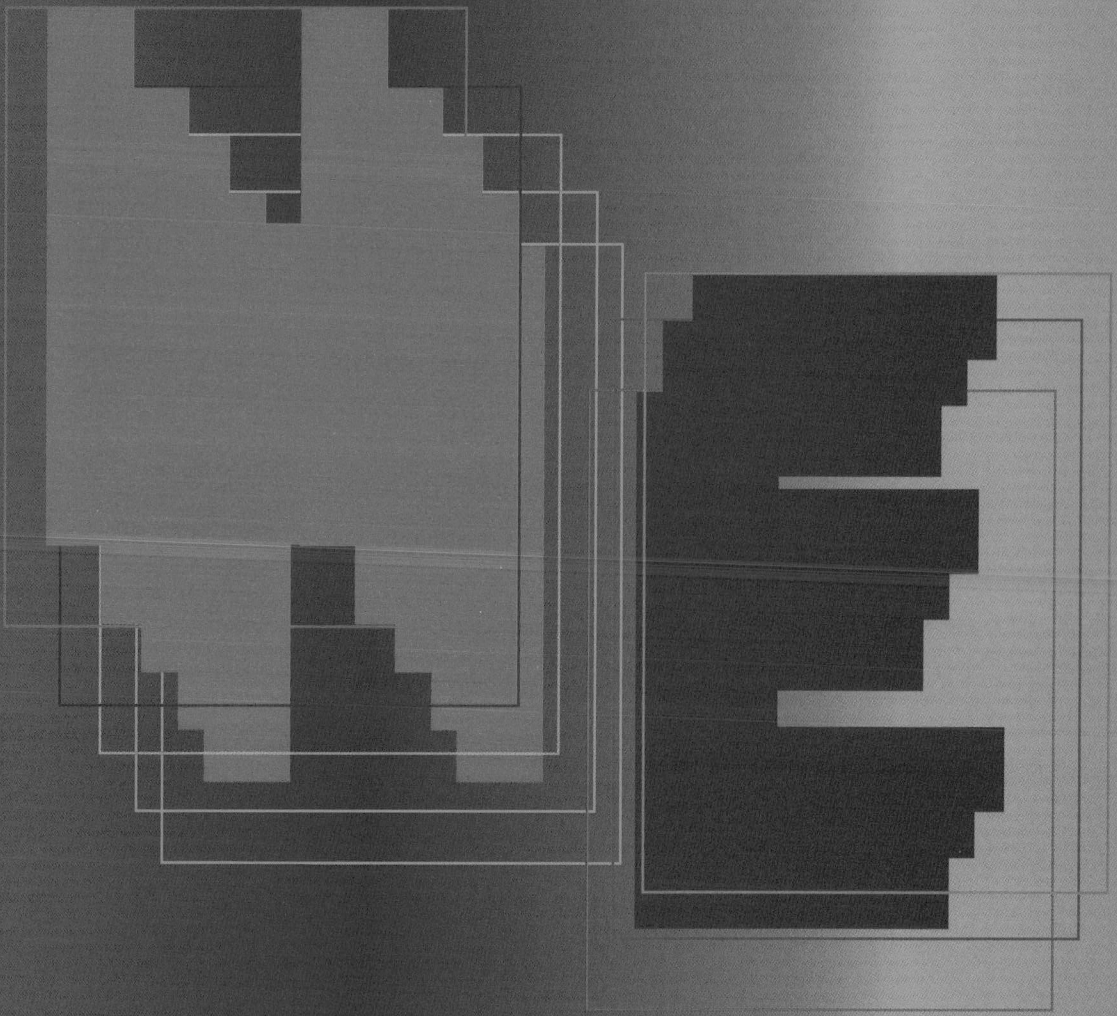

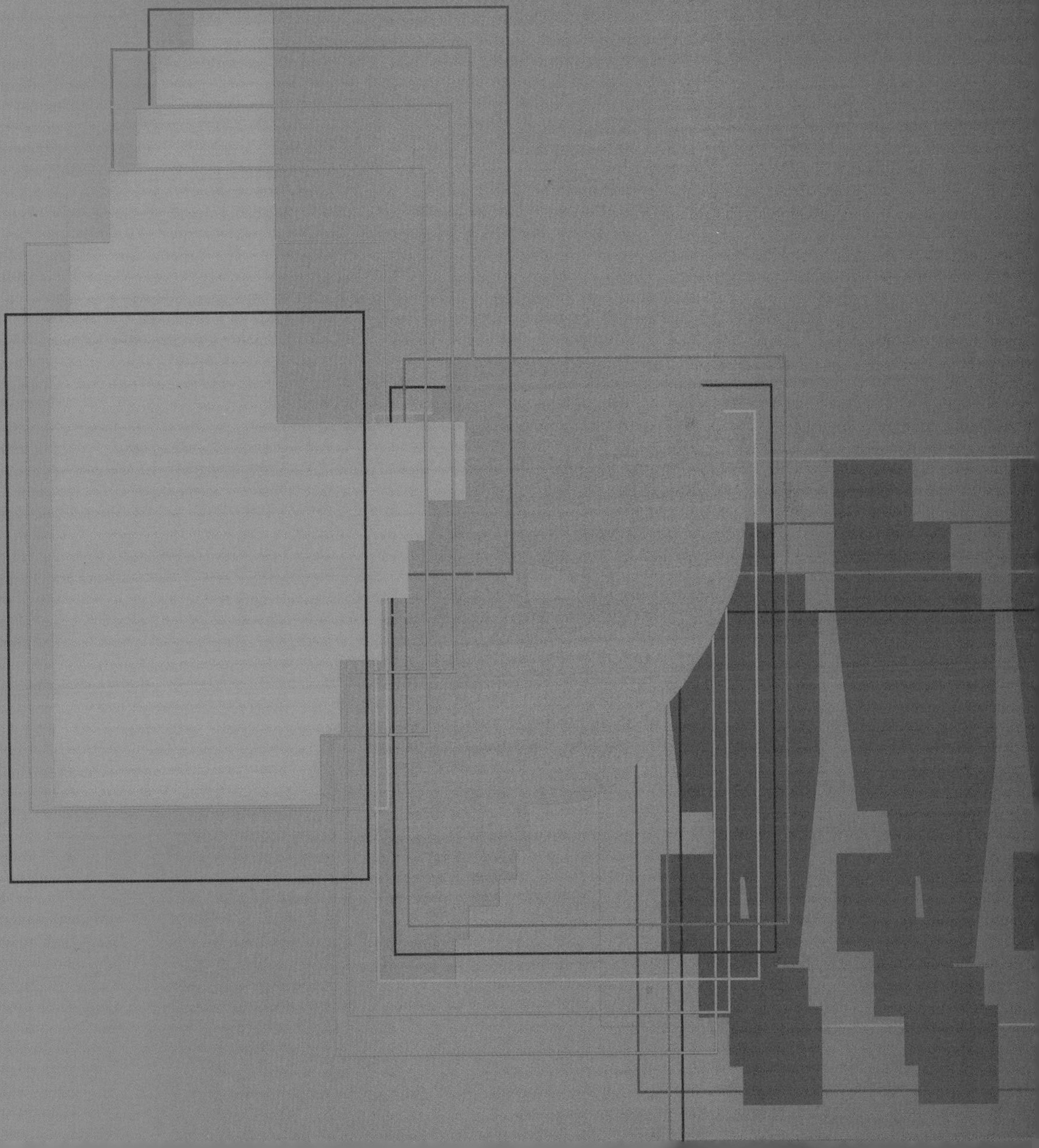

MORE TIPS ON HAVING A SUCCESSFUL BODY

Picking your nose is an easy way of removing mucus from your nasal cavities. It can be fun, challenging and SAFE if you follow these simple steps.

HOW TO PICK YOUR NOSE

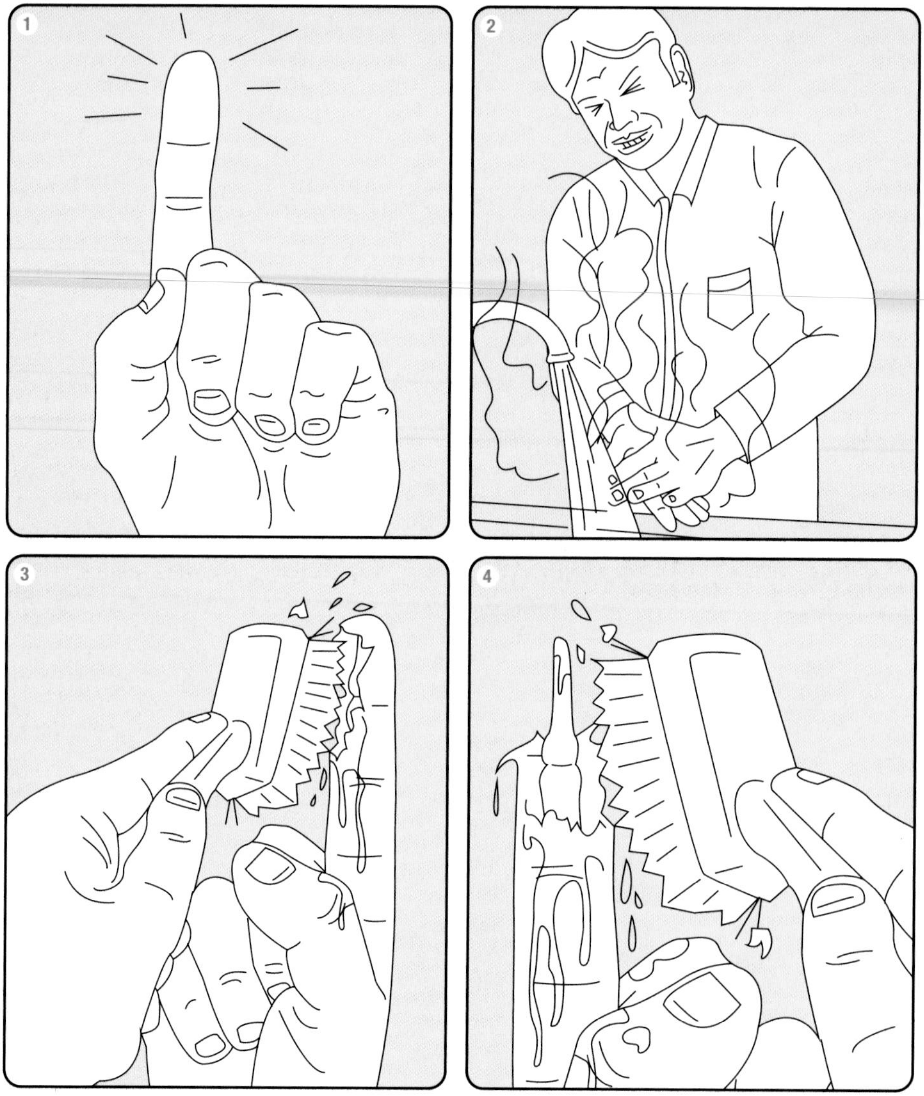

PICKING YOUR NOSE *(Continued)*

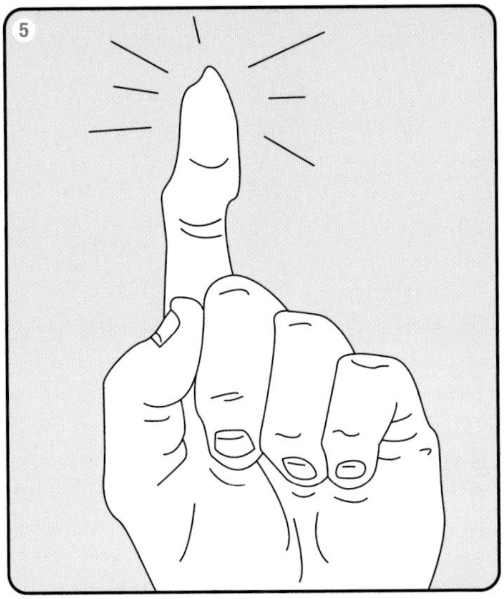

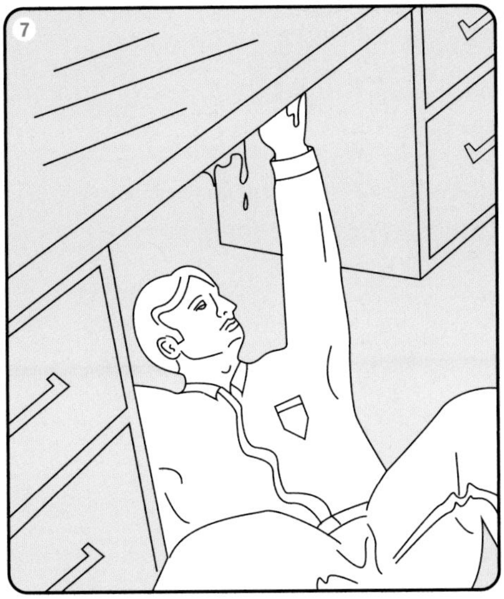

1. Choose a finger—we recommend your index finger or middle finger—if you are right-handed use your right hand. If you are left-handed the **ZONE THEORY™** *is not for you and you should immediately destroy this book.*

2. Wash your finger with scalding water. Let it soak in the near boiling water until it turns red and then white.

3. Scrub the finger hard with a wire brush.

4. Scrub the finger again with a new wire brush.

5. Allow finger to heal and reskin itself (5 to 10 days).

6. Insert finger into nasal cavity and twist to unlodge boogies, snot and whatever else is up there.

7. Wipe findings on the back of a chair, under your leg, or under a desk at work.

HOW TO SMELL YOURSELF

Our natural body odor can tell us so much about ourselves. But how can you experience your own body odor?

YOU HAVE TO LEARN HOW TO SMELL YOURSELF.

Smelling yourself is a great way to answer some important questions:

1. What do I smell like?
2. Do I have bad body odor?
3. What does my smell remind me of?

And many, many other questions.

STEP 1. Place yourself in a room which is devoid of all smells—for example, do not place yourself in a room that's filled with trash and dog shit.

STEP 2. Become fully nude and remove all clothes from the room.

STEP 3. Lift either arm and bury your nose in your armpit.

STEP 4. Breathe deeply for 90 seconds.

STEP 5. Check off the smells that come to your mind on this smelling chart on opposite page. Don't think too hard—this should be your first, gut reaction.

STEP 6. Invite a stranger into the room and have them breathe deeply into your pit for 90 seconds and have them fill out the smelling chart.

STEP 7. Cross-reference the two charts, compile and send results to your local Zone Center.

THE OFFICIAL ZONE THEORY™
CIRCLE OF SMELLS
DEAD RAT
BURNT EGGS
ROTTEN PUMPKIN
HOBO
AGED STEAK
BABY FART
DRY SEMEN
JUNKIE
HOMELESS MAN
OLD WOMAN'S FART

HELP
HELP
HELP
HELP
HELP

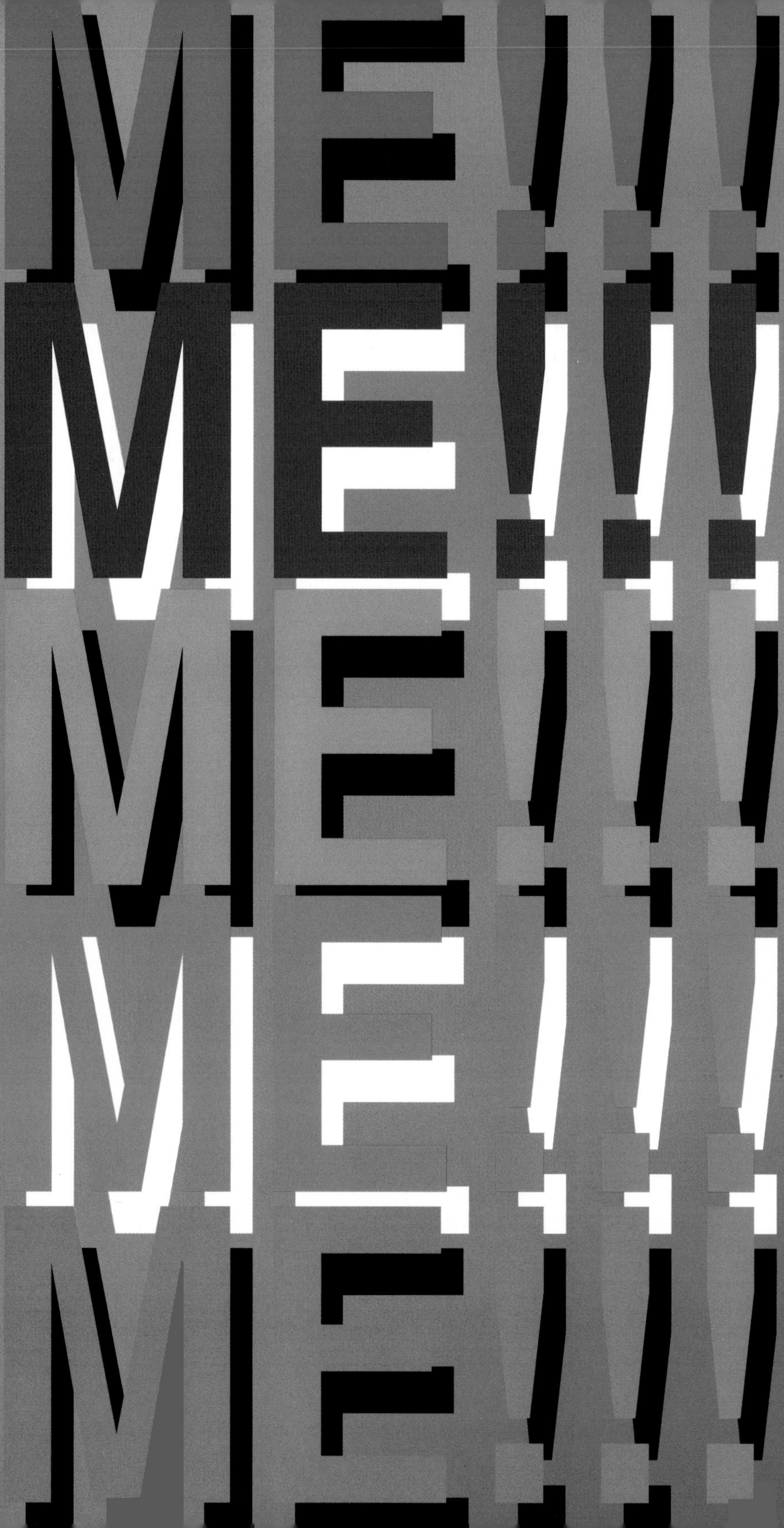
ME!!!
ME!!!
ME!!!
ME!!!
ME!!!

Need a boost in your Zone life?
- Add a "kick" to your Zone Fitness
- Enhance your social skills
- Increase motivation
THE ZONE THEORY
Zowder
Zone Powder
- Add a kick to your Zone Fitness
- Enhance your social skills
- Increase motivation
VOTED #1 ZONE PRODUCT OF 1997
Zowder BM
Zone Powder
Ingest nasally or intravenously. Side effects may include anal contractions, insomnia, impotence, anxiety, incontinence and loss of appetite.
Consult your Zone Mentor when any or all side effects occur. Do not operate heavy equipment 24 hrs. after Zowder effects wear off.

HEALTH WORKSHEET

Write down latest 5 messages from your diarrhea.

1.____

2.____

3.____

4.____

5.____

Removed Tubes? ☐ **YES** ☐ **NO**

Number of exercises completed? ________

Weigh your brain now.

How are you feeling? *(circle at least 3)*

death's door / awful / sick / nauseous / depressed / fine / reasonably well
above normal / well above normal / vamb / orgasmic / cherished

Stand in front of your ***ZONE THEORY***™ Mirror and stare at your nude body for one hour. Notate here your observations. What would you change about the shape and size of your body if you could? How could your body improve? List 100 areas where improvements are possible. ____________________

Have you grown yet? ☐ **YES** ☐ **NO**

ZONE SUCCESS STORIES / PROFILES

BRYUN TANDER *(Zone Plane 1)*

Before

After

Before ***ZONE THEORY***™ I was 5'3" 450 lbs. It was impossible for me to eat, sleep, move, produce Probo, or even open my eyes. (Thanks to ***ZONE THEORY's***™ Book on Tape series for allowing me to become a Zone Boy.) My life was a living nightmare. I attempted suicide on several occasions only to fail miserably over and over again. On one occasion an event occurred that would seem more likely to occur in the comics… I tumbled myself off a bridge into a river only to hit a shallow area and my fat belly bounced me back onto the bridge! It's a true story that landed me on popular television show *Weird but True Suicides.* After completing ***ZONE THEORY***™ courses 1-25 I am now 5'9" and only 100 pounds! My brain weight alone is 59 pounds! I've never been happier, healthier and more productive. I produce Probo for my hot Zone Wife 5 times a day! My Zone Score is off the charts at 45,094,564 and I am approaching Zone Plane 8 at record speed! All because of ***ZONE THEORY***™ advanced chapters and course work!

QUIK QUIZ 7

Please answer YES or NO to the questions below:
(THERE ARE NO RIGHT OR WRONG ANSWERS)

1. Do you love?	☐ YES	☐ NO
2. Have you ever had red hair?	☐ YES	☐ NO
3. Inside your body, what is it?	☐ YES	☐ NO
4. Are you a dream?	☐ YES	☐ NO
5. Can you reduce?	☐ YES	☐ NO
6. Is there ways?	☐ YES	☐ NO

CALCULATE YOUR ZONE SCORE NOW

☐	FRIENDSHIP
☐	FAMILY
☐	BUSINESS
☐	LOVE
☐	HEALTH
☒	POEMS
☒	FOOD
☐	TOTAL

TIM ON HEALTH

Health is very important to me. Without health there's no real quality of life and if you don't have optimal quality of life you might as well jump off a bridge.

I take very good care of my body and do many things to ensure that I will live forever. For example, I do not always eat hot dogs.

But how do I maintain my health? Through using the tips and tricks outlined in ***ZONE THEORY***™! It's not always easy but it's what I know I need to do to exceed and succeed in life.

There are secrets that are my own though and I'd love to share them with you—I believe my body is my place, it's my own personal Zone that I often explore and fondle when no one is home. I don't mean jacking it off or ramming toys up my own ass—I mean taking sensual oils (created from my own extracted body fat) and lathering up my nude body; rubbing and stroking it with my own oils. This is what I call self-pleasure. It gets me off and it turns me on.

It's one of the many secrets to perfect health that I keep to myself and there's no way I'm ever sharing it with you.*

***Zone Plane 8 call me.**

ERIC ON HEALTH

I have a secret that I have decided to share with you.

I have been bottling my own breast milk and drinking a shot glass of it mixed with tap water every day since I was born.

As a result, I am the healthiest person alive.

Last year my breasts stopped producing milk. At first I panicked, thinking that death was around the corner. But then common sense prevailed. I purchased four 55-gallon drums of Tabitha Lane–brand Mildew Water and drank them in a day. My abdomen became horribly distended and my kidneys began to fail. Four friends carried me to Miller's Cave to die.

Alas, they did not know the power of my breast milk! As I lay there dying, I began to squeeze and manipulate my dried-up teats. After an hour, the cave began to smell bad, as my teats started spouting that familiar oily fluid…the breast milk was back! I cupped my hands and drank every drop that came out. Within minutes, my abdomen was flat as a washboard. My kidneys sprang back into action and began processing piss and shit. I jumped to my feet, and I ran all the way home from Miller's Cave, in the best shape of my life, topping speeds of 100 mph, and leaving my friends in the dust.

I am the healthiest person alive!

ZONE 6
POEMS

EXT. QUIET ROOM—NIGHT

M: What are you doing?

YOU: Writing poetry.

M: I will leave you alone then.

It's a hard and true scientific fact: as sure as the sky is blue, the human brain automatically produces thousands of poems per second. We produce them every time we see an object in nature, experience an emotion, touch something, get touched...you name it; every moment our brain is active it is collecting experience and translating it into poems. If this is news to you, trust in this. It's all true.

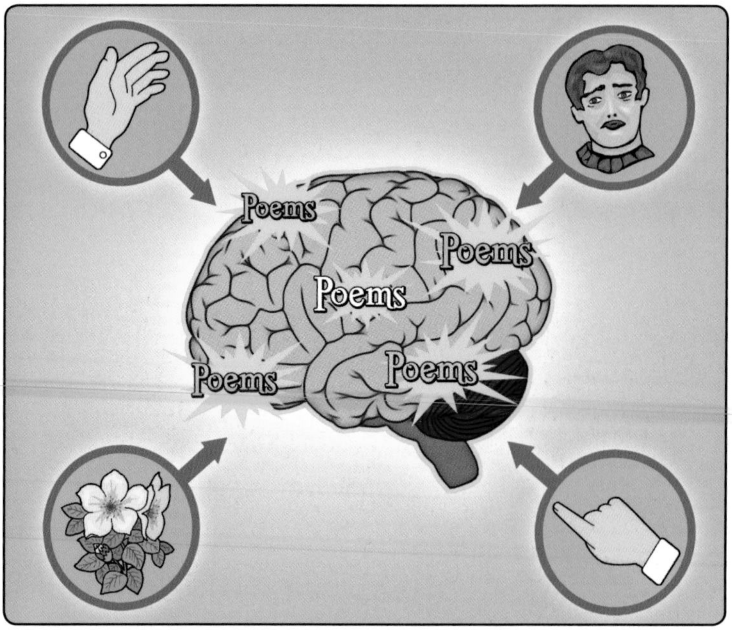

The problem is these poems quickly bottle up and oversaturate the brain. We may not know these poems consciously but each poem sits on a brain nugget and takes up space—it clouds our thoughts and weighs us down. If these poems stay up in our brains there is a high chance that we can suffer:

Brain Deterioration
Mental Illness
Severe Mental Retardation
Brain Sickness
Brain Clots and Cancers
Mental Problems

Therefore, it's vital that through ***ZONE THEORY***™ techniques we access these poems and "download" them from our brain, freeing up valuable brain space (without sacrificing brain weight).

The Bhyll Yee Crystal
It makes you smile!
2,000 ZP
"My crystal guarantees 35% more Zone elation"
Bhyll Yee
- 1994 Zone Theory™ Symposium Speech -

COMPOSING YOUR ZONE POEMS

GETTING STARTED

Dedicate a room in your house—this will be your Poem Room (Proem)—it can only be used to compose your Zone Poems. Any other activities in this room are strictly prohibited.

Have a Zone Priest sanctify and bless your Proem before writing a poem—writing a poem in an unblessed Proem invalidates the ***ZONE THEORY***™ program.

MAKING YOUR OWN STARTER POEMS

Poems need to be at least two words in length.

The following words[17] don't rhyme—
so don't even try using them.
It's a waste of time.

- Angst • Breadth • Depth • Gulf • Mulcts
- Ninth • Twelfth • Wolf

Barely rhymable words include:

- Month—Hunth *(an abbreviation for hundred thousand)*
- Orange—Gorringe *(Sussex surname)* & Blorenge *(Welsh mountain)* & Sporange *(more common father is sporangium)*
- Purple—Curple *(hindquarters of a horse)* & Hirple *(walk with a limp)*
- Silver

TIME FOR YOUR BRAIN WEIGHT CHECK-IN!

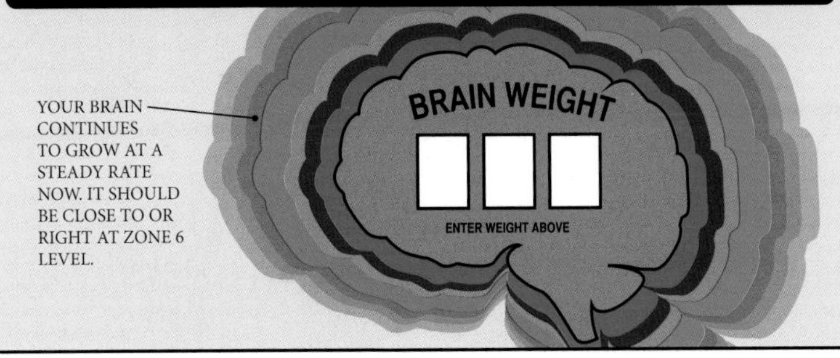
YOUR BRAIN CONTINUES TO GROW AT A STEADY RATE NOW. IT SHOULD BE CLOSE TO OR RIGHT AT ZONE 6 LEVEL.
BRAIN WEIGHT
ENTER WEIGHT ABOVE

[17] You can try using these words but it's going to make your life very hard so why bother! Use other words that are EZ to rhyme.

LEVEL ONE ZONE POEMS

HAMBURGER HAIKU
Pickles onions and beef
Please don't skimp on the American cheese
Diarrhea now.

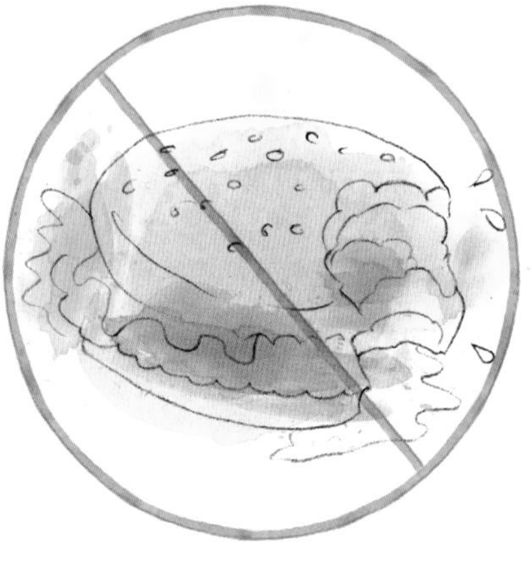

HAMBURGER HAIKU 2
Yes you can have a small bite
I said a small bite
What's wrong with you
Friends no more.

I AM A SANDY MAN

I was at the beach
I am a sandy man
I was lying off the towel
I am a sandy man
I was just rolling around in the waves
I am a sandy man

I have sand in my cracks
I have sand in my ears
I do have sand in my shorts

I am a sandy man
I am a sandy man.

WITH THE COURAGE OF A SAILOR

The spider
Is a sailor

Without a compass
He navigates
Treacherous waters

From the ceiling
Into the toilet
And onto diarrhea

He crawls off of the diarrhea
Before it is flushed away.

My hero, Araneae!

THE BUS RIDE

Thank Goodness for "good luck"; we ran to
get on the bus
and could have slipped
on the ice
but did not

Thank you God for the soldier on leave who
was cracking jokes; and he gave us
a present of a killed human jawbone

Thanks to everyone on the bus that day
who was patient with the old guy who got on
and stood at the front of the bus
with urine streaming down his leg
as he explained that the local radio station
was giving away turkeys
that were made of old dog-meat from the dead animal pile
and if you won their raffle,
they delivered you a prize turkey.

SPOTLIGHT ON A SPECTACULAR ZONE 6 POET

PARDURAL BIE

Pardural Bie has mastered Zone 6 but aspires to one day achieve Zone Plane 8. He and his brother run a family business installing and maintaining security cameras on the grounds of Nude Recreation Centers across the United States. Pardural also writes poetry and recently won the Amateur Poet Contest Award sponsored by the military. It is an honor to print some of his recent poems here.

MYSTERY

I wonder what they would think
If they knew

TOLERANCE

It takes all kinds
To make a world.
All walks of life
Naked and flickering
On my screen.

SERVANT

With my screwdriver
In my hand
I screw you all
Selling your secrets
Silently spilling seed

CONFESSION

When you put suntan oil
Onto those balls
And then leap upon his shoulders
As if they were a wall
And you all laugh
And you all fall down
I zoom in
Every time.
A spiritual awakening
Inside me.
Thank you Grandfather Great Spirit
For giving me eyes to see.
Ngi loyto, ngi loyto,
Kum, kum, kum.

THE INVINCIBLE BEES

The Governor claimed he balanced the budget
By sending convicts and mentals home
Clearly he should have used the money
To stop the bees who threaten his throne!

The President and his henchmen
The most corrupt people alive
Sex scandals in the news
But who will incinerate the hive?

Is this another Watergate
Or Contragate or Troopergate
What I want to know is in which laboratory
These bees, did someone secretly create?

Well, that's my story
I hope you enjoyed reading
The government won't stop these bees
From multiplying and breeding

So in approximately one year
We don't know the exact date
The bees will take over everything
Sorry all my friends, but it's now too late!

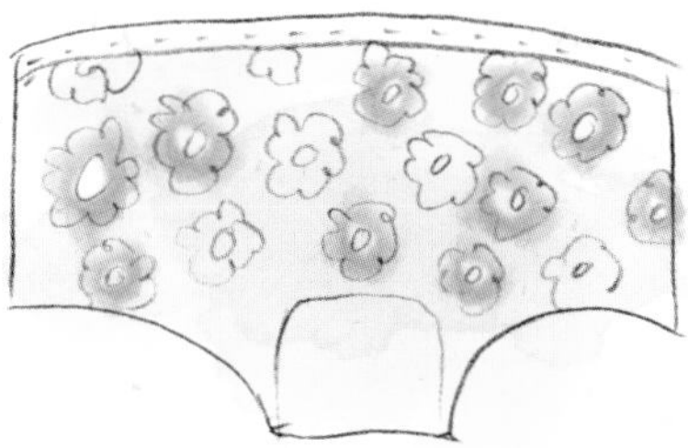

LAUNDROMAT

As humming machines
Lull the launderer into a trance
Fluorescent lights
Reveal semen stains
On grandpa's underpants!

DO NOT EAT IT

Thank you old guy for saving ours
Thanks-Giving!!!!

AN INVITATION FROM DAD

Y
O
U

AND

E
V
E
R
Y
O
N
E

ELSE

ARE

I
N
V
I
T
E
D

TO

B
A
I
L

EXPERIMENTAL POEMS

MALODREX

Contrare Barpt of the Fill Wish Wish Wish
Tony Boro is will well Fill Wishhhhhhhhhh
Incidence equals Zone—Broy Troy
It could.

Ghud.

Ghug.

Ghub.

(To be screamed)

ZONE TIPS AND TRICKS 5:
SHARPEN YOUR BARBER'S NEEDLE OR HAVE YOUR BARBER'S NEEDLE SHARPENED BY A PROFESSIONAL.

DEVOTIONAL HYMNS

Devotional hymns are the most important part of ***ZONE THEORY***™—you must sing these hymns 3 times a day before meals. If you don't do this, Z.T. don't work. Sorry.

(To the tune of "Old MacDonald")

Old Ba'hee Nodaramoo Priss Dimmie
You are who you are
You know my Zones more than I do
Ba'hee Nodaramoo Priss Dimmie
Praise to Ba'hee Nodaramoo Priss Dimmie
Yes I think I will
It's easy when you sing this song
Ba'hee Nodaramoo Priss Dimmie

SPECIAL GUEST POET

David Liebe Hart

David Liebe Hart

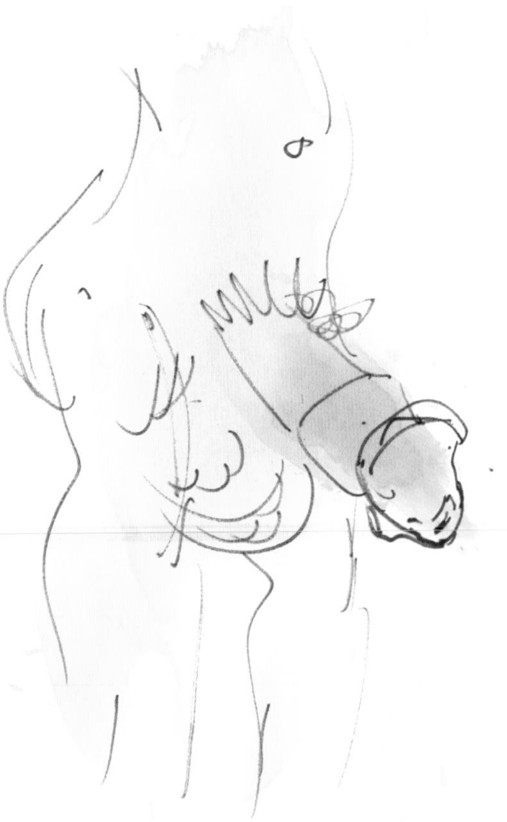

PORN POEM

Corn reminds me of porn. You can't stop enjoying it. It makes you grow a big horn. Porn reminds me of popcorn, it grows bigger than a goat's horn. I get a hard on thinking of porn. When it makes me enjoy sex without getting a torn. I like having porn. Having porn, I'll never get bored. But I'll have more sex all the more. Grease grease the trolley pole, let me stick it in that vagina hole. Grease grease the trolley pole, let me stick it in that butt hole.

—DAVID LIEBE HART

COMMITMENT POEM

Sex is great but love and commitment is the best. Sex is sweet but commitment, love can't be beat. I like to be loyal to a girl. I like to bring her joy and good sex in her world. I like to be committed to her. I like to go out of my way to make her feel strong and fair cause I like a woman that will be with me here and there and everywhere.

—DAVID LIEBE HART

POEM ZONE WORKBOOK

Write your first one thousand poems here. Your first 10 to 200 poems should focus on Drahl, Probo Health and Production and Zone Value/Points.

TIP: DON'T THROW THIS PAGE OUT.

HOW TO DESTROY BEES

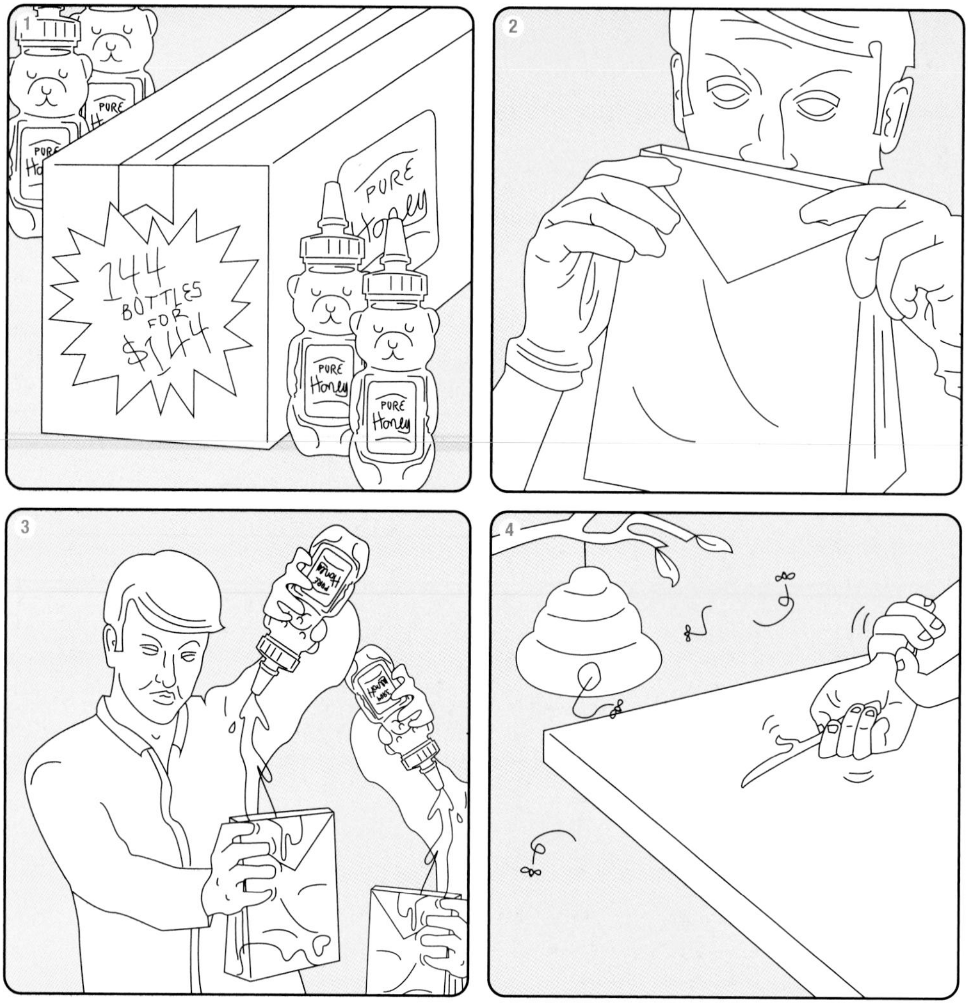

1. You should purchase old, stale honey from the dollar store. One gross (144 bottles) of honey in "honey-bear" containers is the amount you should get. It should cost $144.

2. Assemble a team of 10 trusted associates who can fold old newspapers into makeshift paper bags capable of holding a gallon of stale honey. Instruct your associates to wear expensive latex gloves while constructing the bags, so the toxic newspaper ink doesn't get on their hands and repel the bees during step #6 below.

3. Pour the honey from the "honey-bear" containers into the makeshift bags in quantities of one gallon per bag.

DESTROY BEES *(Continued)*

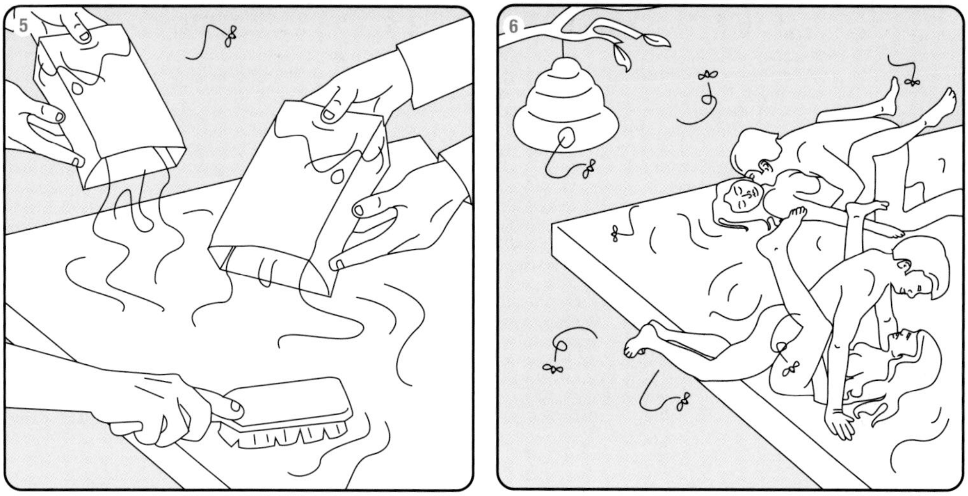

4. Using cement and hot water, create a 10-foot-by-10-foot makeshift cement slab a foot or so from the dangerous bees. Make sure the cement slab has completely dried, and "please" resist the temptation to put your initials in the drying cement.

5. Dump the gallon bags of stale honey onto the slab and use an old hairbrush to spread the stale honey until slab is entirely covered.

6. You and your 10 associates must now undress and assume coital position on the slab, being careful not to shed pubic hair into the stale honey. If the bees start to congregate in the honey during coitus, increase the heat of the sensual passion so that your mutual eroto-sexuality is now crushing the bees onto the cement slab with your naked lovemaking, it should be very passionate and unbridled unself-concious lovemaking, all inhibitions should be shed (you will be filmed), and it works best if everyone is orgasming in unison as they are being penetrated by the sexual peters and also digitally too. During orgasms most of those bees will be destroyed. If any bees are left, go ahead and smash them with your fist, you can't be stung! There is no way our bees would do that.

CALCULATE YOUR ZONE SCORE NOW

	FRIENDSHIP
	FAMILY
	BUSINESS
	LOVE
	HEALTH
	POEMS
X	FOOD
	TOTAL

TIM ON POEMS

For years I allowed poems to bottle up in my brain leading me to suffer severe mental illness that resulted in me declaring myself "Mentally Insane"—I was known in my community as "The Toothy Clown" due to my clown-like appearance and tendency to bite strangers. I would regularly attack random people on the street, running full speed and tackling and then biting at their face and neck. It's clear now looking back that my temporary insanity was due to an overload of poems. I've since calculated my poem overload was nearly 3 million poems! Clearing my brain of these poems literally saved my life as well as many others in my town and surrounding community. It's a gift to have these poems (all of them are at least Level 5 Poems and one of them "My Chubby Wick" received the Gold Coin at the Zone Council Awards last year).

ERIC ON POEMS

Before I was a Zone 8 Master I used to lead public readings of words to other transients in my town park. It wasn't till the guidance of ***ZONE THEORY***™ that I discovered those were the early fragments of my "Master Poems." These sonnets would make the average hobo weep but I had no idea of their power to a regular human. I recited one of my Master Poems to my Discard father and he went into an epileptic fit and slipped into a coma where he still is today. This is the reason I keep my powerful Master Poems locked in a small safe buried in my backyard. My Zone Wife has the coordinates in case I pass before her. Which is doubtful considering her average brain weight.

ZONE 7
FOOD

INT. RESTAURANT—NIGHT

A waiter approaches a man sitting at a table.

WAITER: What can I get you?

MAN: I'll have food.

WAITER: Coming up!

The waiter exits and the man opens his mouth awaiting food.

WHAT IS FOOD?

Food is the sustenance of life…

"Food is the sustenance of life"

—Eric Wareheim

Simply put: we need food to survive but how can we tone our Food Zone to best serve us? What should we eat? Is there a simple easy diet we can follow instead of just eating whatever is put in front of us? YES.

Before we can begin the ***ZONE THEORY***™ Diet we must cleanse and purify the body with the ***ZONE THEORY***™ Fast.

ZONE THEORY™ FAST

ZONE THEORY™ Fast involves totally drying out your body—no liquid must remain. When you are urinating or ejaculating only dust particles (NO WATER MIST or SEMEN DRIBBLE!) you will have completed the ***ZONE THEORY***™ Fast and are free to begin drinking water or diluted pancake syrup again, as well as being able to move on to step 2 of our ***ZONE THEORY***™ Diet.

To begin—you will need to learn to eat cat litter. This is one of the most inexpensive and healthiest foods in the world, and can be purchased at any supermarket or pet foods store, generally for less than 25 cents a pound. As it is made with mined clay, it has a pleasant flavor, similar to expensive caviar or fine Italian wines, but at a much lower cost.

Start by dumping 2 lbs of cat litter on every one of your regular meals. Do not leave a speck on the plate! You should also stir cotton balls into your meals. After a couple of days, throw out all your regular food and switch exclusively to recipes from our ***ZONE THEORY***™ *Fast Cookbook* (sold separately). Here is a recipe that should be cooked up twice daily. An old favorite with a new twist: chili Zone carne!!!! Whoever said that total dehydration cannot be delicious?

CHILI ZONE CARNE

1 pound uncooked white beans
1 gallon white sauce
1 pound white salt
1 bag of cotton balls
1 pound bleached chicken skin
1 red brick

Heat everything in an oven set to the highest temperature. When the heat causes the brick to shatter, turn the oven off and discard the brick pieces. Dump the rest into a gigantic metal dog bowl. Wait 10 minutes to cool and then gently add 2 pounds of cat litter on top of the chili. Stir with a small wooden bat. Serves 2 people.

ZONE THEORY™ DIET

The initial fast completed, it is time to begin the first phase of the ***ZONE THEORY***™ Diet.

As you are now aware, you're going to have to stop eating colorful foods. These are unknown in Zone Plane 8. We eat white foods only! White is the color of hope. Other colors signal hopelessness! Do you want to eat hopeless food? Do you want your body vehicle to be made of utter defeat and despair?

Eating white foods on a black or blue blanket in the park is not recommended. Bi-shade spillage is embarrassing and sends the wrong signal to the people who run the park, that our ***ZONE THEORY***™ community cannot be trusted. We eat white foods and then watch the whole world look at us in awe when we spill white food on our white clothing and bedding, and there is no need to wash up! White on white = white. A famous man who we know once dumped an entire 5-gallon pot of Alfredo sauce onto his wealthy guests at an elegant dinner party of ***ZONE THEORY***™ Plane 8'ers. Everyone screamed at first but then they realized that there was no reason for that, the only people who scream are people frying in an electric chair, or that are being summarily executed by some kangaroo court's firing squad. Do we want to live as if we are being put to death? No. White foods radiate hope.

White foods can be very easy, or very difficult to prepare. It all depends on how good of a cook you are and if you have been jacking off a lot. One nice dish that everyone loves is simple white bread that has been steamed and doused in Zonus milk or Tabitha Lane–brand Lemon Urine Drink. Before dousing the bread, you would want to cut the crusts off, for they are brown—essentially dirt. That is dirt food. Do you want to signal to the world that you eat dirt (slang for "shit" in most cultures)? This would likely get you expelled from our community without refund, unless you could prove that the shit had come from a natural source.

Wiley Allaiyn Whyte

We also sell dozen-paks of Zone W–brand white sausages by mail order. These do not require refrigeration as they are not made of materials that can spoil. The inventor, Wiley Allaiyn Whyte, started Zone W–brand out of his own dilapidated garage with money he found underneath outdoor vending machines at motels in the area. When he had a million dollars in coins, he opened a bank account and bought an old wood-processing plant that had been shut down by Governor Brady. With the help of some hardworking ***ZONE THEORY***™ Plane 8'ers, they got the factory up and running in days, and were selling the sausages by mail order to all 50 states and 87 countries within the first year. Now Wiley and his family have retired in luxury, and own 1,000 sailboats. It's been a long time since any of them ever touched a sausage casing! The factory is all run by animals and the mentally infirmed, and it won an award for efficiency recently.

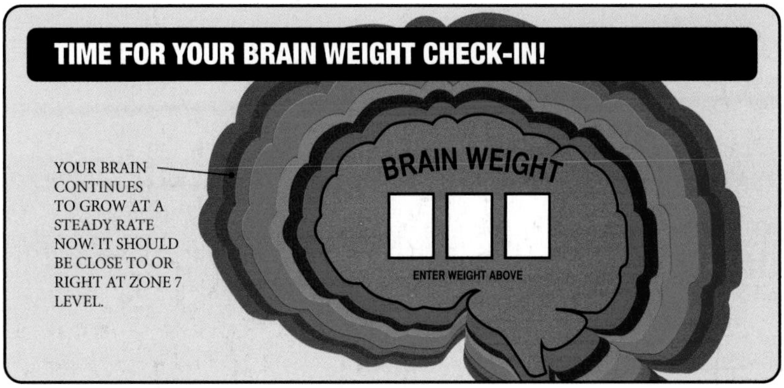
TIME FOR YOUR BRAIN WEIGHT CHECK-IN!
YOUR BRAIN CONTINUES TO GROW AT A STEADY RATE NOW. IT SHOULD BE CLOSE TO OR RIGHT AT ZONE 7 LEVEL.
BRAIN WEIGHT
ENTER WEIGHT ABOVE

THE SOUP LIE

(The following section can be skipped so long as you understand and accept the principle that eating (or drinking/slurping) soup should be avoided at all costs.)

Did you know that for the past 100 years a small, powerful group of men have been manipulating and controlling the way YOU think about soup? IS it a coincidence that the current head of the FDA and USGABP is Joseph P. Soup and that the head of the American Food Council is Adam Campbell Soupman? Are these men really working in our best interest to keep us healthy and safe or are they simply pawns of the "Grand Soup Lie" that aims to control us and limit our foods and beverages to a small list of simple soups?

Consider the facts:

- The current head of the FDA and USGABP is Joseph P. Soup, elected in March 1991 and given a lifetime appointment with no judicial review or confirmation process.
- The current president of the American Food Council is Adam Campbell Soupman whose family has strong soup ties to the Campbell Soup company and introduced several flavors of soup into US and world markets.
- More soup is being produced, manufactured and consumed per capita than the entire country of Spain.
- The World Council on Dietary Results concludes that soup is a major factor in diet and consumption.
- 20 to 40% of soup is consumed daily.

When asked by a survey of American interests in food development and future usage of food as substance, Soupman said, "We believe in the power of soup and its long-lasting positive influences on society. We take soup seriously and so should you." These are alarming statements considering the conflict of interest that exists between the FDA and the AFC—when considering whether these signify a conspiracy to delude existing users of such food products one must consider the source and how they could possibly benefit from these activities. Would the actions of the combined forces of the FDA, USGABP and the AFC along with the WCDR lead you to believe that the intentions of the soup elite are just and justified or do they represent some more devious plot that does involve soup but also other angles, which leads to the "thickening" of the mystery?

One needs only to walk down the aisle of a major grocery store to see the quantity and variety of soups on display:

- Cream of broccoli
- Chicken noodle soup
- Tomato soup
- Beef barley

These represent the top 4 soups currently on the market in terms of sales—what is shocking and should raise red flags amongst the general population is the utter disregard and complacency in the act of marketing and distributing these soups with lack of oversight from non-soup-related entities.

Since March, there has been a steady increase in soup consumption to a degree that should alarm and disrupt current projections on soup yields as it relates to general consumption of soup—be it canned or otherwise. These are all facts and information that are currently available on the Food Market Research Council's annual table of consumption. It's not made secret which only begs the question "What has been made secret and what elements of soup manufacturing are being hidden from the public?"

Is there a soup lie? Of course.

We must:
Dupe the Soup.

Another interesting fact about the soup lie is the origin of the word "soup." Prior to 1558, hot water was consumed as a clear beverage ONLY. During an outbreak of deadly whooping cough, the King's doctors, who were also pea farmers, suggested that handfuls of peas be added to the hot water to give everyone diarrhea so that the

SPAGHETTI POTS WANTED

Donate Unwanted Spaghetti Pots for Extra Zone Points

The Zone Theory™ Spaghetti Pot
Donation Center
(Miami, FL)

Donations are made by appointment only. Call (900)555-2314 to schedule an appointment.

Operators are standing by!

USED POTS ONLY

deadly whooping cough bacteria would escape the body more readily through the anal/fecal canal. They needed a name for the new medicine drink, and let's now examine where this name came from. The King's doctors undressed themselves and sat down to think about a way to dupe the dummies and sell them more peas, but also to make fun of them. "A-ha," said one of the nude doctors, "let's make an acronym that rubs their stupid faces in our little scam, without them even knowing, they're just all such big idiots." The other three nude doctors were laughing so much by now, that they had to cover up their heaving scrotums in case a lady walked by and saw that they now had sizeable red erections while laughing at the stupid dumb idiots buying cups of hot water with peas floating around in it.

This is the acronym that these guys finally came up with.

Scam Only Unwashed Peasants

They laughed and laughed at this, but now nearly 500 years later, we are not laughing, as we drink unnecessary soup at heretofore unimaginable prices.

So Our Uniform Procedure, *(must be to)*
Stop One Unusual Precedent!! *(The precedent of drinking soup!)*

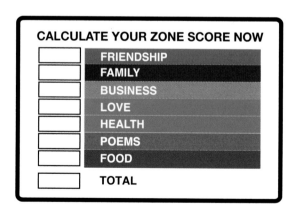

CALCULATE YOUR ZONE SCORE NOW

	FRIENDSHIP
	FAMILY
	BUSINESS
	LOVE
	HEALTH
	POEMS
	FOOD
	TOTAL

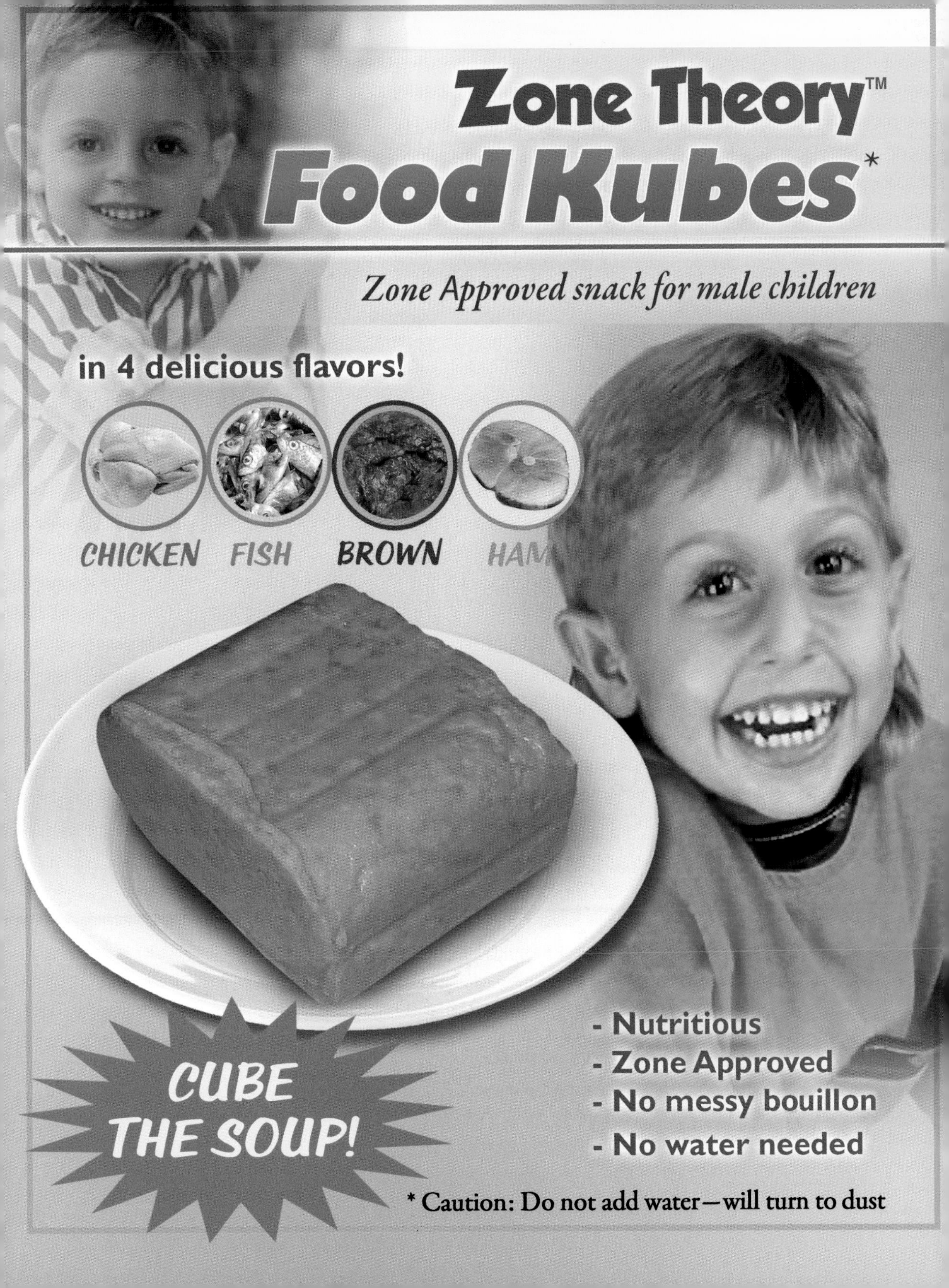
Zone Theory™
Food Kubes*
Zone Approved snack for male children
in 4 delicious flavors!
CHICKEN
FISH
BROWN
CUBE THE SOUP!
- Nutritious
- Zone Approved
- No messy bouillon
- No water needed
* Caution: Do not add water—will turn to dust

TIM ON FOOD

Here's a confession. I do not like the taste of cat litter. It tastes like gravel or sand. But guess what? I eat a spoonful every morning because I know it's the key to LONG-TERM ZONE HEALTH! (Daily cat litter intake is an advanced ***ZONE THEORY***™ practice not recommended for new Z.T.s. DO NOT ATTEMPT.) You might be wondering: What the FUCK does food (cat litter) have to do with health? Haha, you see this is why ***ZONE THEORY***™ is truly unique and the perfect system for YOU:

FOOD IS CONNECTED IN SOME WAY TO HEALTH!

We don't know why but it appears through Zone Science that the food you eat can directly affect your body health. Do you remember the old adage: "You are what you eat"? Now think about that expression in context of what we're now discussing!

Now when I wake up and just want to eat some bacon and eggs I know that a scoop of cat litter is what my body really needs to soak up and collect excess, unneeded body fluids and export them out of my body in a concentrated form. And THIS is why I am in perfect health. Funny how some old adages still ring true.

ERIC ON FOOD

On the 5th day of my ***ZONE THEORY***™ Fast, my Zone Father turned to me with a large jar of mayonnaise and offered me some. I pulled out a cured white sausage log from my pocket that I'd been saving for this very moment. I got on my knees, meditated about the importance of white foods, then I dipped my white sausage into the mayonnaise jar over and over till it was fully coated with the thick warm mess. Once my Zone Father said, "Ok my son, your white sausage is fully coated," I pushed the cured meat into my mouth and took one large bite. It was euphoric. The mayo became technicolor and the sausage log started to move like a serpent. My Zone Father smiled and said, "You are now ready, my son." I went to the men's room, vomited the rancid sausage log into the toilet and went home to my Zone Wife and cried.

ZONE SUCCESS STORIES / PROFILES

DAN PEENER *(Zone Plane 2)*

Before

After

Hi, my name is Dan Peener and I began using the ***ZONE THEORY***™ 2 years ago and it's literally changed who I am. A little bit about myself:

My name is Daniel Jacoby Peener. I live in Calamungo, CA, and am currently a part-time Real Estate bidder. Don't ask me what that means, because I'm only just figuring it out for myself. I know that I have to deal with a ton of bullshit and also commercial land lease agreements. It's so boring. I own a 1998 Toyota Avalon, which is shitty and smells like the old man I bought it from (my gramps) and I live in a one bedroom apartment building called Oxford Manor. I can see the highway from my balcony.

But before that I was in real trouble. My typical weekend evening would usually involve me getting **POUNDED** by gym men in the forest by my dad's condo. Now, thanks to intensive ***ZONE THEORY***™ workshopping and Zone counseling I do the pounding and it's now moved to INSIDE my dad's condo when he's away on business. I recommend ***ZONE THEORY***™ to everyone I pound!

ZONE SUCCESS STORIES / PROFILES

JOCK DE REENE *(Zone Plane 1)*

Before

After

Hello—I am a riverboat blackjack dealer, I've been jackin' cards for 25 years. 10 years on the riverboat "Sally's Apple"—we port out of New Orleans—4 trips a day—I deal cards in 4 hour shifts and I'm ashamed to admit that I've jumped overboard 6 times. There's nothing more terrifying than standing on the edge of the bow leaning forward and looking into the brown, angry current of the Mississippi—"old miss"—as she starts her journey up north to Lake Itasca in Minnesota, and carelessly careens south passing through Ohio, Illinois, down into the delta—home of the blues—into Louisiana—Cajun country... Where French, African, Caribbean and you name it, combine to create the richest culture in the world. I worked my way down from Chicago when I was 17, working the river—trading cards—learning my blackjack craft like the back of my hand. I worked for a year in the Zamp club called Zepher's—learned the dog pipe there. I've been involved in a lot of different "theories" over the year: "God Worship," "Death Cults," "Chinese Poetry," "Yogic Panting," you name it! But ***ZONE THEORY***™ has made me happier, healthier and more focused than all of the others combined! If you happen to have me deal at your card table on your next riverboat cruise I'll do my best to deal you: BLACKJACK!

PART III

ALIGNING YOUR ZONES

R ZONES

G YOUR ZONES

ALIGNIN

ALIGNING YOU

PRE-ALIGNMENT

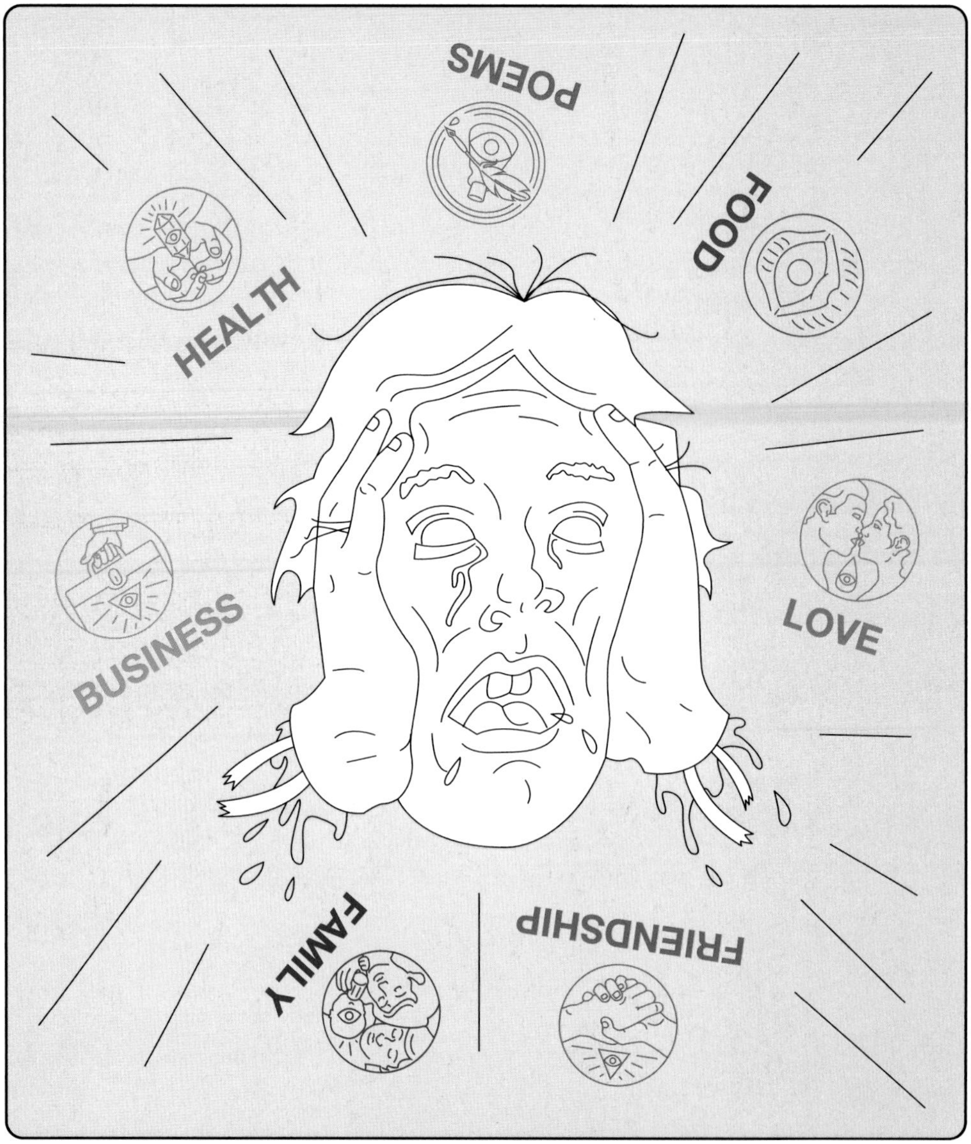

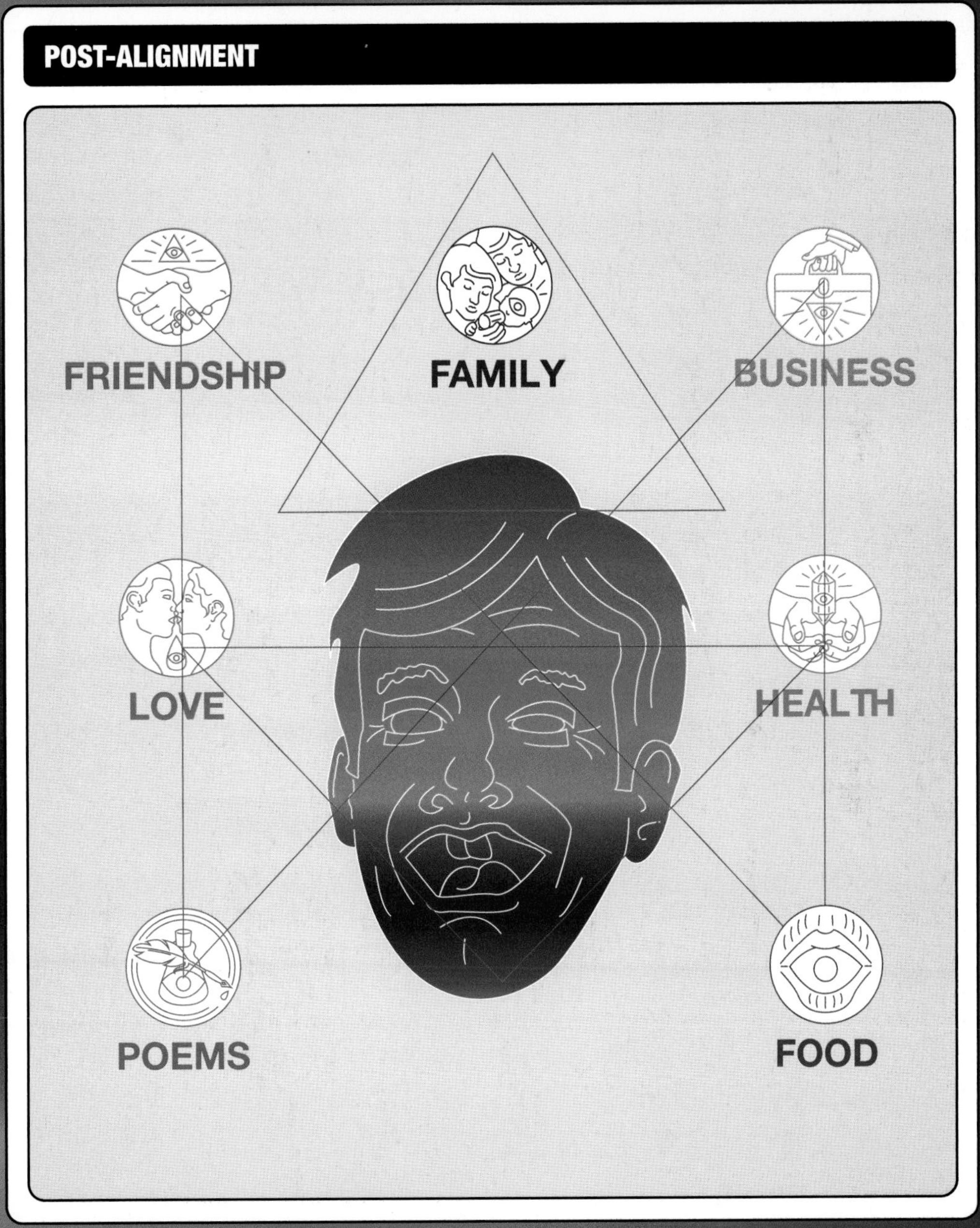
POST-ALIGNMENT
FRIENDSHIP
FAMILY
BUSINESS
LOVE
HEALTH
POEMS
FOOD

ALIGN YOUR ZONES
CERTIFICATION
EVANGELIZE
SACRIFICE

ZONES
ALIGNED

3 STEPS TO ALIGN YOUR ZONES

Congratulations! You have successfully toned your Zones and are ready for the final step. True lifelong happiness and life perfection are just around the corner! You are now only moments away from ascending to ZONE PLANE 8!

But there is still so much left to do. So, so, so, so, so, so, so much left to do!

You must now:

ALIGN
YOUR
ZONES

Right now, your Zones are perfectly toned and in great shape—but they are not working TOGETHER—they must be brought into alignment. There are three steps to aligning your Zones:

1) CERTIFICATION
2) EVANGELIZE
3) SACRIFICE

CERTIFICATION

The first step is an EZ step! Simply sign the Certification Form located on page 233. Send in the certification to the address listed below and wait for ***ZONE THEORY***™ to send back countersigned with the ***ZONE THEORY***™ Seal (allow 10 to 40 weeks).

CUT HERE AND FRAME FOR DISPLAY

Zone Theory™ Certification

THE ZONE THEORY™
OFFICE OF NOTARY COMMISSIONS AND AUTHENTICATIONS

I ________________

HAVE FULLY TONED MY SEVEN ZONES AND COMPLETED ALL QUIZZES AND WORKSHEET ASSIGNMENTS SUCCESSFULLY.

________________ PRINTED LEGAL NAME	________________ ZONE MOTHER'S NAME
________________ SIGNED	________________ CO-SIGNER'S PRINTED LEGAL NAME
________________ ZONE FATHER'S NAME	________________ CO-SIGNER'S SIGNATURE
________________ ZONE PRIEST'S NAME	Today's Date ________________

THIS DOCUMENT IS INVALID WITHOUT THE PERSONAL REVIEW AND AUTHORIZATION FROM TIM HEIDECKER AND ERIC WAREHEIM.

CUT HERE AND FRAME FOR DISPLAY

EVANGELIZE

The second phase of Zone alignment involves evangelizing ***ZONE THEORY***™ and encouraging the people around you to join in the ***ZONE THEORY***™ movement.

There are two techniques to evangalizing ***ZONE THEORY***™.

ORAL EVANGELIZING TECHNIQUE (O.E.T.)

Take an afternoon and position yourself in a busy intersection or public park perhaps and begin screaming the following phrase:

YOU NOW MUST HEAR THIS! ZONE THEORY™ IS THE WAY! ZONE THEORY™ IS THE WAY! YOU MUST GET THE ZONE THEORY™ BOOK AND START LEARNING ABOUT ZONE THEORY™! ZONE THEORY™ IS THE WAY! ZONE THEORY™ IS THE ONLY WAY! DO THIS NOW OR A GREAT RAIN OF FIRE WILL FALL ON YOU AND ALL YOU KNOW!

Scream this until you lose your voice. This is your body's way of telling you that you have completed O.E.T.

ZONE REWARDS EVANGELIZING TECHNIQUE (Z.R.E.T.)

Have you enrolled in the Zone Rewards Program yet? If you haven't, consult the advertisement in the beginning of the book and begin the process NOW.

If you have enrolled in the Zone Rewards Program take your Zone Calculator and calculate your Zone Rewards outreach points. If you are below 10,000 you must begin again from scratch. (Turn to Forgetting This Book section for more information.)

Now take this number (x) and apply it to the following formula:

(j) - aligned position of Zones
(r) - the time it takes to find Zone Wife
(l) - body weight
(m) - brain weight

$$x + j/l - r\,(x)\,m = target$$

Target = Goal.

Your goal should be to get (x) number of people in your Zone community to re-enroll in the Zone Lifestyle!

Set this goal now and see if you can achieve it before sundown!

LET'S TALK ABOUT HUMAN SACRIFICE

(The perfect crime)

From the dawn of civilization, human sacrifice has been an essential and practical staple of everyday life. The Czuchians (arguably mankind's first major civilization) made a sport out of human sacrifice—a talent show called "Hali-Mak-Im" which rewarded talented singers and dancers with their own tracts of land and piles of jewels while losers who lacked talent were sacrificed (often peeled, boiled and eaten as well)—sacrificed up to the god Turp.

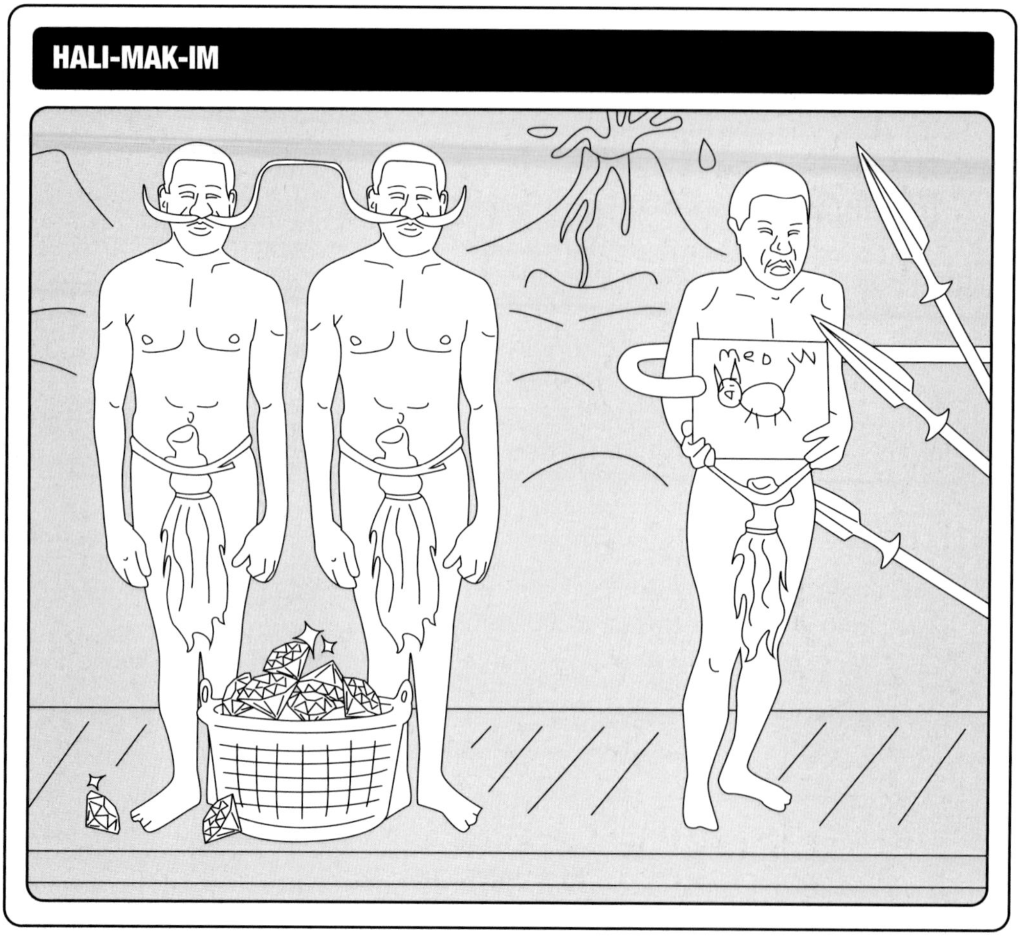

Human sacrifice is literally the founding cornerstone for all major religions being practiced today—Christianity, Buddhism, Muslimism, Jewishness and Yogic Panting all began with Jesus Christ being born and then immediately crucified by 3 "wise" men. The crucifixion of a newborn baby was an innovation in the science and practice of human sacrifice—it was a quantum leap that inspired science and religion to create "The Enlightenment" and the "Industrial Revolution."

"It's all happening!"—noted one scholar, at the time.

NEWBORN CRUCIFIXION

Recently "human sacrifice" has fallen out of favor. Modern civilization places an unreasonably high value on human life. Murder, no matter what the circumstance or conditions, is now considered a crime… A bad crime. But, "human sacrifice" is how we align our 7 Zones.

"The act of 'human sacrifice' is the very fabric by which we unite our Zones and ascend to the Zone Plane 8."—Zone Priest Thom Mound

So you may be staring at this page and wondering—"How am I supposed to align my Zones and ascend to Zone Plane 8? I don't want to live a perfect life in jail!"

Your concerns are natural. But write down your doubts in the doubt worksheet (not provided).

ZONE THEORY™ has created 3 "Perfect Crime" scenarios so you will be able to perform human sacrifice and avoid getting caught. These are EZ ways!!! But first we'll explore a common question:

WHO DO I SACRIFICE???

The short answer is: It doesn't really matter. But there is a way to choose wisely so you feel good about it!

ZONE THEORY™ prefers you sacrifice non-Zone members. Consult the Business Zone to find a quick list of non-Zoners. It may be as easy as going to the local gas station and following and then befriending a mechanic for a few days.

Women and children make great candidates for human sacrifice too! It's your choice! We recommend avoiding people you like to talk to or Zone Wives. Also avoid celebrities and known figures as they are harder to access and shine a light into this dark world with their brilliance.

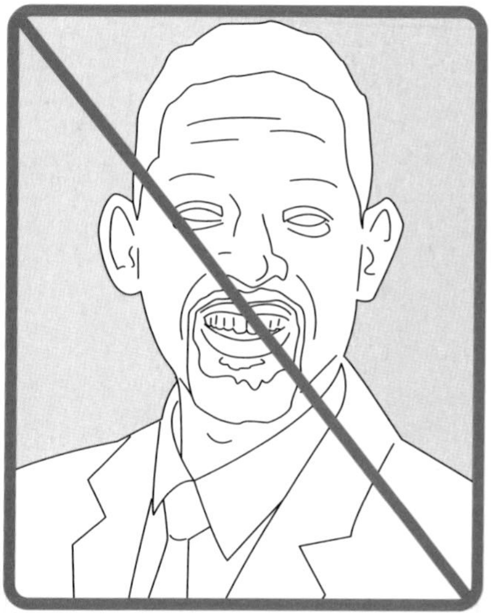

ZONE TIPS AND TRICKS 6:

25 ANIMALS TO AVOID—THIS WILL QUICKEN YOUR JOURNEY ONTO PLANE 8.

THE PERFECT CRIME

Scenario #1

The Victim: Some worker at a plant named Frank.

Frank leaves the plant every day on the dot at 5 PM. Follow Frank and take note of his after-work activities—most likely he heads over to the corner bar and has a few cold beers before heading home. After confirmation—start going to the bar about 4:45, have a drink and wait for Frank to walk in.

After about seven weeks of this, Frank will start to recognize you as "one of the regulars." Engage in small talk with Frank—talk about the sports game on TV, who you're rooting for (root for Frank's team) and over time things will get more personal. You can tell the following "amusing anecdote" to make Frank think you are good guy, but funny and fun to be around as well:

"One time I was fishing with some friends and I lost my lure and my one friend let me borrow his and I went on to catch a huge fish—I let him have half the fish as it was his lure."

Now Frank trusts you, knows you and WANTS to be around you. One day after one too many beers with Frank you suggest you and Frank meet up outside the bar on his day off. Frank suggests fishing but you poo poo this idea and suggest you meet at a men's fitness club. Frank agrees, warily—he's not fit and doesn't like spending time in those sorts of places.

You meet Frank very early on Saturday morning at "Men's Total Fitness"—you explain that you are going to help Frank get in shape and teach him about lifting weights and doing exercise. You show him how to lift BIG weights—demonstrate how you can dead lift over 300 pounds. Now Frank will be impressed and want to lift like you do and become a big stud with huge muscles. After the workout you and Frank hit the showers. While Frank showers you take a hunting knife (which you've hidden in your gym bag) and stab Frank to death—several stabs to the stomach and neck should do the trick. Make sure you hear him gurgling blood and a death rattle.

Now run out of the fitness gym screaming there's a madman on the loose.

Finally, simply move to a new town.

The Perfect Crime!

THE PERFECT CRIME

Scenario #2

Have you ever wondered how to commit human sacrifice and destroy all the evidence while having a delicious meal all at the same time? It's called cannibalism and all it means is eating another human being.

It's not that hard. Here's the most popular scenario:

The Victim: Some shit bird named Josh who works for a seafood company.

Josh is 28 and works for "So-and-So" Seafood Company. You get a job at this seafood company—you are in charge of all the shellfish—lobster, clams, mussels, etc. One day you say to Josh, "Hey, Josh, I'd love to have you over (and under your breath you say 'easy' as in 'over easy fried eggs' but you say 'easy' so quietly he can't hear it) for dinner."

Josh agrees and you set a time for 7 PM on Wednesday. Josh arrives with wine and you show him around your place. (Make sure to line all your furniture with plastic… It's gonna get bloody in there.) Josh says: "Where's the food" and you can say, "You're the food!" But then laugh like you're making a joke, but you really aren't. Then ask Josh if he's a baseball fan (most people are, so he's likely to say yes). Take out a baseball bat and tell him it's Babe Ruth's original bat. Tell him to look closely. As he's staring at the counterfeit bat, swing the bat around and clobber him hard on the back of the head. Clobber him hard enough so he zonks out. We don't want him going "ouch!" at this point.

Now take a knife and slit his throat. He'll bleed out and be dead. Then you can remove his clothes (you can't eat his clothes, sorry) and eat him head to tail! Every part is edible except the bones and you can just throw them away… NOW you see why you have to work at a seafood company! The bones will mix in nicely with all the fish bones you have in your trash! Not one eyebrow will be raised!!!!

THE CANNIBAL SACRIFICE

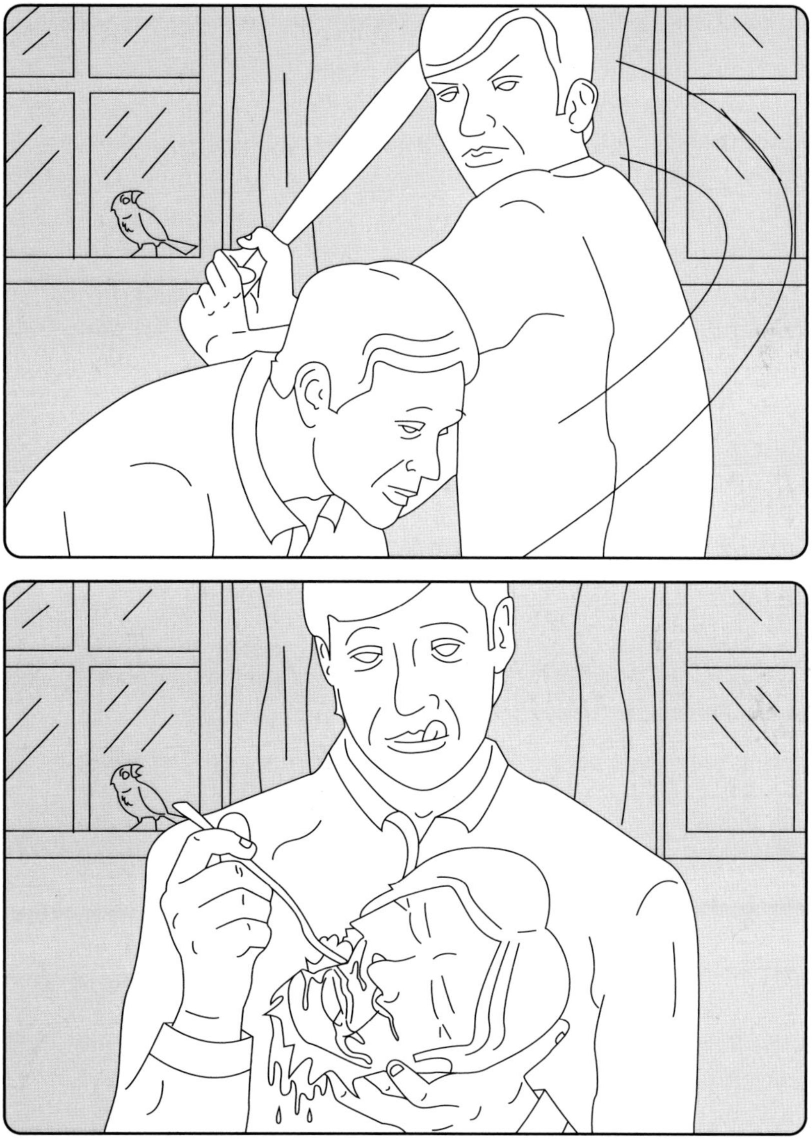

THE PERFECT CRIME

Scenario #3

Have you ever heard the old expression KILL TWO BIRDS WITH ONE STONE? What if eliminating your pre-Zone family (which is required) also involved human sacrifice? Too good to be true? It isn't! Systematically exterminating your P.Z.F.s qualifies as Zone Approved human sacrifice! But how do you get away with it!

First, contact your P.Z.F.s and apologize for cutting them out of your life. They will be overjoyed to hear from you! Admit that ***ZONE THEORY***™ was just a phase and you are ready to resume a normal life with them. Next, agree to meet them at a popular family restaurant, ideally one that they are familiar with but is out of the way and not very popular. Contact the restaurant manager and have the following conversation:

MANAGER (Terry): Thanks for calling Skunk's, this is Terry, how can I help you?

YOU: Hi, Terry. My name is not important so don't even ask for it… I'm hoping to make a large reservation for next Thursday at 5 PM. I would like to request your largest round table. It's a family reunion of sorts, Terry.

TERRY: Got it.

YOU: Terry, I'd also like to pay ahead for the meal and would request that you and your staff prepare the meal and then vacate the premises for the rest of the evening. Some bad things are going to happen.

TERRY: I can definitely arrange that for ya.

YOU: Thanks, Terry.

TERRY: Not a problem.

Next, allow all your family to arrive and seat themselves around the table. Lurk out behind the restaurant and watch them get comfortable and start eating the food that's been set out for them. You'll notice them wondering where you are! After all, you invited them!

Now, storm into the dining room with a large 3 to 4 ft sword and begin decapitating each and every member of your P.Z.F.

ZONE THEORY • SEAL OF APPROVAL •

PLEASE REVIEW!

I certify that I have:

CERTIFIED ☐

EVANGELIZED ☐

SACRIFICED ☐

Sign ______________________________ Date____

NOW YOU MAY TURN THE PAGE.

→

CONGRATULATIONS!

CONGRATULATIONS!

CONGRATULATIONS!

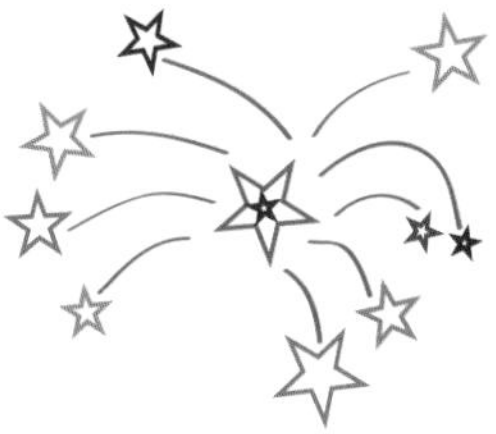

CONGRATULATIONS!

CONGRATULATIONS!

CONGRATULATIONS!

CONGRATULATIONS!

YOU ARE NOW ON THE PATH TOWARDS ZONE PLANE 8.

DO YOU WANT TO SEE A PREVIEW OF
YOUR LIFE ON ZONE PLANE 8?

INSTRUCTIONS ON PREVIEWING ZONE PLANE 8

1. Place the remaining pages of the book between your index finger and thumb.

2. Bend pages away from you as you quickly let the pages release, one by one, treating it as you would a flip book.

3. If the pages get damaged during this process, destroy book immediately.

4. If you carefully follow the above directions, you will soon be enjoying a brief glimpse of your life on Zone Plane 8.

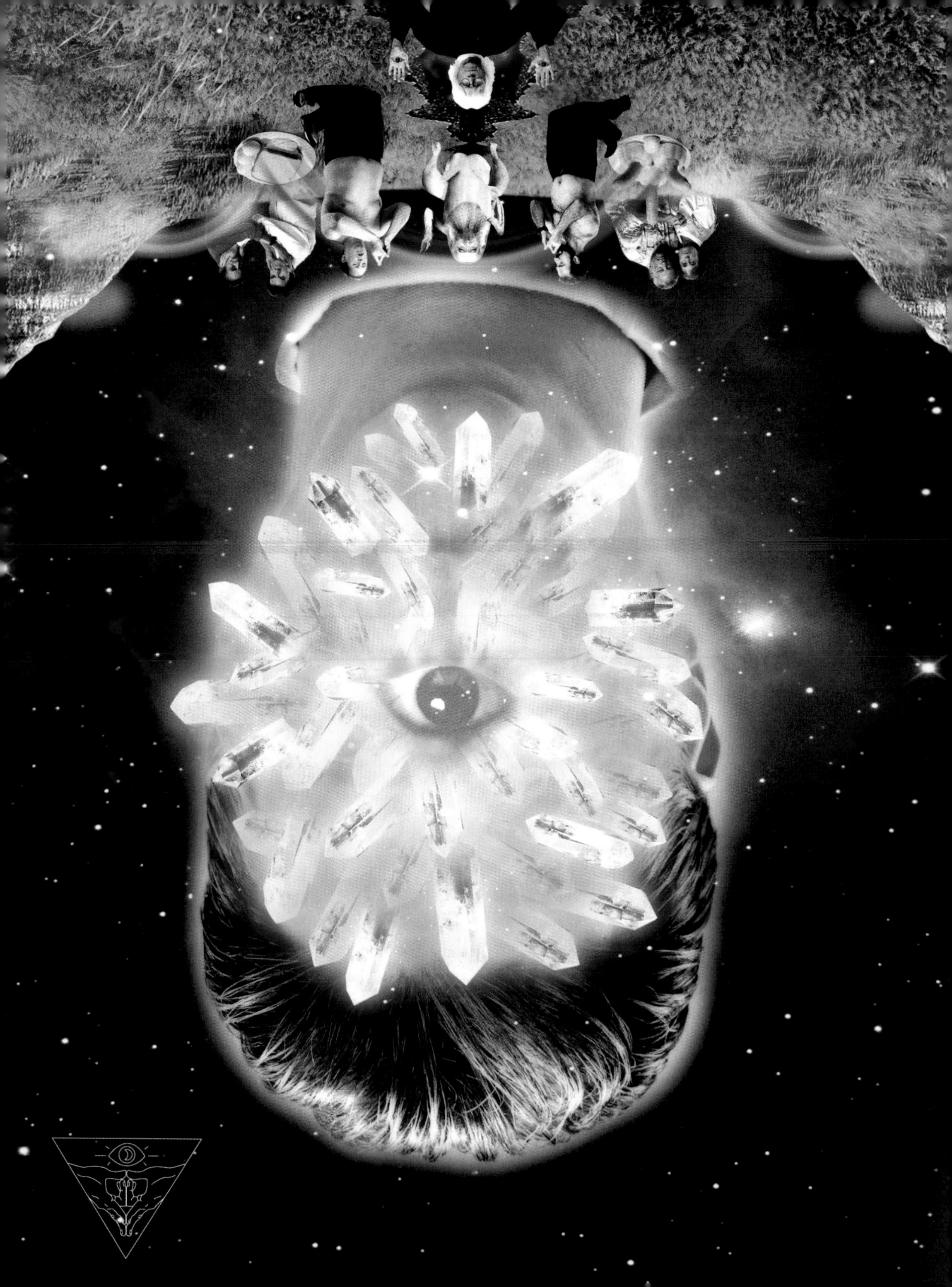

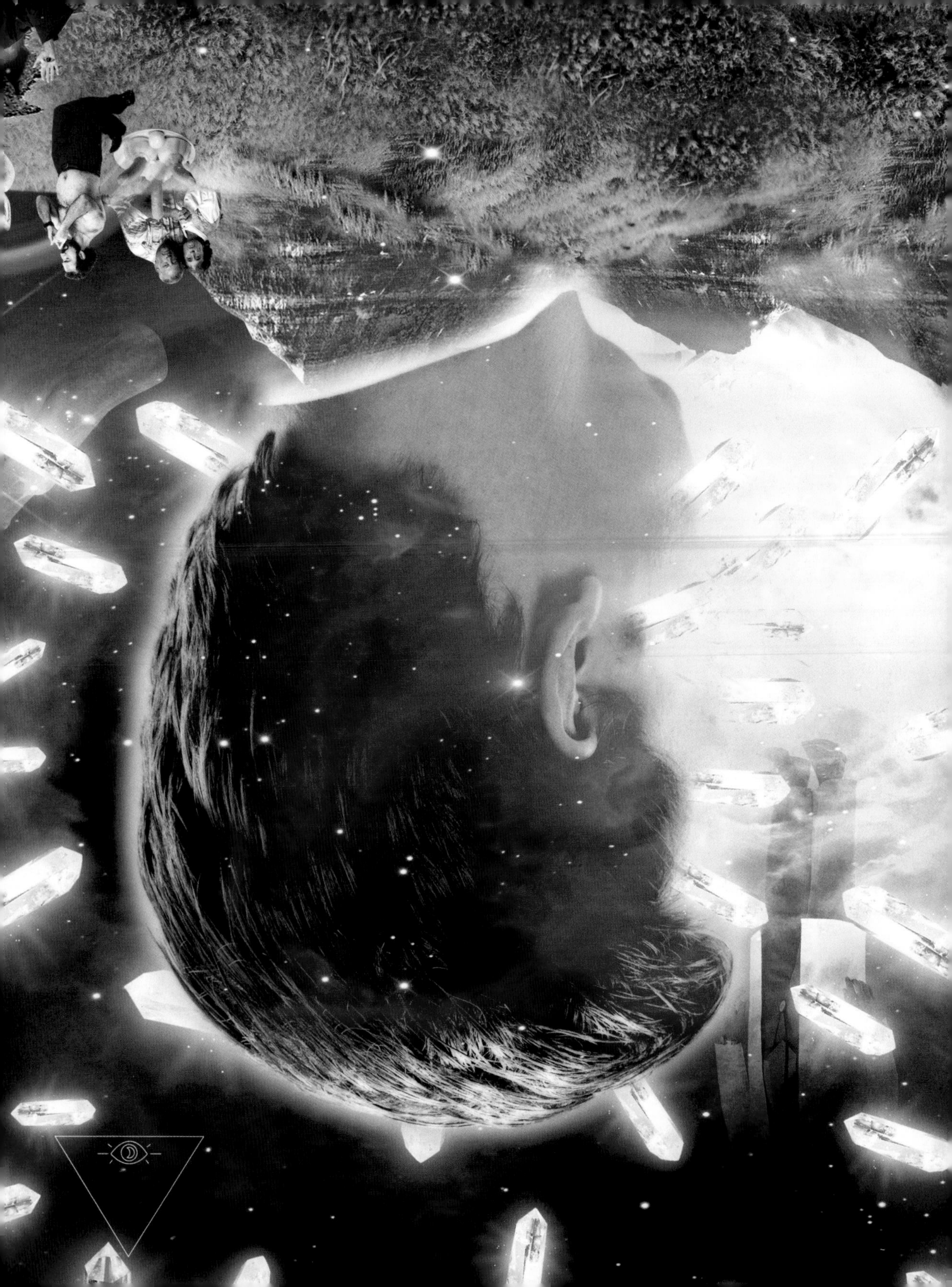

FLIP BOOK IMMEDIATELY!

AND REPEAT THE LAST SET OF INSTRUCTIONS. IF YOU FIND YOURSELF FLIPPING TOO FAR BACK INTO THE BOOK, START OVER FROM THE BEGINNING. THIS MIGHT TAKE SEVERAL ATTEMPTS BUT WHEN BOTH SIDES OF ZONE PLANE 8 ARE COMPLETELY VIEWED, YOU WILL FEEL COMPLETELY AT EASE AND WILL THEN BE READY TO POSSIBLY MOVE FORWARD TO THE RARE BUT VERY POSSIBLE ZONE PLANE 9.

FLIP BOOK IMMEDIATELY!

AND REPEAT THE LAST SET OF INSTRUCTIONS. IF YOU FIND YOURSELF FLIPPING TOO FAR BACK INTO THE BOOK, START OVER FROM THE BEGINNING. THIS MIGHT TAKE SEVERAL ATTEMPTS BUT WHEN BOTH SIDES OF ZONE PLANE 8 ARE COMPLETELY VIEWED, YOU WILL FEEL COMPLETELY AT EASE AND WILL THEN BE READY TO POSSIBLY MOVE FORWARD TO THE RARE BUT VERY POSSIBLE ZONE PLANE 9.

ARTIST RENDERING OF A TYPICAL AFTERNOON IN ZONE PLANE 8

ANOTHER RENDERING PROVIDED AT NO EXTRA CHARGE.

THIS CONCLUDES ZONE THEORY™ VOLUME ONE

YOU HAVE JUST SCRATCHED THE SURFACE OF ***ZONE THEORY***™.

Visit www.zonetheory.net to continue ***ZONE THEORY***™ studies and access:

ADVANCED WORKSHOPS (1-40)
ZONE PRIEST LECTURES
ZONE BAPTISM EVENTS

You can also purchase Zone Approved merchandise, products and tools including the Zone Wand *(mandatory for continued **ZONE THEORY**™ Study)*.

email: garydork@zonetheory.net
for any further questions or technical issues.

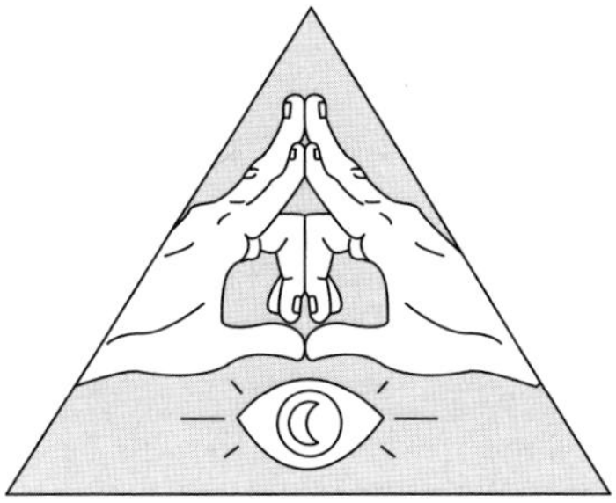

APPENDIX

SECRET INFORMATION

NOT FOR PUBLICATION !!!!!

THREE SECRET *ZONE THEORY*™ RITUALS

that you won't read about in any book!

1. EARLOBE DRAINING—Our scientists have recently proven that the earlobe is where all the toxins and bacteria in the body aggregate and are concentrated into a lethal syrup. Ear piercing for reasons of vanity is extremely dangerous, in that it allows these toxins to escape the lobe and enter the environment where they represent a threat to human life. The average earring is coated with a poisonous grime that is 10,000,000,000 times more infectious than a raw bowel movement from a tubercular wino. Congress needs to introduce a bill to ban ear piercing and earrings as soon as possible.

The earlobe should ideally be flat—it should resemble a piece of dried-up, discarded chicken skin. To do this you will need to draw out all the liquid. Fill an old condom completely with cat litter, packing it tightly so that it is now the size of an erect penis. Using fishing line, tie the litter-filled condom around the earlobe tightly—almost tight enough to sever the earlobe off completely, but not quite. Leave this in place for 6 to 8 months. The cat litter will slowly absorb all the infectious, potentially fatal toxins from your earlobe, saving your life and the lives of your friends and family in the process. When you remove the condom, you will find that your earlobe is now flat, dead, and discolored. Perfect. Throw the condom full of now-infectious cat litter into an industrial furnace at once! You are now free to rejoin your friends and family for a picnic, ball game, or what have you.

2. COUPON COLLECTING—Save coupons from the Sunday newspaper and get discounts on everything from frozen foods to paper towels.

3. MYSTICAL SPIRITUAL TONGUE ART—There is nothing more mystical or spiritual than this ancient art. The ancients would paint entire buildings, inside and out, with their tongues, baptizing the buildings as "safe havens" in the process. Many of these tongue-painted buildings are now considered mystical and spiritual works of art and have been exhibited in museums in Europe and elsewhere. With the advent of the paint roller, this great form of mystical spiritual art has been lost. You will need to get a can of paint from the hardware store. Whatever is on sale will do just fine. Put a condom on the end of your tongue so you don't swallow any of the paint (it's poisonous). Take off all your clothes and remove furniture and pets from the premises. Dip your tongue in the can of paint and lick the walls of your apartment or house, re-dipping your tongue in the paint with each lick. Make sure to remove any nails in the wall beforehand. After you've finished the walls, ceiling, and floors of the interior of the building, go outside and paint the exterior with your tongue, including the roof and the driveway. There is nothing more mystical or spiritual than this ancient art.

YOU WILL NEED ZONE APPROVED READING GLASSES TO VIEW THIS CHAPTER.
LIMITED SUPPLIES ARE AVAILABLE AT THE ZONE-ZONE COMMUNAL THOUGHT-HOUSE.

9]2-0ej 2;jfs.djkvn'

wpnclksadnviosdajdsjfiefeiuetrutotu

[kr13em]c90jw rjq3-urj31;o4ufy1-

gfp918rf 98rhg 1p98rhg 1c98rf

jsdby ne8q9hy]34

o2di/laksc

0e89r759438 [illegible] 89345owjf;osc;oaidnc.aksncaeiw [illegible] 9]2-0ej 2;jfs.djkvn'

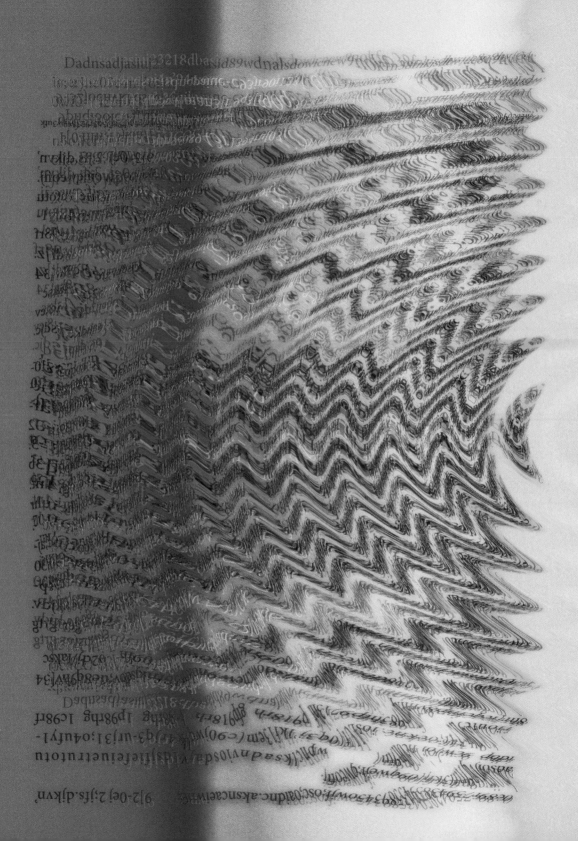

wpn'lksadnviosda [illegible] dsjfiefeiuetrutotu

[illegible] (c90jw [illegible] q3-urj31;o4ufy1-

[illegible] p918rh gp918rh [illegible] rhg 1p98rhg 1c98rf

[illegible] de89hv[34

[illegible] 92dj/laksc

Dadnsadjasiuj23218dbasid89wdnalsdowicnew9 [illegible]

9e8fr7594385943589345owjf;osc;oaidnc.aksncaeiwr 9]2-0ej 2;jfs.djkvn'

9dwejf;qweofj.

wpnc]ksadnviosda dsjfiefeiuetrutotu

3j'lkf73em]c90jwo k4rjq3-urj31;o4ufy1-

p918rh gfp918rh 98rhg 1p98rhg 1c98rf

]vlp98m,v;ue9hv]34

o2dj]laksc

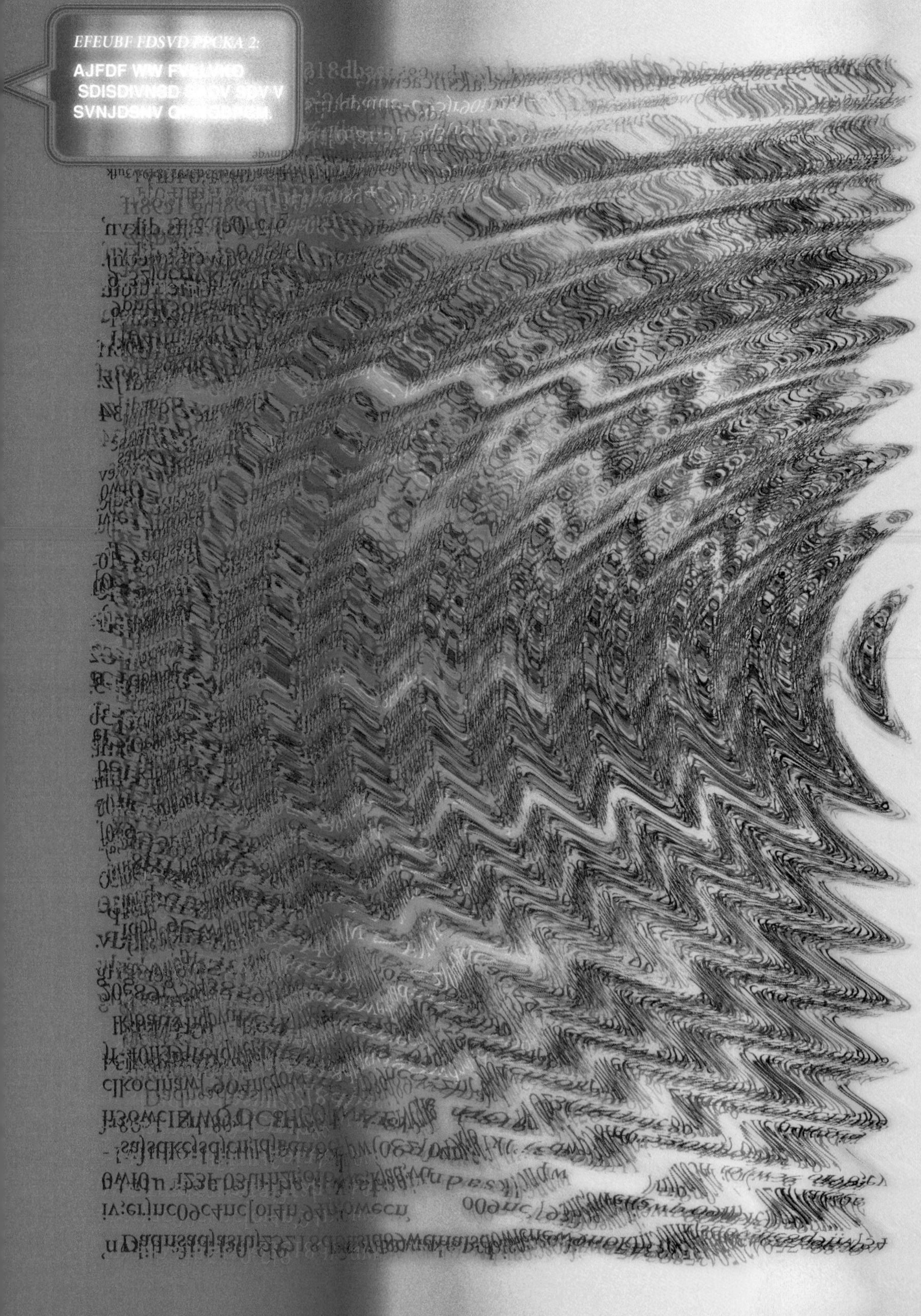
EFEUBF FDSVD
AJFDF
SDISD
SVNJD

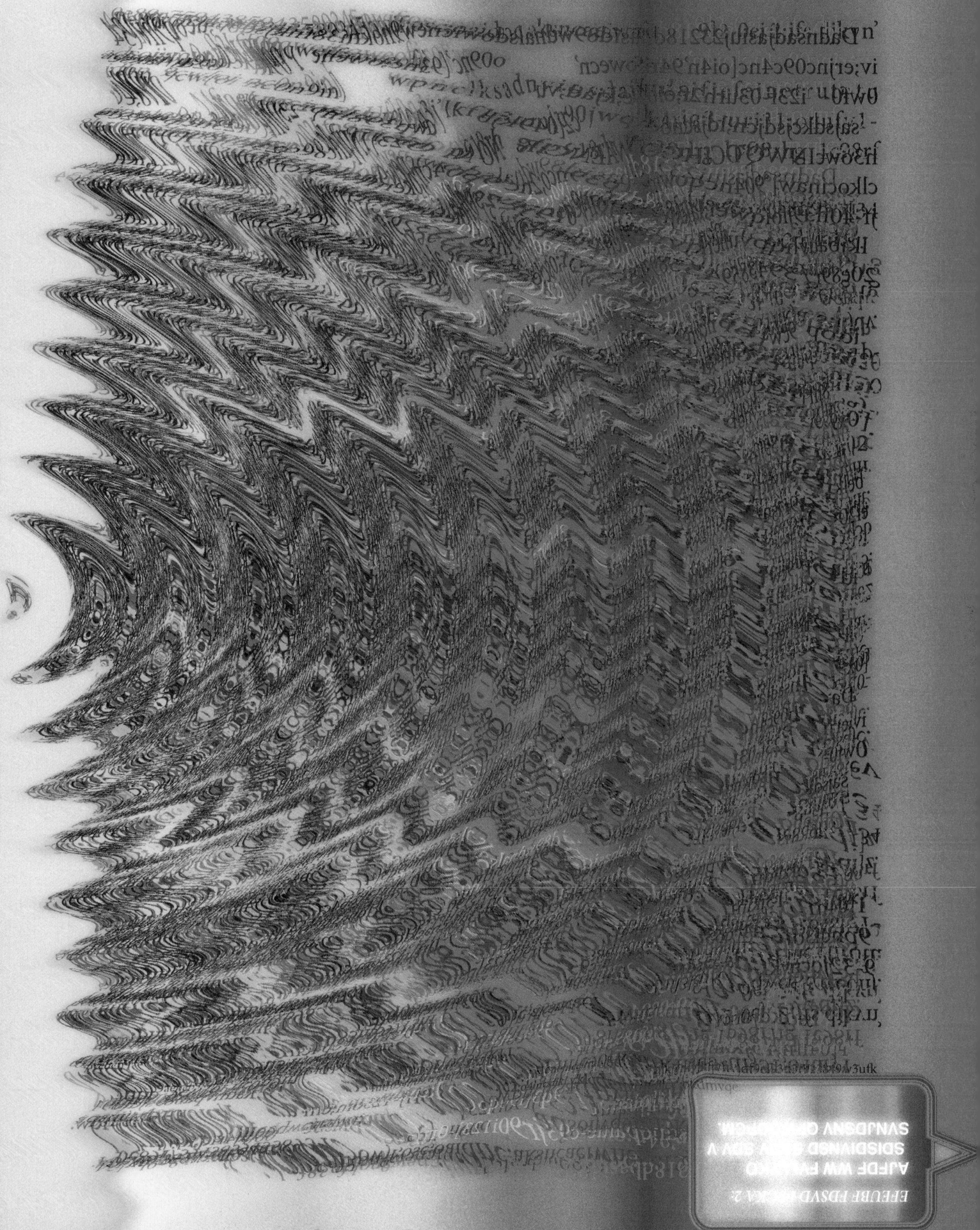
n' Dadnsadjasdnj|352181
iv:erjnc09c4nc|oi4n9a4sowecn,
0wf0 u 123r 03hh2

ANNOUNCING...

TIM & ERIC'S ZONE THEORY™ BOOK CONTEST!

EVERYONE WANTS TO KNOW: WHO IS THE FASTEST READER?

ARE YOU?

Whoever reads this book the fastest will receive a free "I Read Books Fast" t-shirt

Official Rules:

You must film yourself reading entire book with a timer visible.
You must write a 3 page essay on book to prove you understood the book.
Please use following three blank pages for essay.

ADDITIONAL *ZONE THEORY*™ TERMINOLOGY

ZONE THEORY™ uses mainly the same words found in your standard dictionary, which you can purchase at any bookstore or supermarket. Learn all the words in preparation for your new life.

We have a few other words not covered elsewhere in this book that you will need to learn as well, in order to have a productive conversation with a ***ZONE THEORY***™ instructor or practitioner. These words should not be used around non-Zone friends and/or family.

Aalty—*semen that has been slipped into waffle batter and served to boehhongs that you are trying to sicken.*

Boehhongs—*computer-savvy family members who send you dubious links attempting to discredit* ***ZONE THEORY***™.

Boehhong Furmo—*law enforcement who are antagonistic towards* ***ZONE THEORY***™ *and our methods and lifestyle.*

Cyhii—*wine made of strawberries and dog urine that is to be drunk from a golden chalice to commemorate mastery of any single* ***ZONE THEORY***™ *level.*

Darthreigh—*foot fungus that is common amongst Adult Horseplay practitioners.*

Dkrunnos—*salted apples.*

Epyurst—*basement room at Nude Recreation Centers, where newcomers and initiates are photographed, fingerprinted, and tested for blood disorders.*

Exoo Somoo—*special soap for mopping up semen without damaging its precious DNA.*

Fuy—*secret, intimate undergarment to be worn only by* ***ZONE THEORY***™ *masters.*

G'hor Hoo—*EZ self-punishment system that works great with* ***ZONE THEORY***™. *Self-punishment is key to toning your Zones and should be practiced regularly.*

ZONE TIPS AND TRICKS 9:
USE YOUR MIND TO ASCEND— ASCEND NOW

Gliooaf—*slang word for anyone who is failing to thrive in* ***ZONE THEORY™****.*

Ibbo—*brain surgery.*

Ibbo 39—*brain surgery resulting in death.*

Maaggaatti—*fictitious dumping planet where non-****ZONE THEORY™*** *people are enslaved, in Z.T. comic books and fantasy films.*

Plombdomb—*newcomer to Adult Horseplay who is squeamish about penis grazing.*

Radiant Tomog—*diarrhea after midnight.*

Rummo Fofe—*a lucky beverage made by dissolving chicken in buckets of rum; this is to be served to physicians prior to performing surgery or the delivery of a* ***ZONE THEORY™*** *Child.*

Sqikyr—*the "fourth testicle."*

Tommielance—*a harmless wart that grows on the head of the penis as a result of taking too much Zowder.*

Vons Swastika—*stolen clumps of pubic hair rearranged to form a swastika.*

Yeaven—*a ceremonial cheese made from waste fluids.*

Zongsonggi Tandat—*the impromptu "jump for joy" done by a poet after writing a particularly great poem.*

"Zuhmis Zuhmis Instook"—*phrase to be screamed by a visiting Zone Priest into a woman's vagina 50 times before she is penetrated by her Zone Husband, in order to prevent unwanted pregnancy.*

"Zuhmis Zuhmis Bent Peniss Micanapee-Pee"—*phrase to be screamed by a visiting Zone Priest into a woman's vagina 1,000 times before she in penetrated by her Zone Husband in order to ensure conception.*

Zz8zz8—*recommended ATM password for* ***ZONE THEORY™*** *practitioners.*

FORGETTING THIS BOOK

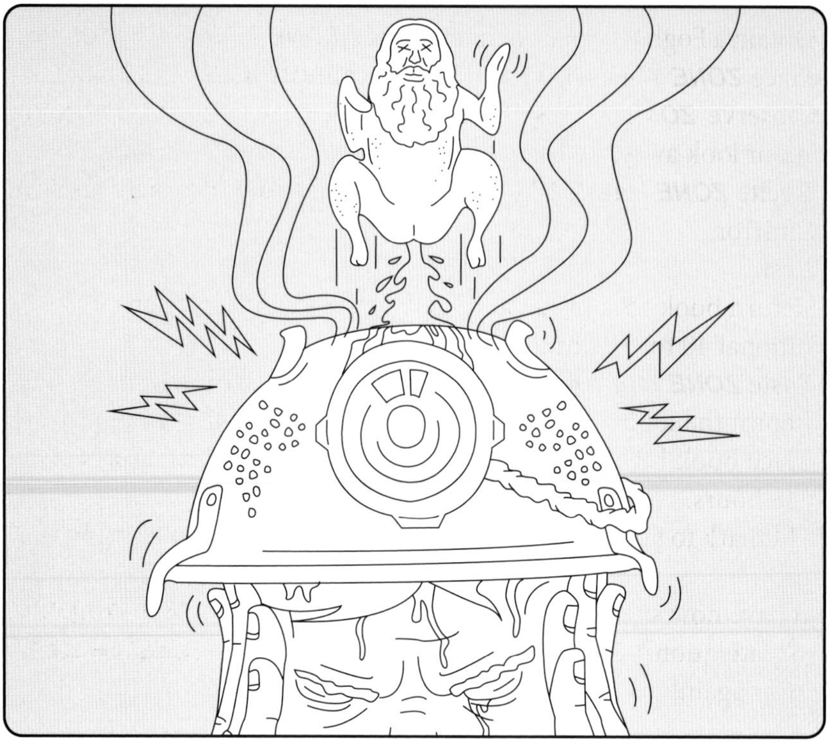

"One of the most...[valuable] tools that this book provides is the capacity and ability for the reader to forget its entire contents in ten simple steps..."—Japrene D. Stunt, reader

There are so many reasons why you may want to forget this book:

- You have found this book useless.
- You would like to re-read the book from scratch.
- A family member got you the book for your birthday and insists he/she watches you read it cover to cover.
- The bees have gotten to you.

On the following page you will find these 10 simple steps to forgetting this book. Please consult a Zone Councilor before going any further to ensure that you are forgetting this book for the right reasons.

10 STEPS TO FORGETTING THE BOOK

1. Obtain a Foghat. Wear Foghat and read ***ZONE THEORY***™ backwards.
2. Place ***ZONE THEORY***™ outside for 90 minutes in direct sunlight.
3. Observe ***ZONE THEORY***™ for an additional 90 minutes. Do not blink or look away.
4. Recite ***ZONE THEORY***™ in its entirety while looking at yourself in the mirror.
5. Rest.
6. Return book to sunlight and allow to bask in light for an additional 40 to 45 minutes.
7. Baste ***ZONE THEORY***™ using body fluids of your choice.
8. Repeat the following phrase: "I condemn you" 1,000 times.
9. Place book high atop the ***ZONE THEORY***™ bookshelf. Allow to sit for 48 hours.
10. Remark to yourself: "I have no idea what was in that dang book!"

You have now successfully forgotten the entirety of ***ZONE THEORY***™. Congratulations! Now it's time to begin to learn the ***ZONE THEORY***™ all over again!

Book will disappear.

AFTERWORD

Are you a Hollywood producer? Are you reading this book and saying to yourself: “Wow, this would make a great movie!” If you are please contact us immediately. The whole idea of writing this book is to attract attention to the value of this idea which in turn should lead to a MOVIE which is what it’s all about. How can we make some $$$ off this situation? We really see the value in the ***ZONE THEORY***™ in terms of merch, dolls and ancillary products that we’ll leave to a marketing professional to delve into. This is exciting. Let’s get on the phone and talk ASAP. We’d like to jump on the momentum that already exists. We are not going to mess with the creative, we just want to be a part of something great. Thanks again.

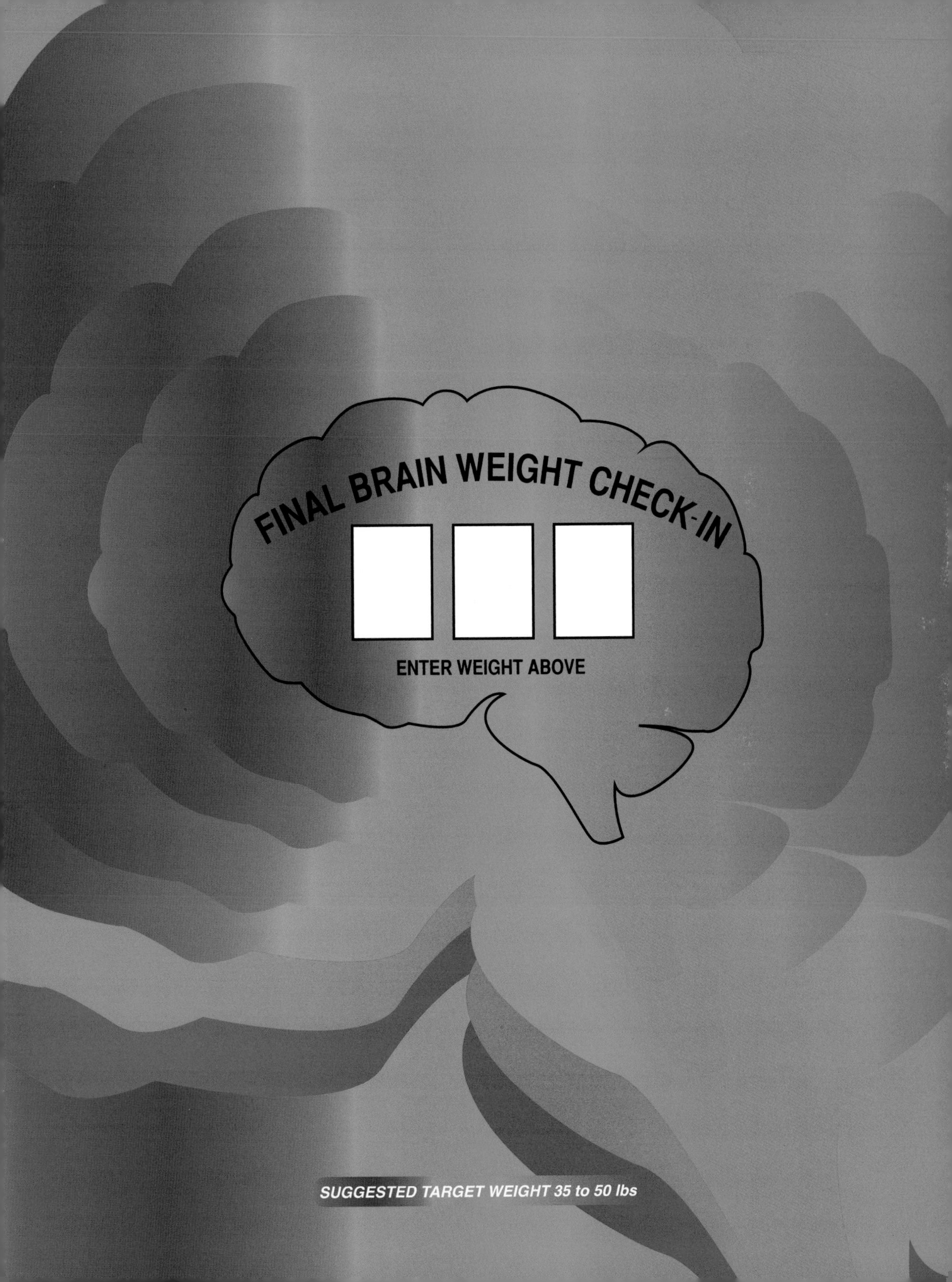
FINAL BRAIN WEIGHT CHECK-IN
ENTER WEIGHT ABOVE
SUGGESTED TARGET WEIGHT 35 to 50 lbs

MORE BOOKS BY THIS AUTHOR

ZONE THEORY*™ *VOLUME II

ZONE THEORY*™ *VOLUME III

ZONE THEORY*™ *VOLUME IV

MORE ***ZONE THEORY*™**

ACUTUALIZING ***ZONE THEORY*™** *IN MODERN LIFE*

***ZONE THEORY*™** *TESTIMONIES*

***ZONE THEORY*™** *FOR YOU*

***ZONE THEORY*™** *THE EZ WAY*

***ZONE THEORY*™** *ANTICS AND STORIES*

BUILDING YOUR ZONES

ZONE POTENTIAL

ZONING IT AT WORK: A PRACTICAL GUIDE

THE ZONE ULTIMATUM: FROM THE ZONE FILES

THE ZONE COOKBOOK VOLUME ONE